CALIFORNIA BREWMASTERS

Portraits and Profiles of the Golden State's Brewing Icons

CALIFORNIA
BREWMASTERS

Portraits and Profiles of the Golden State's Brewing Icons

Interviews and Photography by Nicholas Gingold
With a Foreword by Steve Wagner, co-founder, Stone Brewing Co.

Published by Georgian Bay Books, Inc. (an imprint of Georgian Bay, LLC)
San Diego, California
www.georgianbaybooks.com

Text and Photos © Nicholas Gingold
Publisher & President: Bruce Glassman
Design: berniergraphics.com
Proofreading: Jessica Knott

ISBN: 978-0-9896142-2-1

First Edition
Printed in the USA

Acknowledgments

I dedicate this book to my parents, Donna and Jeff, who have always stood behind me and encouraged me to follow my wildest aspirations. I thank them for their endless displays of love and support, without which this book would have never seen the light of day.

There are many, many people that contributed to the success of this book. I thank my family: my sisters Kristin and Kate, for all their help and support on this project, and my brother-in-law Michael; my beer obsession is all his fault. To Sam, the coolest nephew in the world. To my good friend Sean, I couldn't imagine a smoother two-weeks of brewery tours and shoots up North without your assistance.

To the brewers: Thank you for your time in front of the camera, your openness with my questions, and for your enthusiasm towards this project. To the entire craft beer industry, I thank you for welcoming me in with a full pint and open arms.

To my publisher Bruce Glassman and Georgian Bay Books, thank you for believing in this project and for your guidance. Together we're getting the good word out to the fine people of the craft beer world.

To my Kickstarter backers: All 197 of you. We did it, and it's all thanks to you!

A special thank you to the breweries (and one beer bar) listed below whose generous support of this book went above and beyond. Thank you!

INSIDE

74	Todd Ashman FiftyFifty Brewing Company	
78	Matt Brynildson Firestone Walker Brewing Company	
82	Jesse Houck Golden Road Brewing	
86	Dan Gordon Gordon Biersch Brewing Company	
90	Chuck Silva Green Flash Brewing Company	
94	Ben Cook Hangar 24 Craft Brewery	
98	Paul Segura Karl Strauss Brewing Company	
102	Kyle Smith Kern River Brewing Company	

106	Tony Magee Lagunitas Brewing Company	
110	Tomme Arthur Port Brewing and The Lost Abbey	
114	Dave McLean Magnolia Gastropub and Brewery	
118	Arne Johnson Marin Brewing Company	
122	Brian Hunt Moonlight Brewing Company	
126	Denise Jones Napa Point Brewery	
130	Don Barkley Napa Smith Brewery	
134	Tom Nickel Nickel Beer Company	

Foreword
by Steve Wagner

Co-founder, Stone Brewing Co.
President, California Craft Brewers Association

California is seen worldwide as a hotbed of craft brewing creativity and exploration. A number of contemporary styles, now ubiquitous across the globe, originated here, including the West Coast-style India pale ale (IPA) as well as its even more formidable imperial siblings, the double and triple IPA. New World takes on Belgian styles, wood-aged brews, and more, also harken back to The Golden State. Much has been written about the amazing quality and variety of California craft beer, and deservedly so. But, what about the brewers who are responsible for starting this revolution and continuing it today? California's talented and adventurous brewers have pushed the envelope, but who are they, where did they come from, and where are they going? This book provides a unique glimpse into the lives and thoughts of some of our most creative and successful brewers. Hopefully the profiles and photographs within these pages will inspire you and excite you anew about what is happening in the "cradle" of craft beer.

One of the major reasons California has the most craft brewers of any state is because of the long-term vision of some of its founding breweries. Fritz Maytag, who saved San Francisco's Anchor Brewing Co. from extinction, established the country's first craft brewing company. He was also responsible for ensuring a state regulatory environment in which small brewers could thrive. Ken Grossman, founder and owner of Chico-based Sierra Nevada Brewing Company (the country's largest craft brewer) has carried the torch from early on. He has worked tirelessly to protect and add to the rights of his fellow craft brewers. These men were leaders before there was anything to lead, and every California brewer who's followed in their footsteps has benefited from their efforts, myself included.

When we established Stone Brewing Co. in 1996, my partner, Greg Koch, and I looked to the efforts and contributions of our craft beer forerunners. We regarded them as standard bearers, examples of how to do things right and responsibly. Today, we are proud to be members of the California Craft Brewers Association (CCBA), an organization dedicated to giving craft brewers a single, unified voice in protecting their interests in the state. I currently serve as the president of the CCBA, and I'm particularly proud to have assisted in initiatives that resulted in beneficial legislation and other regulations that protect the rights and privileges of craft brewers.

In many ways, the success of the CCBA mirrors the triumphs of our state's breweries. Though each company operates in its own unique way, we are connected via an overarching and very real sense of camaraderie. While members of other industries resort to cutthroat competition, the greater percentage of brewers make the active, concerted decision to collaborate and work together for the greater good of one another, and for our profession as a whole. We do this on a state level, but also in a regional fashion, with brewing companies from individual counties and cities banding together to make a difference. In many cases, that strength-in-numbers approach is facilitated through brewers guilds. These guilds amplify the energy and impact of their members while they raise the visibility of breweries in succinct geographical areas. They also help brewers forge significant and lasting bonds with their communities.

Good intentions and good will, however, can only account for so much. Without high quality beer, there is nothing. Luckily, that is what we are known for. It's the reason California is the birthplace of craft brewing in the United States. Whether it's those massive IPAs or Germanic lagers or Belgian-style sour ales (or just about anything else a craft beer enthusiast's mind can conjure), California brewers are doing it, and doing it right. It's that commitment to quality and to each other that has fueled our ascent for decades. That very same commitment will be the foundation of the countless innovations and successes that lie ahead for us and the craft beer fans we so happily and humbly serve.

Introduction
by Nicholas Gingold

There are fleeting experiences in life that impact us deeply, moments we glide through without realizing their significance at the time. Whether it's a chance encounter that leads to an unlikely friendship, or a new experience that throws us head first into a new community, these experiences and encounters shape us. They ripple out in immeasurable ways, causing consequences that continue far beyond their beginnings. Often, it is not until much later that we look back on those moments and see their true effects. I'm lucky to be able to look back on a recent series of moments and experiences that changed my life. And it all has to do with that great social lubricant we know as beer.

If you enjoy good beer, then you have likely had that "a-ha" moment when it comes to craft beer. If your drinking history is anything like mine, your formative drinking years were plagued by fizzy yellow rice water that lacked flavor, definition, or true value. It did the job when it came to beer pong, sure, but, for the most part, it left a bad taste in my mouth. It pointed me away from beer instead of toward it. I was unaware that, brewing all around me, the men and women of the craft beer industry were silently plotting the hostile takeover of my taste buds and would forever hold me hostage.

It was my brother-in-law Michael's fascination with craft beer that brought me into the fold. We bought two tickets to the very first Firestone Walker Invitational Beer Festival in Paso Robles, and, on a hot summer Saturday, my "a-ha" moment happened. I tried my first sour beer, Oude Tart by the Bruery, and could literally feel that wild new taste go from my mouth to deep within my brain, and end with a cartoon-like mushroom cloud feeling of pure enlightenment. Wow . . . that was different. That was good! I immediately got in line two more times. Hell, I hadn't even been able to stomach an IPA at the time; but with that one taste, my world opened up to the great craft beers being poured all around me. That first "a-ha" moment made me realize that somehow I needed to attach my passion for journalism and photography to the craft beer industry.

Many conversations and many beers later, the thought crossed my mind that we had plenty of books about the beer itself—be it a guidebook to breweries, books about beer styles, or books on rating beer. They focused on the beverage, but they left so much more behind, ignoring the element

that made me a fan of craft beer culture in the first place. Go to any craft beer festival and you can tell that it's the people that make this industry special. I'm talking about the people responsible for every recipe, the people that spend their early mornings fixing a fermenter or a bottling line, and fellow beer fans who talk endlessly about beer characteristics and nerd out over the newest collaborations. These are the factors that make the craft beer community special. I decided that if I wanted to pursue a project about beer, it had better be based on the people.

The result is what you see before you: *California BrewMasters*, a book of interviews and portraits profiling some of California's great brewers. The idea was to meet the faces behind the beer; to make you, the reader, like a fly on the wall in the midst of a conversation. In doing so, you'd learn about these brewers' personalities, their thoughts, and of course, their beer. I wanted to showcase where they work and live, to peel back the curtain just enough to bring about an understanding of who they are and where they come from.

I think this "craft" movement is here to stay. More and more, people all over America are supporting local, quality-oriented, small businesses that provide the types of flavors and variety that cannot be produced by large corporations. And if this movement is permanent, shouldn't we be talking to the pioneers of such a transition? The landscape of American drinking could forever be changing, and I hope we can view books like this as a way of honoring and learning from the men and women who paved the way.

So, why focus on California specifically? This book takes us to more than 40 breweries throughout the state, from San Diego to Fort Bragg. I'll come right out and say it: California is responsible for craft beer. It may have been possible for the movement to begin elsewhere, and it may have had seedlings in other states, but the industry as we know it started right here on the West Coast. It began with the fine folks at Anchor, Sierra Nevada, and New Albion, among other trailblazers. Some of my favorite interviews in this book talk of the days when equipment was welded out of old dairy tanks and great beer was conceived and created by those who found a way to make it happen despite a lack of resources. As a native Californian, this is the tastiest state history I could ever think to study. And it's living history available to us today in a glass.

A few notes to consider: The list of brewers we included is largely based on the recommendations of the brewers themselves. It is in no way a complete list, because that would be impossible. As I write this, there are more than 400 breweries in California; for every brewer featured in this book, we could have easily added another three that are just as deserving. I do think, however, that this is a wonderful cross-section of brewers and breweries, all of whom represent great California beer. This is just the tip of the iceberg. I invite you to challenge yourself as I have tried to do: Pick up a beer you've never tried before. Then another. There is so much out there to explore, and so little to get bored by.

So crack open your favorite Golden State brew (be sure to pour it into a clean glass!), take a nice big sip, and join me in conversations with some of the finest folks you'll ever meet: California BrewMasters.

Peter Zien
AleSmith Brewing Company

Peter Zien has been at the helm of AleSmith for nearly 15 years. As an award-winning home brewer, a grand master beer judge, and a serious hobbyist, Peter has utilized a wealth and diversity of experience to make AleSmith the exemplary company that it is.

Nick: Ok, Peter, tell me how you started brewing—how you got interested in brewing and home brewing and bring me to where you are now.

Peter: It is a long story. My roots for enjoying good beer go way back. When I was in tenth grade, well before I was of legal age to drink, I had a 300-bottle beer collection in my bedroom. I built shelving for it because I considered these like art. Like all of us, we all started our drinking a little early. I was drinking those beers back in the late 70's, best stuff I could get my hands on.

My dad was 50 when I was born. When they retired they were taking my sister and me to Europe. At ages 12, 13, 14, 15, those formative years, I was getting to taste some of the world's best beer. I came from an open house where my dad figured it was better to offer me a drink than to send me out on the street to go find it.

Fast forward, It was about 1994 when I bought a home brew kit on my birthday as a birthday present to myself. I went down to Ballast Point Home Brew Mart and I bought that kit from Tom Nickel who was working there at the time, who is now the owner of O'Brien's Pub [and Nickel Beer Co.]. I bought it because my dad and I would go fishing every year in Canada and I'd make him stop at breweries. I've always been a beer nerd and a beer nut. One of the stops, August-Shell brewing, had the free magazines out. One of them was on how to make your own beer, and that was it; it was as simple as that.

> **"When I was in tenth grade . . . I had a 300-bottle beer collection in my bedroom."**

Then I found out there is a little sub-culture here in San Diego of home brewers. By 1996 I found QUAFF, the home brewing club and became active with that club. By '98 I was vice president, and in '99 I became president of that club. We did a lot of great things under my presidency. We were the first San Diego home brew club to ever be named "National Home Brew Club of the Year" at the American Home Brewers Association. We also were California's "Home Brew Club of the Year."

I gained confidence; I was brewing a lot. I'm a style brewer. I was trying to nail these styles and before you know it I had met a lot of the professional brewers in town. I am the second owner of AleSmith, and all this had happened by 2002. That's my little beer history, in a little capsule there.

Nick: Going back to home brewing, do you remember the first beer that you ever tried? Do you remember how it came out?

Peter: As a home brew, absolutely. I can tell you pretty much most of the 135 batches I did. I kept meticulous records. I have them all. The home brew kits, they set you up a lot of times with your first beer being an IPA. They figure your errors will be hidden behind the wall of hops that they send you home with. My first beer was an IPA. I still have a bottle of it. It was bottled on July 5, 1994. I'm also kind of a pack rat so I have almost every beer I've brewed since, at least a bottle of it. It's a great hobby. You can make world-class beer pretty quickly.

They tell you it doesn't have to be rocket science, but it can be. That's, I think, where it appealed to me. I took it to the next step quickly, a couple extract batches, and I was in the mini-mashes, and then I was into all grain by batch eight or nine. I just wanted to learn more. It was the blend of art and science that I'd been looking for my whole life.

When you look back at my records you can see the styles were usually brewed in a row. You could see four or five milds, I made four or five saisons. That way you could really

> **"It was the blend of art and science that I'd been looking for my whole life."**

explore the different styles and how you want to put your little spin on them, being careful maybe to do only one or two changes per recipe so you know what did what.

Nick: Do you have any wisdom to impart to new or possible home brewers?

Peter: Yeah: think outside the box. Don't just blindly follow recipes. Use them as templates to get yourself started. Always have an eye towards how you and your abilities can make something different and something new to the world. We're all different. We all have different perceptions in the way we taste.

Another little thing I would tell home brewers is: taste and smell and look and listen to everything you put into your home brews. The home brew shops will let you taste things, smell it. The grains should taste fresh and crunchy, not stale. It should have a bread-like flavor. Your hops should smell citrusy and nice and fresh, no cheese-like aromas. Use your olfactory as your laboratory and that will take you far.

Nick: Thank you for that. Speaking of cheese, you're a cheese-maker?

Peter: Yes, I am.

Nick: Tell me a little bit about how you got into that. Does that influence your beer? Or does your beer influence your cheese at all?

Peter: I like to make a lot of different things. I bake and I like to cook and make cheese and make mustards and pickle olives. When I started working here, home brewing fell to the wayside. I brewed every batch of beer here at AleSmith from 2002 through 2004. In those years, the last thing I wanted to do on a weekend was to home brew again.

But an interesting thing was happening here. At the end of the brew day, I always had a few thousand pounds of grain to give away to farmers and we'd haul it out back in these trucks. Farmers would come in and get it. This goat farmer one year, she brought me a gallon of milk out of the blue. I thought, "Oh . . . They're feeding it to their animals and here's a nice story. I'm making cheese with the milk from the animals that eat the AleSmith grain."

I found quickly that cheese-making scratched the same itch as home brewing for me. It was a great replacement for my now lost hobby of home brewing that I wasn't doing anymore. I just love it. I've made some of the cheeses with our beers. I have the name CheeseSmith registered and it's a dream at this point.

Nick: I wanted to ask you about this Grand Master Beer Judge certification that you have. Can you explain that and what that means? You're the only guy in San Diego to have that.

Peter: Yeah, in Southern California I'm the only Grand Master level judge. There's a program, the Beer Judge Certification Program. They offer an exam where you can become a beer judge. They have different levels. You move up in levels. Every time you go to a judging event, you're given a point and you move up and up and up.

I have the second highest score on record with the program. Out of 6,000 people I have a 98 on my tasting portion. I take beer judging very seriously. If you're having fun, you're probably not doing it right. It should feel like work. You're filling out these score sheets and by the 10th, 12th beer, I'm really a big believer in giving these brewers honest feedback. Not just pointing out things, but offering how to correct it. That's the difference in a quality beer judge: they have to be able to tell you how to fix things.

Nick: Let's talk a little bit about your recipe and brewing process. Do you have any overriding philosophies?

Peter: We're trying to give you a full-flavored experience here, with the freshest ingredients we can possibly get. Money is no object when it comes to what's going to go into our beers. If I want something, I'm going to find it somewhere in the world and we'll pay what we have to. I think an example of

that is the specialty Speedway Stouts we do. I pay over two hundred dollars a pound for the coffee that passes through the body of an Asian palm civet, and it's collected off the jungle floors. There's only a certain amount per year. The Decadence that we made last year had a couple grand worth of Vermont organic maple syrup in it. Every fleck of grain and hop is the best we could possibly get. We're never going to cut a corner on any AleSmith beers, so I think that's how we're able to keep producing beers that people enjoy and that get acclaim from our peers.

Nick: Do you start from, "I have this in mind and I'm going to take steps A, B, and C to get there," or is do you say "I want to try something like this" . . .

Peter: I think it would be the former way you described it. We definitely come up with a style we want to do. For the Decadence Anniversary we rotate a new style through that label every year. That's when we have to pick the new beer to make. We put my brewers together and we sit in a circle. We'll go out and buy every commercial example of that style we can find, four or five at least to taste. We're going to see what we like about certain other ones and what we don't. We know the result we want. We're going to find the steps we need to get there.

Nick: Obviously, this attention to detail and quality has lead you guys to some pretty amazing accolades including the "Best Small Brewery Award."

Peter: I'm very proud of my gang, absolutely.

Nick: What are some of the accolades that you're most proud of and what do they mean for you?

Peter: As a home brewer I was very interested in competing. I gained 400 different medals that are honors during my home brewing.

I found out it was a little tougher to win medals at the professional level. AleSmith's done really well and I'm very proud of our awards that we've gotten at the World Beer Cup and Great American Beer Festival. I believe we're the second-most medaled brewery in San Diego. First place would obviously go to the Pizza Port chains that do so well. We're right behind them. I think we have 13 or so medals from GABF and close to that same number from World Beer Cup (more have been won since this interview was recorded). For up-and-coming breweries winning medals is incredibly important; you want to at least get your name out there, and have your brewing associated with a quality high enough that you could win a medal.

Whether we win medals or not, we're still AleSmith. We still show up to work on Monday morning. We still know what we've got to do. We still make some of the world's best beer.

Nick: In the past five or so years we've seen this wave of breweries opening up and the general public taking a much greater interest. The culture is really expanding. Are you seeing this as well? How do you like it? Is it good for you guys?

Peter: Absolutely. I'm seeing more and more people converting to microbrews from mass produced beers. Personally, I love it. All these breweries opening up. We're all helping each other. The more the merrier. There's plenty of room. This is a big, big town. It's a big beer drinking country, 75 million beer drinkers—plenty of room for all of us.

The way I see San Diego is sort of like restaurants in San Francisco or New York. There are many great ones. They can all survive together. People are going to go around to the better ones, so you always want to bring your A-game.

Nick: What do you attribute this to, why now? Why are people suddenly interested in craft beers all of a sudden when they weren't ten years ago?

Peter: I guess that's a complicated question. First of all, you have to look to what's happening in the food segment with restaurants, too: the farm-to-table movement. People are more excited about high-quality food. They want to know where it's from. For years I think America worried about feeding the world and we took our eye off the ball for quality a little bit. We learned to make fields of wheat grow forever and all of a sudden we became a white bread nation where, "Oh it's food, just eat it." Then we started realizing, tomatoes don't taste as good as they used to. Anyone from our parents' generation will tell you that.

These farm-to-table restaurants got really in vogue around the same time craft beer started to heat up—in the early 2000s. I think the beer is wrapped up in that, in this search for higher quality. The mass-produced beers that hit you with all those commercials, people are starting to give these microbrews a try and then making a decision for themselves.

Nick: My last question for you, I've asked this of everyone so far: What's the one thing you've never been asked in an interview that you've always wanted to be able to say?

> ## "This is a passion-driven business. I do this because I love to brew and it's not about the money at all."

Peter: Wow, that's a great question. I didn't think anyone could ask me something that I couldn't answer. I think there's a misconception out there that brewery owners make a lot of money.

I've never been asked, "How much do you make?" I make nothing; everything I have is in this brewery. Because we produce alcohol, we're taxed very heavily. It's just a very tough business. I guess I'd just like people to know that this is a passion-driven business. I do this because I love to brew and it's not about the money at all. There are way better ways to make money in this country, and I've been part of some other projects that enable me to do this. Don't ever think someone's brewing beer just because they want to make money off you. This is a passion project.

Patrick McIlhenney
Alpine Beer Company

Patrick McIlhenney is the co-founder and owner of Alpine Beer Company.

Nick: I guess my first question for you is about starting this business. What got you into brewing?

Pat: I started off in my formative years wondering why people drank the macro beers that were available out there. I didn't find any joy in drinking them. It wasn't until I came across a fancy European beer that I discovered that there was more to beer than just being bland. I was into good beer at a very young age. Too young to actually mention.

It wasn't until I was in the fire service, working in Northern California (Mendocino County) that I discovered Mendocino Brewing Company. That was my first exposure to really good craft beer and something different and flavorful. It wasn't until about a year later—1983—that I discovered you could make your own beer. I started home brewing with an intent of someday opening my own brewery. Not just the casual home brew. I purchased scientifically, I took notes, I submitted the beers to judging, made the adjustments, and would submit again until I was winning awards.

> **"I started off in my formative years wondering why people drink macro beers that were available out there. I didn't find any joy in drinking them."**

Then I would move on to another style, trying to perfect it. I would submit it until I was winning a really good prize for it. By the time I felt I was ready, I had 8 core recipes under my belt. Finding the equipment was easy. But finding a location was a little harder. It took over a year to find a location in Alpine. I never felt that the mainstream beers were worthy of drinking and, once I realized you can make your own, look out.

Nick: Were you from here?

Pat: Southern California. Grew up in Oceanside and then high school years in Lakeside down the road. All the kids went to the same high school in Lakeside. All the kids in Alpine went to the same high school because there's one up here. I met a lot of people from Alpine and just fell in love with this town.

Nick: Do you remember the first beer that you ever attempted? Do you remember how it turned out when you start home brewing?

Pat: The first beer was a pale ale and it was really good. The second beer was—I don't remember, but I do remember that it was terrible. I attribute that to getting cocky and thinking, "This is easy I can do this."

Nick: Give me a sense of how you go about creating a new beer. What are the steps you take, if you can walk me through that process.

Pat: Well, if we're going to delve into a new style that we haven't done before I'll research all the beers of that style and I'll taste as many as I can. I'll talk to people I know that make them. I get all the insight I can and then I actually have a predetermined outcome that I want to achieve. It may not be the cookie cutter example of that beer style but it will fit parameters generally. I amass the proper ingredients, develop a recipe that I know fits the style guidelines, and put our twist on it, whatever it may be. There's a lot of thorough research ahead of any new beer.

I actually developed our IPA hop profiles based on scientific analysis. In a lab, they take the actual aromatic hops oil compounds and they analyze them. They'll tell you what percentages of each one of those individual hop compounds there are. These are the compounds that produce the aromatics and the flavors that you like. In the right proportions, they come across phenomenally. If they're not in the right proportions then it's muddled and bitter, not as stellar as it would be if certain percentages of individual hop oil compounds reached certain threshold limits.

Myrcene is probably the hop oil compound that has the biggest influence on your sensory analysis when smelling it. If there's too much myrcene and it's not balanced by a legitimate amount of caryophyllene then it's going to be off. I know what the certain percentages are, and no one's ever going to learn those from me except people that work here. What makes our IPAs so good is that those individual compounds are in the proper percentages and the right mix, and we complement them with the ones that fill the holes. If it takes more than that, three or four different hops, that's what we do. That's how we build our IPAs. No one else has a clue about how that works. They go "Oh, we're going to do all high myrcene hops. Yippee!" What does that do with your cohumulone and your geraniol and your linalool? Are you just throwing it together because you think it's cool? No, there's an absolute purpose for the amounts and types of hops that go into our brews. Nobody else does that—that I know of.

> **"Just know there's more to hops than just bitter or aromatic."**

On that same note, the microbiology and sanitation class that I took was one of the biggest boosts in my knowledge. There's the art of building the recipe, knowing what ingredients contribute and how to proportion it out correctly. Then there's the science part of it. Microbiology. Knowing how to use wort, knowing how to keep microbes from intruding on your lovely liquids. That's a whole other field of intense science that you

have to know. It's a balance between art and science, and having background in both of those are really essential for the whole overall control of your outcome. Just know there's more to hops than just bitter or aromatic.

Nick: Are you home brewing a recipe before you make a larger production quantity?

Pat: You would think, but I haven't home brewed in so long that I actually consider this system my home brew system. We haven't had any real "dogs." The only issues we've ever had have been related to yeast and sluggish response or a contamination. That's 3 batches in 10 years, not too bad.

Nick: Do you have a favorite then? Of the beers that you guys created?

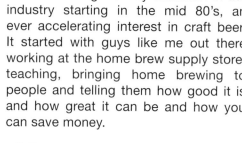

Pat: Well, picking your favorite beer is like picking your favorite kid. Honestly, at any given time, any of our beers could be my favorite beer. The situation, what I'm eating, who I'm with, what I'm doing later, all factor into what would be the best beer for that particular moment. I do like IPAs obviously. I think we're probably best known for them, but I also like a wide variety of beers in general. We make what we like.

I think the winning combination of focusing on quality and not putting your money into telling people that this is good beer is really a much better way to go. Money, I feel is better spent focusing on quality than marketing and trying to convince people that this is good. You know just as well as I do that if your friend tells you something is really good you're more likely to believe him than you are a commercial or an ad. Word of mouth advertising is our backbone.

Nick: What else do you attribute your success to?

Pat: I would have to say it's the beer. Certainly not my attitude, I'm grumpy and aggressive and don't take shit from anybody. I don't care if you don't like that, so it's obviously not that making people appreciate our beer. I think it's just our focus on quality—that should shine through in the beer.

Nick: What are you seeing these days as far as trends?

Pat: We are seeing an ever-increasing interest in craft beer. I would have thought we would have maxed out in our little town here, and with all the people that live around here. We thought we would have our steady customers and very few new ones and that's not the case. We have new customers all the time. What do I attribute that to? I think most people that get in to craft beer are better educated, more intelligent, have better sophistication, and a better sense of taste. They know the economics of craft beer and know that it's probably a better deal than just a shitload of macro beer.

I saw throughout my affiliation in the industry starting in the mid 80's, an ever accelerating interest in craft beer. It started with guys like me out there working at the home brew supply store, teaching, bringing home brewing to people and telling them how good it is and how great it can be and how you can save money.

"I know in San Diego the work that we have done is paying off."

I know in San Diego the work that we have done is paying off. We're seeing that, if we stick together as a beer community—focus on education and telling people what makes craft beer different; it's tasty, complex, pairs better with food than wine—all those things are true and people are realizing it and learning.

Nick: What do you see in this industry five years, ten years from now?

Pat: While I always like to be optimistic—there's plenty of room out there—I also know that the cream will rise to the top. If you aren't making quality beer you won't be around very long. That's just the nature of the business. When you are in a region where there's nothing but really good craft beer around you and you aren't keeping up, people just won't patronize you. If people are passing you by in the quality department, you will be selling your equipment and moving on—going back to your former day job.

> **"If people are passing you by in the quality department, you will be selling your equipment and moving on—going back to your former day job."**

Nick: What do you guys see for Alpine? What's next for Alpine moving forward?

Pat: We are trying to expand and it's in response to the demand that's been projected at us. I can't emphasize enough how much demand there is for our beer out there because we get phone calls, emails, bribery attempts, solicitations, you name it. It's being thrown our way to get us to try and sell people beer and of course that takes more beer being made.

Nick: Are you worried that if you were to take someone on like a private investor that you'll lose what's so cool about this company that you built?

Pat: Not at all. That's because I have specific growth designs. A plateau that is extraordinarily low by most people's standards. I don't ever intend to lose the craft beer qualities of our beer. It will always be a hands-on brewery. That's just because I know what got us here and I'm not going to fuck that up.

Nick: You seem to focus a lot of your business on staying local and being part of the local community. Is that a strategy?

Pat: Well, it doesn't make sense for us to focus sales on areas we can't sustain or where there aren't going to be returning customers. What pays our bills are our repeat customers. There's nothing more complex than that. I'm going to take care of the people that are taking care of us. I started Alpine Beer Company to sell beer to the people in Alpine. If you come from outside the area, great. Just know that our focus here is on the people that are going to keep our lights on.

Nick: Is there anything that no one's ever asked you that you've always wanted to say in an interview?

Pat: No. I'm not all that flamboyant. I have principles, pretty straight on stuff like that, but if I wanted to say something I would've already said it by now.

Mark Carpenter
Anchor Brewing Company

Mark Carpenter is the brewmaster at Anchor Brewing Company in San Francisco, a company he's been part of for more than four decades.

Nick: So, take me through your history; bring me back to the first time you remember being interested in beer.

Mark: I've been a beer drinker for as long as I can remember. As long as I was able to drink alcohol, it was beer. If I was ever in a city that had breweries, I'd always try to visit those breweries because they were just fun places to be and to visit. In 1970, I took a tour of the Anchor Brewing Company. It was at 541 8th Street at the time. In 1971, I thought that Anchor might be a fun place to work while I figure out what I'm going to do with my life. I actually went by and asked for a job and I just happened to be at the right place at the right time.

I got to meet Fritz Maytag. We talked and we got along and he wound up hiring me. At the time there were a total of five people at Anchor: Fritz's secretary and three of us in the brewery. We didn't brew much beer those first years. I think the first year was about a thousand barrels, but we had a 57-barrel brew size, so we were brewing once every three weeks or so. It was a perfect environment for learning brewing. It was really an unbelievable opportunity. Then the brewery started to grow. Fritz had a lot of trouble selling the beer at first, but he started to build quality in the beer and got out there and sold it.

I think 1974 was his first profitable year. We really started to grow after that and realized we were going to outgrow that building. In 1977, we found this site that was the Chase and Sandborn Coffee plant, but it's a beautiful building. It really looks like a brewery when you approach it, so it was the perfect choice. Fritz bought the building and it took us until 1979 to actually move in. Our first brew here was August 13, 1979.

Nick: So you've been here for 43+ years.

Mark: Yes.

Nick: During that span has anything really changed in terms of how you guys operate?

Mark: At the old brewery, we only made Anchor Steam Beer. Over the years, as we started developing all these other beers—our barleywine, our liberty ale, our wheat beer—so many of them were the very first of their varieties in America. Liberty ale—probably the most copied beer in the world—uses the Cascade hop as an aroma hop. This really became a West Coast flavor in pale ale, but now it's since moved around the world. Now you can find Cascade hops in beers brewed in England and on the continent, which I find just amazing that we're exporting our hops to Europe.

What's changed over the years is just the number of beers that we've done. The brewery has grown quite a bit, adding a lot more employees. Fritz always wanted it to be a very traditional brewery in the sense of having a copper brew house, using only whole hops, and open fermentation. In the early days when we didn't have any competition from other craft brewers, our competition was the big brewers and we had to set ourselves apart. Some of the ways we did that was to go all malt because all the big brewers used corn or rice.

It was those types of things that set us apart from the major brewers, and still today: It seems to now set us apart from many of the craft brewers that are all stainless steel and pellets and whatnot. We try to be a traditional brewery wherever we can. We obviously are modern wherever it's important to be modern.

> **"Liberty ale—probably the most copied beer in the world—uses the Cascade hop as an aroma hop."**

Nick: So, did you guys think at the time that you were going to be trailblazing? That this path would eventually lead to American craft beer? What was the feeling inside the brewery during those beginning years?

Mark: I didn't see what was coming. That's for sure. At the time when I started with the brewery, there were three other breweries in San Francisco, Lucky Lager, Burgermeister, and Hamm's—all big brewers and no small brewers on the horizon. Fritz really did see what was going on. Very early on, as early as 1973, I questioned why we were doing these other beers, and he said that down the road there's going to be lots of small brewers around the U.S.

Fritz really did create it. I think he really did create this entire industry. If he had never been around, would it have happened? Maybe, but in what form? Probably not the same form it is today. Steam beer set the path for more unusual brews. I think had Fritz not been here, the revival would have been more continental type beers, maybe some English ales.

Nick: What is Fritz like?

Mark: He's just an amazing guy. He's very thoughtful. I've never met a man who had such a long, clear vision of where he wanted to go and stuck to his path. Early on, he passed up many opportunities to grow faster, but I think he felt he wasn't ready. He wanted to grow at his own pace.

Nick: Throughout your career, has he given you any brewing advice that stands out in your mind more than anything else?

Mark: Fritz was the brewmaster here until he retired and so we worked very closely together. He just had a very scientific approach. If anything, he taught me the importance of a good scientific approach. Fritz always said: "we don't make beer, we just get all the ingredients together and let the yeast make the beer."

Nick: A lot of brewers say brewing is a perfect mix between science and creativity. Do you put yourself on one end of that spectrum?

Mark: I think, yeah, it is between science and creativity and I don't think that brewers get the credit that they deserve. Maybe it's a bit of jealousy, but the winemakers seem to get all this credit for being real "artists," but brewers don't. For one thing, with a winemaker, every year their wine can have a different flavor because it's the production of that year. Brewers have ongoing products, though. When we make more batches, it's different malt, different hops every year, yet we have to make sure our products taste the same. If you bought an Anchor Steam and you go to get another one, you don't want to hear, "well, this is the 2012 Anchor Steam. You like the 2011."

> **"Fritz always said: 'We don't make beer, we just get all the ingredients together and let the yeast make the beer.'"**

Nick: How do you go about creating a new beer in terms of the recipe formation? Is there a certain way that you tackle a new recipe?

Mark: It mainly starts with the idea of the beer that we want to create. Then we'll try to research if we're doing a beer that already exists. For instance, our mild that we recently did: I knew I wanted to do a mild and I didn't want to do an American version of the mild. I wanted to do an English mild, a classic English mild. You start to research about milds and then

you make your choices. We used sugar in our mild because many small (and large) English brewers do use sugar. They would make fun of Americans for using corn and rice, but they would use sugar. They'd been doing it since the 1700s, so I guess it was okay. If you do it long enough, it's okay. I did want to use sugar. I actually used a dark invert sugar, and malt.

We come up with a recipe that we think is going to give us what we want. We don't have a pilot brew house here, so we work pretty hard at getting the recipe that's going to work for us. Then we make a beer and it'll be our full-size batch of beer. If—when we taste it in the cellar—if we've really missed our mark, we can go back and correct with the second beer and then blend those to where we want it and go on from there. With the mild, when I brought it up to the lab to taste it—I was thinking, "okay now, I've got to look now for what I want different or what's wrong." As soon as I tasted it, it just hit me that it was a mild. I could have closed my eyes and been standing in an English pub.

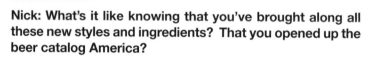

Nick: What's it like knowing that you've brought along all these new styles and ingredients? That you opened up the beer catalog America?

Mark: I think that we're proud of it. There're so many good creative brewers out there who have taken those styles and gone on to make even better versions of that style. Plus tastes in those styles change so much. When we first made our Liberty ale it was just a radically hopped beer. People would drink that and they'd say, "oh man, this has so many hops. We can't drink this." We haven't changed the recipe, but by today's standards it's pretty tame.

Nick: It seems like California has been one of those states that's been an epicenter for craft beer growth. What do you think it is about California that has made this possible?

Mark: It certainly started in California, and I think that has to do with the West. The West is just more open to new stuff. California's always been, I think, more creative than the East Coast. The whole micro-brewing movement took a long time to take hold in the east. Now it's going nuts.

Nick: Can you discuss why you guys use open fermentation and why, in your opinion, there aren't more breweries going that route?

Mark: We do open fermentation because it's traditional to our brewery. Steam beer was always made in shallow open fermenters and so we stuck to that. When it came time to put in an ale fermenter, yeah we did a traditional ale from them, much deeper, but a square open fermenter. We do it because that's traditional to brewing. I think there are many drawbacks

"The west is just more open to new stuff. California's always been, I think, more creative that way than the East Coast."

with open fermentation, especially the cleaning. They have to be hand cleaned. I think most brewers don't want to invest the space for open fermentation and don't want to invest in the labor to do open fermentation. They go to unit tanks. It just makes life easier.

Nick: So what are the advantages?

Mark: There are a couple of advantages to open fermentation. When I'm walking past the fermenters in the morning, I can see if I have a problem right away. I don't have to wait to see a lab result or something. I can walk into the fermenting room and smell it and tell if everything's going okay.

Nick: What's exciting you right now in beer world?

Mark: Just all the different beers coming out now. I mean, it's all over the map. At first, small brewers did English ales, all different varieties. Then they started inventing a lot of goofy beers, most of which were apricot, chocolate ale. Then that trend went away and the brewers started to look at Belgian style beers and more Belgian styles were brewed. There are more German styles being brewed now, but still that's the lowest category. Also they are using bacteria and barrel aging, so there's just going to be all kinds of experimenting.

Nick: Are you guys playing around with anything like that?

Mark: We've done barrel aging because we have our whiskey barrels, but we've done it in a much smaller way than most brewers because we've only used our own barrels. We get them right when we empty the whisky out of them so they still have a lot of whisky in the wood. Our barrel-aged beers do have a great flavor. We haven't don't any sour beers or bacteria beers. It's not to say we won't in the future: we just haven't gotten around to it yet. We have a couple of ideas for things we want to do in the future that may be a little different.

Nick: Anchor is under new management as of recently?

Mark: Yep. Three years.

Nick: Has that affected how the brewery operates at all? Are you guys kind of excited about your new partnership?

Mark: Yeah. The new owners are Tony Foglio and Keith Greggor. Both are great guys and I think they have a long vision something like Fritz's for the brewery. They do want to grow

it. Fritz was always happy if we were just growing a tiny bit. I think Keith and Tony would like to see it grow a little more than that. They asked us to create some other beers, which we have. It's going just great.

Nick: There are plans for some expansion, then?

Mark: Oh yeah. We can expand here. We still haven't filled this place. It may look like it when you walk around, but we're going to put in some more fermenters. We'll be growing here, but we're also looking for other sites around the city for maybe a second location. We also own the property across the street, so we could always expand over there.

Nick: Keeping it in this area is important?

Mark: Yeah, I think so for our brewery. I've seen a lot of our competitors going to the East Coast—places like North Carolina. Maybe somewhere down the road we would do that, but we're still a pretty small brewery. I think our growth will be here in the city for the foreseeable future.

Nick: What advice would you give to the next generation of brewers just coming up?

Mark: Get as much science education as you can. So many young people come to me today and ask "how?"—they want to get into brewing and they want to know how to do it. They've graduated from college and they're a communications major and that's fine, but you really do need a scientific background, even more than I have. I was really lucky working for Fritz. He sent us to various schools around the country, but the more science, the better.

Fal Allen
Anderson Valley Brewing Company

Fal Allen is the brewmaster for Anderson Valley Brewing Company located in Boonville, California.

Nick: Tell me about when you first remember enjoying craft beer. And how did that take you to where you are today?

Fal: I grew up in Hawaii where there wasn't a lot of beer choice or beer diversity. There weren't a lot of beer choices or diversity anywhere in the U.S., but it was particularly bad in Hawaii where everything had to be shipped in. The first craft beer I remember having is probably Watney's Red Barrel. It was from a home brew friend of mine. He made his own beer, too and that was my first introduction to the concept of being able to make your own beer.

Many years went by and a lot of beers in between before I started home brewing, which I did in the early '80s some time, '83 or '84, and I home brewed for a few years.

In 1988 I got a job at Redhook. I worked days for Redhook and nights at a bar. The brewmaster there at the time, Rick Buchanan, took me under his wing and I got to do a lot of different jobs around the brewery.

From there, in the 1990, I went to work for Pike Place Brewery. It was a very small four-barrel brewery, in Pike Place Market. Fortunately, for me, the guy who owned it, Charles Finkel, had all these great connections. He was a beer importer and had been since the early '70s. He had all these connections with European breweries and all these beer people in what was then a very nascent industry of craft brewing.

He understood beer and he knew a lot of people. We traveled to Europe and met with them. I met a lot of industry people that I never would have otherwise. He was friends with Michael Jackson (the writer, not the singer), and I got to meet Michael. Later, Michael and I became friends. I don't think any of that would have happened had I not worked for Charles Finkel, so I was very, very fortunate to work for him.

In 2000, I came to work at Anderson Valley Brewing for about five years. The previous owner and I did not work well together, so I left in 2004 and took some time off. In 2005 I got in job in Singapore working for Asia Pacific Brewing, which again was very lucky. Going to Singapore and working there changed a lot of things for me.

Going to Asia was really a great experience. It reinvigorated how I felt about my career. When I arrived, there was no brewery, just a big field of grass. I helped design and build the building and designed the equipment, helped with the installation and later I designed and brewed the beers. I was their brand ambassador for the first four years.

Asia Pacific brewing is very big—they have 30 other breweries in Asia, so they had a good amount of money to spend on the project. I became their R&D brewer for some of their experimental stuff, which was interesting and a lot of fun.

They sent me to different places, like Vietnam and India. It was a great experience.

I loved my time in Asia but it was nice to come back to the United States after five years there. It's an exciting time to be in the industry now. I was very fortunate to come back to Anderson Valley. I got a lot of experience in Asia and I learned a lot about myself and about other people.

Nick: How did being in Asia influence your brewing or brewing philosophies?

Fal: I was able to design the equipment and brew the beers—that was a good experience. They wanted beers that were unusual and they wanted to incorporate the Asian cooking tradition with the European brewing tradition and fuse them together.

I learned a lot about Asian spices and cooking. Because I grew up in Hawaii, I thought I knew a lot about Asia—but really I knew very little.

The food in Singapore is probably the most diverse in the world. Eating is the Singaporean national pastime. They take eating very seriously in a way that Americans don't understand. In Asia, eating is a lot more than just about putting something in your stomach. There's always a social piece tied to it. I tied all that into my brewing.

Nick: Tell me about your recipe development process. Is it ingredient driven or is there an end product in mind and then you go through ingredients that will fit that?

Fal: Both. It depends on the beer. Sometimes somebody says, "Let's try this in a beer." For example, we have a beer that has lemongrass in it. So we built a beer around the idea of using lemongrass without being overpowering. Other days somebody says, "I want to make this style of beer," so we build a beer around the style.

When I design beers at other breweries, and at this brewery, we do it as a team. I think that way you get better beers.

Nick: Are there characteristics that you like all of your beers to have?

Fal: We want to achieve balance and we want our beers to be clean. I think everybody wants that, but not everybody achieves it—we don't always achieve it. Not every beer is a homerun. For example; we wanted to brew a beer with redwood tips, . . . So I called Brian [Hunt] one day and said, "Would you mind if we did that? It's your idea and we don't want to steal that from you." He's said, "No, no, it would be cool. Why don't you come down, I'll show you what I do." We went down and visited Brian, talked about it and he showed me what he did. We came back up to Anderson Valley and brewed a redwood batch, got it ready, packaged it, and brought it to our test panel. The owner was like, "I don't know. I don't get it. I don't get the redwood."

The second batch had twice as much redwood and he said the same things, "It's good beer, but I don't get it. We have to have some reason for people to drink this beer. It's redwood—so we have to be able to taste the redwood." We ended up brewing four different batches of this beer, each with more redwood—the fourth was too strong and the three previous not strong enough—so we thought; now we have these four beers, we don't know what the hell to do with them. They were good beers all, I don't want to dump it down the drain. . .

Our lab manager, Andy, said, "Why don't we blend them and sour all of it." So, we took these beers and like they do in Belgium we soured half of it in stainless and half in wood

and then blended them back together after about nine months. Now, I think it's fantastic. It's one of the most interesting beers we've made in years. We took what could have been a loser and made a winner out of it.

Nick: What do you look for in beers?

Fal: If a home brewer asked me: "How do I make my beers better?" I'd tell them, "You have to be super clean. A lot of times the flavors are all jumbled together and you don't really get clear distinct flavors. I think your flavor should be like a wave; hops, then malt, instead of just this jumble of flavors, which some beers can have. We try and look for distinct variation in the flavors so one gets different experiences as they drink the beer.

We also try to keep our beers dry. A lot of beers are sweet and I think that takes away from their drinkability.

Nick: Do you think there's a craft beer revolution underway in America today?

Fal: I wouldn't call it a craft beer revolution. The revolution already happened. It's a second wave, no doubt, or even a third wave. It's a great thing, but I wouldn't call it a revolution. The revolution was when guys like Ken Grossman started brewing and changed the way people think about beer. That was the revolution because those kinds of beers were just unheard of at the time. People didn't know you could make beer like that: they didn't get it. Mike Hale, Ken Grossman and a handful of other guys—they were true the revolutionaries.

Nick: Why the surge in popularity now, though?

Fal: When I started brewing, we'd go to beer events and they were predominantly middle-aged, overweight white guys who were home brewers and that's all there was.

When I got back from Asia a couple of years ago, I went to an event in San Francisco. It had to be nearly half women, which is pretty awesome. Mainstream beer in general has ignored women, but not craft beer.

And all those middle-aged white guys, they all had kids and the kids grew up drinking their dad's craft beer. Now these kids are 21 to 35 and the demographic of the craft beer drinker has changed. The median age used to be 40 or 45 and now it's like 26 to 35. It went from being mostly Caucasians to a much broader spectrum of people. It also went from being mostly men to about 40% women.

Nick: Can you explain your logo?

Fal: What happens when a bear and a deer mate…?

Nick: What do you get?

Fal: A Beer.

Nick: Exactly. I want to talk to you about Anderson Valley being environmentally conscious. Is that very important to you guys?

Fal: It is definitely important to us. It's important to me personally and it's important to the owner, Trey White, and it's important to everyone who works here. I think being environmentally responsible (I hate the word *sustainable*) it's a great thing. Everybody should be doing it, and one of the best reasons is because it's not just good for the planet, it's also good for your business.

Anderson Valley brewing put up 648 solar panels. It costs us infrastructure to put it up there but it paid for itself in a few years. And now we're producing about 40% of our electricity—basically for free.

Part of the reason we do some of these things is because we have to. Other breweries have options that we don't. We don't have municipal sewer. We don't have municipal water or municipal waste collection of any sort. We generate all of our own water. We treat all of our own wastewater, then we use it to irrigate our crops or our ornamentals around the brewery. We try to recycle everything we can so we don't have to truck it out of here and put it in a landfill.

Nick: Let's talk about the Boonville Festival. Tell me a little bit about it and why it's important to you guys.

Fal: It started out as just a gathering of friends, a few brewers from around the area getting together to have beers, but it has morphed into something else, something much larger.

In the beginning, the first one was held here at the brewery. It was just like, "Hey, let's get together and have a few beers. We'll invite some of our brewer friends." Then it became a bigger thing and other people started coming and we moved it down the street. And now it's quite a big festival. We get about 85 breweries to come out each year.

The previous owner wanted to take all the money that we generated from the festival and give it back to the non-profits in the area. Today, we generate about $100,000 every year and give it back to the community, and I think that's a great thing and that's one of the main reasons we keep doing this festival, even though it is so much work.

Nick: Let's talk about you, now. What is it about beer that keeps you getting up in the morning and coming here to brew it? Why is beer so special?

Fal: One of the reasons I chose this profession is because I really like making something, although I don't physically brew as often as I'd like anymore. I enjoy making beer and I enjoy making stuff. One of the things that I used to really enjoy when I got off my shift at Pike Place was that they had a little pub. I'd go up and sit at the end of the bar and I'd listen to what people had to say about the beer. It was really gratifying to see people enjoying what I had been making, so I think that's what keeps me going.

Nick: Tell our readers something interesting they don't know, would you?

Fal: Are you familiar with Boontling?

Nick: No.

Fal: The Anderson Valley was so isolated that its people developed their own language called Boontling. It is a real American lingo, like Creole down south.

Boontling is so unique that they used it as a code language during World War I, like they used Navajo during World War II.

> **"Boontling is so unique that they used it as a code language during World War I…"**

If you're not from the valley, you would never know what people speaking Boontling were talking about. The brewery tries to keep that tradition alive because the tradition of speaking it is dying out—there are not a lot of Boonters who know much Boontling anymore and can speak Boontling, so we try to keep it alive with the beer names we have.

Nick: What are some examples?

Fal: Most of our beer names like Boont Amber. Boont is the word for "Boonville" in Boontling. The Poleeko Pale Ale; *Poleeko* is the word for the next town down called Philo. Hop Ottin', Ottin' means hardworking, so Hop Ottin' is a hardworking hop. There's a bunch of them. We go little crazy with some names. We have one called Feather Leggy Bull Rusher.

Nick: Oh?

Fal: Oh, yeah. "Feather Leggy" is someone who is talky or arrogant. And "Bull Rusher" is an orphan, so Feather Leggy Bull Rusher is "arrogant bastard."

Nick: That's awesome. That's really cool.

Fal: Oh, yeah. We wanted to name a beer Arrogant Bastard, but we knew that Greg would be unhappy with us if we did, so we did it in Boontling.

Jeff Bagby
Bagby Beer Company

Jeff Bagby has been brewing for nearly 20 years and is one of San Diego's most award-winning brewers. Recently, he started his own enterprise, Bagby Beer Company in Oceanside.

Nick: What were your first experiences with craft beer and how did you wind up here today?

Jeff: The first time I really experienced craft beer was in college. It was there that I realized craft beers tasted much better than the crap beer we are drinking out of kegs or cans. So we paid attention to that. This was '93. I went to UC Santa Barbara.

My favorites back then are still some of my favorites now: Anchor Steam, and definitely Sierra Nevada Pale Ale, which was throughout college. Junior and senior year of school . . . at Santa Barbara we would have a keg of Sierra Nevada Pale Ale on tap at our house the entire time. The only other beer that was ever on tap was our home brew.

> **"If you'd asked me back then, "Are you going to pursue this? Are you going to become a brewer professionally or anything like that?" I would have laughed my ass off."**

It just started like any kind of hobby or interest does. You want to learn about it, you want to see it, you want to explore it, you want to see who's making it, and how it's made. I just fueled this energy into, "Well, maybe we can try and make this stuff." We started at the bottom. We bought a kit at Home Brew Mart at Solana Beach back when it was just south of Pizza Port. We experimented with the extract, read, learned, and visited breweries. We were 20 years old asking to talk to brewers, asking to talk to anybody that would listen to us or answer our questions. This is before the age of the internet and email. You couldn't Google a beer name, it took some time, it took some phone calls. It took writing letters (believe it or not) to get information, to get a coaster, to get a t-shirt, or to get somebody to just go, "Cool, you're a fan of our brewery. Here's some info. Here's a catalog, here's the menu, here's the coaster."

Then we really got into home brewing. By the time I was in my junior and senior year, we had our own beer on draft at our house. We were using all-grain, we were experimenting with all the different new [yeast] strains and different hops that we could get our hands on. It was really good and fun.

If you'd asked me back then, "Are you going to pursue this? Are you going to become a brewer professionally or anything like that?" I would have laughed my ass off. Back then, I had no idea in the world I'd be where I am today. I was just a fan of beer and thought brewing was really cool.

When Stone Brewing opened, they were looking to hire a driver. I actually went to their first-ever public tapping at Pizza Port in Solana Beach. I think there were 10 people there. Later I went in and interviewed with Greg Koch. I sat down and after interviewing and talking about my experience and what I had done, he said, "Honestly, this is perfect." He said, "You're into beer. You already heard of us. You had our first tapping. You're familiar with the craft beer industry. You're totally hired."

I drove a beer truck for a couple of months and then I went to the Strong Ale Festival at Pizza Port in Carlsbad. I went with Steve Wagner who was the co-founder of Stone and he said, "I know you're really interested in beer. You're interested in the process." He invited me to come in and talk with the brewers, Lee Chase, and himself and ask some questions and see what was going on. He's said, "How'd you like to come in and work in the brewery. We're going to need another person and we're only growing." I was like, "Dude, I'll be there whenever you want me there."

That was my first experience in professional brewing. That was at the end of 1997. I became more and more involved in the brewing side. At Stone I learned: I could brew a batch on my own, I could filter a batch on my own, learn how to operate the four-head bottling machine that they had back then—they only did 22-ounce bottles. I was a part of the design of the first Old Guardian and some of the anniversary beers. It was an exciting time and it was cool to be a part of this thing that was obviously growing and was doing well and was slowly making its name in San Diego.

I left Stone, and took a job at the Y which, even though I knew Stone was growing, the opportunity at the Y seemed bigger and more promising to me for a career. But I only worked at the Y for maybe nine months. It just wasn't working out for me. I didn't like it at all.

After taking a little time off, I got a job working for White Labs, and that was great. They were awesome and we're still good friends.

Then an opportunity came up to get back into a brew house, it was with Tomme [Arthur] in Solana Beach. I want to say that was around 2000, or so. I was involved in cleaning, filling, and delivering kegs, brewing, events, everything. That was good, I learned a lot from Tomme. That was an amazing experience for me, but it was tough. I did not make much money at all for a long time. Eventually I got a bartending shift at Solana, which helped out, and I just loved it. It was a fun job, close to where I lived, and I just enjoyed doing what I was doing, and was learning a lot. I was much more comfortable in the brew house, making recipes and handling the brewery. I also handled the brewery when Tomme was gone.

Nick: Were you starting to think about recipe development at that point?

Jeff: Definitely, yes. What can we do with different types of Belgian beer? What can we do with hops? And what can we do as IPAs and pale ales? The only thing that we didn't do much there was lager. I kind of brought that in, or tried to bring more of that in, when I finally got to Carlsbad. Lagers are slower and take up space and tank time.

At this point, I felt confident that I could become a head brewer for somebody—the industry still wasn't as crazy as it is now. Not a lot of people were hiring head brewers, but it turned out Tom Nickel, another good friend of mine who I had met through Pizza Port channels and beer channels, was working for Oggi's at that time. Tom told me they were looking for a brewer. The owner was really cool and so I took the job. I was the only person doing anything with the beer there, so everything that happened was me. It was the time where I really got to hone in on recipes and what I wanted to do, including selecting the ingredients I wanted to use. I got to just play around while, at the same time, I could polish up

their house beers the way I wanted to and experiment a little bit and just be a head brewer. It was great.

Then a position at Pizza Port Carlsbad came up; It was more opportunity for me, opportunity to make more beer, opportunity to be in charge of people, to have an assistant to grow and to help out. They needed somebody full time and they wanted somebody who was familiar with them and the company. It was a win-win for everybody and it was exciting. Gina [Marsaglia] had been so awesome in letting me do what I did there—I'm proud of the beers that I made and the people that we hired.

After I had been at Pizza Port for a while, I began to seriously thing that I can do this on my own. It came to a point where I told Gina and Vince, "I have to do this. I have to see if I can do it." I'm the type of person that wants to run my own place and I want to do this on my own. They respected that. It wasn't like there were any bad feelings there, it was just, "Okay, I understand that. Go do it." That's where we are.

Since then, I've learned a lot about commercial real estate, about licensing, about investment, business plans, banking, you name it. I knew that was coming, I was fully prepared for long waits and disappointments. This is the second property that we were really serious about. We lost the first one. That was a big blow—we lost a lot of time and money. It was hard to swallow, but then I talk to other people about how many locations they had gone through before they found their spot.

Nick: You've been responsible for a lot of GABF medals. What do you attribute those successes to?

Jeff: Awards are an interesting thing. They're definitely an affirmation of your hard work and of your abilities—especially the GABF, because you're being judged by many of your peers. Other brewers, other industry people, are the ones judging those beers and they're completely blind. There's no bias there, especially if you have a beer that's won medals over certain years on more than one GABF—or more than one color medal. That is a pretty clear indicator that beer is really good. It wasn't a fluke, it wasn't a one time thing, it wasn't just one single batch of beer. We made this beer and then we made it again, and again.

I don't know, obviously, it's fun to win and it's an amazing feeling. The first time I won a brewer of the year award it was with Tomme in Solana Beach. Then I won with with Tom Nickel at Oggi's. But the first big one that really hit me hard was the 2009 one in Carlsbad. It just it floored me and it blew me away.

> **"I always strive to make each one of my beers better."**

I'm a modest person, but a lot of guys worked for me. I have a philosophy about making beer and the way it should go. The resources that I've had, the dozen or so people that I called mentors, people that I've learned from, have helped me out along the way and there's a long list of those people. I tried to learn from them and then apply that in my job and in my brewing and then I tried to pass it on to the guys that worked for me. A lot of those guys have gone on to do great things on their own.

Nick: What exactly is your brewing philosophy?

Jeff: Attention to detail. To me, I always strive to make each one of my beers better—fine tuning things and process, paying attention to ingredients, making sure that our malt was the best it could be, making sure our quality was the best it could be, learning how different yeast strains work and how their lifecycles go, and learning at what temperatures they ferment and produce the most desirable results.

Nick: When you're coming up with a new beer, is it more ingredient based for you or is it more style-driven?

Jeff: I would say, when I look to build a new beer, I look for a base style. I say, "We're going to make some sort of pale ale. It could be extra pale, or American strong, or Imperial IPA, or just IPA. It could be an English IPA, or a hoppy Belgian pale ale." That's very, very broad. You start with that and then you go, "What do we think would work well with what? And our end goal is what?" Tomme tought me this: you look at the beer in layers. You look at your aroma, how does it smell?

How does it look when you get it in a glass? Is it going to be bright, is it going to be slightly hazy, is it going to be black as night, or is it going to be bright and clear and light colored?

You look at it first, and then you consider how it will feel. Is it going to be heavy? Is it going to be carbonated by the CO_2 bubbles? Is it going be thin? Is it going to linger in your mouth? Is it going to fall off real quick? Is it going to have alcohol warmth? Is it going to be light in alcohol? You just look at all the elements and, knowing your ingredients, you can pinpoint different things that you know are going to produce certain results. You work backwards, you look at beers that you've made before and you pull out elements from them. "I like this percentage of this malt in this beer with this yeast at this time, et cetera, et cetera." Or this hop aroma and this hop bitterness with this yeast, different things like that. That's how I create new beers.

Nick: Is there any topic we haven't discussed that you would like to cover?

Jeff: I guess I just want people to know how thankful I am for this industry and to be a part of it. The only reason I'm where I am now is because of the friends that I've made along the way. They've taught me more than I ever could learn in a classroom or from a book, and that's a big thing for me. They've passed it on to me and hopefully I've done that to some of the guys that have worked with me. That seems to be the tradition that I learned long ago in this industry and I'm extremely thankful for that. I definitely wouldn't be where I am without it.

Colby Chandler
Ballast Point Brewing and Spirits

Colby Chandler is the specialty brewer and executive director of Ballast Point Brewing & Spirits/Home Brew Mart, a company he's been with for more than 17 years.

Nick: Tell me what first piqued your interest in brewing.

Colby: My Father went to the University of Washington in the 70's, so they were always into the local craft beer scene around there. I don't know how craft it was, but Rainier, Olympia—that was their local brand. My dad was in the Navy. He traveled to Europe a bunch so he was always shipping back beers from Europe, which got me into those bolder flavors. They moved back to Seattle right around the time I could drink legally. I remember going to Big Time Brewery & Alehouse in Seattle and they'd literally have three IPAs on tap—that was probably '88 or '89. I was like, "Oh, what's this? You got another one. What's that?" And they were all really good. It's what I had been looking for, this nice hoppiness in the beer. So that got me into craft beer tasting more and more. I lived in Hawaii for about 11 years, then I moved to San Diego. I had a family friend who was home brewing. I was in the restaurant business at that point, I liked home cooking, and thought it would be an easy transition for me to cook up some beer. So I started home brewing. I home brewed for about three years before I got a job at Home Brew Mart. A year later, in 1997, I was offered a full time position and was the third brewer to brew at Ballast Point Brewing. The original brewer, Peter A'hearn, and then Yuseff Cherney were before me.

Nick: And how did you get the luckiest job of becoming the specialty brewer?

Colby: I like creating different types of beers. Being able to brew stuff that I can't find on the market—that's what drives me. Home Brew Mart customers and expanding ingredient selection provided a lot of inspiration, too.

Nick: Do you remember the first home brew that you tried to make and how that turned out?

Colby: It was an extract pale ale (MacTarnahan's Amber clone). It was from Ocean Beach Home Brewing Supplies. Basically, I remember the instructions were written out on the back of a business card. And it was horribly over carbonated but you could definitely taste the hops in there. It wasn't perfect—probably not finished out and not done fermenting—but it was good. It definitely got the bug going.

Nick: What was your first specialty beer?

Colby: Probably Crystal Pier Double IPA. I remember the first time serving it—it was at the second annual Strong Ale Festival at Pizza Port in December of 1998. I think we added a little bit of Belgian candied sugar in there to boost up the alcohol. It was a hoppy 8% ABV beer with all Crystal hops. So the first couple of runs of it was called Crystal Pier Double IPA. Today that beer is known as Dorado Double IPA.

And, back then I had never had a double IPA. I had heard of Russian River Brewing's Blind Pig and Pliney the Elder, those may have just started to be brewed but I don't think I had had it yet.

Nick: What's the wisdom you like to impart to home brewers?

Colby: Learn the process before you start messing with the ingredients and the recipe. You have to make clean beer before you know what a hop tastes like, otherwise you're tasting off flavors and things in the beer. People always come in as beginning home brewers at Home Brew Mart and they say, "Hey, I want to do a triple IPA," right off the bat. It's hard enough for us to do a triple IPA. Let's learn the ingredients, learn the process a little bit, learn how to wrangle the yeast and manage them and then go from there. Then we can start building upon your knowledge to make recipes a little bit better for you and start customizing your beer. Keep it simple and follow a recipe.

We're 22 years at Home Brew Mart right now. So, there's a reason we've been around so long. We're selling good recipes. We don't sell premade kits, so you can tweak it whichever way you want for the most part. But until you know that this is a clean beer, you fermented it right, it's clean and everything was sanitary; then with that one recipe then you can use that as a template. My favorite thing was to get a recipe that I really liked, just change the hops, just do all single hops, and then you know exactly what all those hops taste like. Just like a chef, you have to taste your ingredients and work with them.

> **"Just like a chef, you have to taste your ingredients and work with them."**

Nick: Do you have any overriding philosophy or principles that you follow when you're trying to come up a new beer?

Colby: Different ways to get to the end product. Jack White, the owner, plays bagpipes for the House of Scotland and they do the Scottish Highland Games in Vista here in San Diego County. Jack wanted a beer that we could serve at the Games and serve at various places like at the ballpark and other events. So we did Piper Down Scottish Ale, that's how Piper Down came about. I had a recipe that I was playing with that we moved into a Scottish ale and it's been around ever since.

In 2006 we split up into two breweries, the production brewery and the original here at Home Brew Mart. A couple of the hard workers from Home Brew Mart were winning home brew awards, one was the manager and the other was my assistant brewer. We had a small fermenter that we could just play with a little bit. They both had a great IPA recipe. One of them won gold with a single IPA, the other with a double. I looked at their recipes and they were real similar. So we combined the two. I put in some hops that I really liked, and brewed it on the big system. That was Sculpin IPA. So that's another way to go about it.

Nick: You did a beer based on the palates of the different native populations here, right?

Colby: For that particular beer I wanted to do something with ingredients that you would have found when Juan Rodriguez Cabrillo landed on Ballast Point in San Diego harbor. To do that, I did a lot of research on the Kumeyaay People that populated Mission Valley, from the ocean all the way up to Mt. Laguna. So I started researching what ingredients they were eating and what they were making teas and things out of. And then I slowly started narrowing down those flavor profiles into what I thought was a certain style. I wanted to do a play on a farmhouse ale—like a Kumeyaay farmhouse ale. So elderberries, elder flowers, manzanita berries, white sage, they were all thick around water springs. I got honey from Hillaker Farms so it's a local honey from East County. Pine nuts by harvest at a secret Costco location in Mission Valley. (I'm not going and picking pine nuts out of pine cones because that's a little ridiculous.) And then I'm also using a barley that's grown in California just because I can. And then a hops from Star B Buffalo Ranch and Hop Farm which is out in east county as well. So I'm trying to take as many local ingredients and indigenous ingredients to do something that, theoretically, would be close what was going on back then.

> ## "Everybody figured if we make better beer drinkers, we're all going to do better in the long run."

Nick: Do you have a name for that one?

Colby: It's part of our seasonal San Salvador Series, Summer Saison. And then the other one that I did was the winter black lager, where I picked coastal black sage, California bay leaf, and I used Carlsbad Aquafarms luna oysters.

That's the winter version of the San Salvador Series, so I have a couple more seasons to kind of play with. It's all a matter of if I want to stay as indigenous as I can or if I want to start doing stuff that just grows wild or local. I know I want to do something with Julian apples, but I'm not sure.

Nick: When was the decision made really to ramp up the specialty brewing? No one else that I know really has that.

Colby: Well, it goes back to the roots of the Home Brew store because we opened Home Brew Mart in 1992. In 1996, we installed the equipment that started Ballast Point Brewing Com-

pany. And then we got up to about 6,000 barrels down here before we split off in 2006. We had a couple little fermenters and I was playing around with different styles. So, when we actually split, and the other production facility started going full bore, I started to look at all these recipes that I had stockpiled and had played with. Now, I had all these fermenters down here that weren't designated for production beers anymore, so I was able to ramp it up a little bit. I was still brewing the Wahoo Wheat and the Black Marlin down here for years, so that gave me two other fermenters to play around with that were smaller. I could easily sell what I made to Liar's Club and O'Briens (the two best craft beer bars at the time) and some of the early beer bars around town. And then some of those beers just started getting cult followings as we started increasing production up there. They started moving some of them into the seasonal rotation of the stronger 10% specialty beers. So, yeah, it was sticking with our roots—Home Brew Mart and the creative flavors available—and the fact that I don't want to drink the same beer all the time.

Nick: What accounts for the incredible popularity of craft beer—and especially San Diego craft beer?

Colby: I know, I mean everybody gives credit to Stone and the local home brewing scene for the most part. Stone packaging in bottles and getting it out while having San Diego on the label was definitely the first spotlight on the area. There had been a couple of awards won by La Cruda Brewing and PB Ale House, and they were slowly sprinkling in award-wise, but never really dominating at that point. So then you started getting breweries like AleSmith and Ballast Point opening up right around the same time as Stone. Stone had a much larger budget than any of us at that time, so they got the big kick out of the gate.

Then the breweries in town really started working together with the San Diego Brewers Guild. Suddenly we were in a position to promote San Diego as a beer destination. Everybody figured if we make better beer drinkers, we're all going to do better in the long run. That started moving us forward as a brewing community, and a good consequence was that brewers started knowing other brewers by name and became friends with a common goal. So everybody was able to help each other. Do you need some ingredients? Did you ever think about doing it this way? Can you tell me how to gelatin this? Can I borrow some hops? You could start picking the brain of everybody and it was really easy to share information. I think everybody's beer got better because of it.

I ran the San Diego Brewers Guild for six years with a great team. I was the president. So I helped bring on the brochure/location map—there wasn't a brochure at that time. There wasn't a website, which I fixed. There was also no beer festival that highlighted only San Diego Beer. So I started the San Diego Brewers Guild Festival and ran it for the first six years of the Guild Fest. And then like I said, everybody got together and it became a tighter community. We started winning awards, too. Now, all of a sudden, San Diego is branded as a great place where good beer comes from.

> **"I think there needs to be more talk about beer and food pairing, or using beer as an ingredient."**

Now you're seeing a lot of home brewers and people that work for breweries opening up their own breweries. Now there's a level of experience that wasn't around when we opened up. We almost have the perfect circle . . . you have the home brewer, basically. He starts home brewing and then he opens up his own brewery or craft beer bar. And then, from there, the brewery starts selling to bars that are craft-beer-centric. Those bars start educating the public about the craft beers and where they're coming from and giving customers different choices. Pretty soon they start to hear that you can brew this at your house. They become a home brewer. So then the circle just starts feeding on itself.

Nick: You've been doing this, you said, for 17 years. So, what is it that still gets you up in the morning?

Colby: We have great customers. Home Brew Mart is one of the happiest stores in San Diego. I mean you can't go in and get a beer and go shopping in too many other spaces in the county for sure. So all that makes it easy to come in for the most part. It's nice to hear that people like your product.

Nick: What is it that you've never been asked in an interview that you've always wanted to say?

Colby: I think there needs to be more talk about beer and food pairing, or using beer as an ingredient. I just think that San Diego is way ahead of other cities in that regard. I think the more we can get chefs to realize how close brewers are to chefs, the better the beer and food scene will become. We're like a chef where we can pull ingredients from all over the world and put it into a finished plate, but our plates are an upright glass instead of an actual plate. So, I think the more that chefs get on board with beer and see that a beer can hit any wedge of the whole flavor spectrum—that they can pretty much throw out any food and we can pair a beer with it—then they're going to transmit that enthusiasm to their customers, which, in turn, will get them into craft beer. Maybe those customers would never go out and have a pitcher of a certain type of beer or a big hoppy IPA, but paired with the right food, that might hit. It might trigger that light bulb to go off a little bit. I think the more we get associated with food and chefs and restaurants, the more people will see that—not only can their food be enhanced by pairing it with beer—the beer can also be enhanced by the food, too. So, I would like beer to be a part of more of those conversations.

Yuseff Cherney
Ballast Point Brewing and Spirits

Yuseff Cherney is the head brewer, head distiller, and chief operating officer for Ballast Point Brewing & Spirits. His roots with the company go way back to Home Brew Mart, where Yuseff was the first official employee.

Nick: Tell me how you started brewing. How did you get into all this?

Yuseff: About 22 years ago or so, a friend of mine showed me that it was possible to make beer. There was one store around, in El Cajon, called Beer and Wine Crafts. We headed out there and got a batch. I actually brewed about three batches in a row in succession without tasting the first one, which was a mistake because by the time we got around tasting the first one we realized that it wasn't really what we're after. At that point, we already had craft beers like in Sierra Nevada and Anderson Valley, so I knew there was something better that could be brewed than what I made out of those canned kits.

I was going to the liquor stores and loading up shopping carts full of beers, and sitting down with my friends at a table with a notepad and actually critiquing the beers. Of course, there was pretty much no Internet to put that critique on, so it was just for us. (It was more so we wouldn't buy the same crappy beer twice.) I was going to college at USCD at the time. They have a little craft center there. It's an extension from the university. I was working in a jewelry studio there to make some spare money while I was going to college, and they asked me if I wanted to go ahead and teach a beer brewing class. So it forced me to get really involved in home brewing because I didn't want my students knowing more than me! There were a lot of pre-med and biotech and chemistry majors and stuff from UCSD. So I did a lot of reading in those early years.

One of my first students was Chris White. He's the founder and president of White Labs, one of the biggest yeast suppliers in the business. Back in those days, we got together after the class and hit it off. We ended up brewing at home together and then working on yeast in his laboratory in the wee hours of the morning trying to get some products that we could sell at our home brew shop.

"A lot of breweries, once they get to a certain level, they kind of lose the playfulness of brewing."

In the middle of all that teaching and graduating college, I actually met Jack White, who is no relation to Chris White. He had just started Home Brew Mart down in San Diego (in 1992), which was only the second home brew shop in the region. I went in and met him, we just hit it off, and I was hired the next day. So, fresh out of college, I jumped right into a home brew shop, partnering with Chris White, making yeast on the fly at a lab, and marketing it as Home Brew Mart Ale Yeast and Home Brew Mart Lager Yeast. It was the first readily pitchable yeast to be sold. From there, Chris ended up branching off into his own business, and Home Brew Mart kept chugging away making sales until we had enough money to fund Ballast Point Brewing, which opened in 1996. So that's how I got started—in a big nutshell.

Nick: What were those first three home brew batches? How did they turn out?

Yuseff: I think I was trying to brew like an English style ESB. I like the hoppier beers—pale ale and stuff—and that's what I was after. The home brew shop that gave me the ingredients—they were big on using canned malt extract that was pre-hopped. They also liked using corn sugar as an additive, which, if you know anything about beer, is not really used at all in the craft brewing industry, except maybe to jack up the alcohol. They were using it at a rate of almost half and half, and the resulting beer tasted more like apple cider than it did beer, fermented apple cider.

It's funny, if you talk to a hundred brewers my age, they'll probably all tell you the same thing: That *The Joy of Homebrewing* revolutionized the way they brewed. Every time I see Charlie [Papazian], I shake his hand ever so softly because he's always got a bandage around it because everyone crushes his hand. He definitely made his mark. I mean, I read that book cover to cover multiple times. The tables in there for calculating IBUs and extraction rates and everything—that's exactly where I got my knowledge of how to start doing formula and recipe formulation.

Nick: Talk about how you go about coming up with a new beer. Do you have any overriding principles or philosophies that you always use?

Yuseff: Well, there's a few different ways. Luckily, now we have an experimental brewery and a production brewery. The experimental brewery is run by Colby Chandler, and he's our specialty beer brewer. That's all he does is try to come up with new beers. So that's a big plus for us. A lot of breweries, once they get to a certain level, they kind of lose the playfulness of brewing. They're focused on making two-hundred-barrel batches so they don't say, "Okay well, what if we wanted to do something really crazy?"

But there are other ways. I mean, back when I was doing recipe formulation, typically you would start at a style of beer you like. It's not necessarily that we can make them better, but we might put a twist on them. When you look at Calico Amber Ale, it has an ESB style. That's what it is, but the hopping is in no way an ESB. It's robustly bitter. It's got California or West Coast hops in it. It's a twist on the traditional style of beer. I looked at Fuller's . . . I like Fuller's, but it's a little too sweet. So I thought, let me change that a little bit. Any beer you make is inspired by something, whether it's another beer or even a food. Colby will go and taste some crazy food somewhere and he'll come back and make a beer to go with that food.

Nick: How often would you say that you introduce a new beer?

Yuseff: I don't know. We're introducing new beers that are maybe just a twist on our old beers. Like we'll have Black Marlin Porter, which has been around forever, but then we'll come out with cocoa nib, chipotle Black Marlin. So if you count that as a completely new beer, then it's probably every other month.

If you look at at the tasting bar, we've got about 20 different beers on tap, everything from like the Indra Kunindra, which has cumin and curry and toasted coconut and kaffir lime, to Barmy with apricots and honey. Even tweaks on styles like India Pale Lagers—not an IPA but an actual lager. I think that's one of the hallmarks about Ballast Point in general: we do make a very wide variety of beers. We're not out to make 12 beers and have 9 of them be IPAs. We want to drink varied beers ourselves, too. When we get off work and have a shift beer, at the end I might want a helles. I might want a smoked lager. I might want an IPA. And to have 20-something taps to choose from—and have them be varied from two-three percent all the way up to ten and a half—is nice. You can't drink seven percent beer all day long everyday your whole life.

> **"Any beer you make is inspired by something, whether it's another beer or even a food."**

Nick: Ballast Point has won a ton of awards. What are the accolades you're most proud of?

Yuseff: Well, the GABF and the World Beer Cup is what every brewer aspires to win. Probably our biggest award so far was at the World Beer Cup in 2010. We won the best small brewer category with multiple gold medals that count toward the overall. Taking that medal home in Chicago, that was probably the crowning glory there. For our Calico Amber Ale, we won gold at the GABF, and then six months later won gold at the World Beer Cup. Back to back. So that was definitely one I was jumping up and down about.

Recently, we won back to back at the European Beer Star for Sculpin. All of our beers kind of originated out of home brewing roots, but this one was actually a collaboration of the brewers down at Home Brew Mart. Colby and Doug and George got together and created this recipe. They all had IPAs, and they fused it into this one. Sculpin now is almost like a cult IPA. It's so popular.

So we won the gold medal in Europe, which is kind of weird in itself that they're actually recognizing IPAs in Germany. That really drove the point home for me. To be up on a stage in Germany, accepting a silver medal for an IPA brewed in California with famous German brewers on one side of me was mind boggling.

Nick: What do you attribute these successes to?

Yuseff: I think what it boils down is that everyone that works here is proud of what they do. The passion for the craft and the dedication to everything that we're doing here shows through in the beer. When people come up with recipes, it's not geared to focus groups and stuff like that; it's what we want to drink.

Nick: What do you think about the state of craft beer today? Is there a whole new boom going on?

Yuseff: Well, I think in the '90s there was definitely a boom. My friends built brewing equipment, so I was intimately tied to how much they were selling. The same guys are still around selling brewing equipment these days, and they are like, "This is nothing like the '90s. This is even bigger."

I think the thing that's driving the boom—especially here in San Diego—is the tasting room aspect and the ability for a

brewery to sell the beer out on tap at their retail locations. So a lot of the small guys are making their business more as a tasting room than a delivering brewery. I sometimes wonder if that's a viable business plan. For us it wasn't. We couldn't just survive on the tasting room alone. We needed to sell beer out the back. That was our business model, so we ended up doing self-distribution, which is another reason why there are so many breweries in California: because you're allowed to do it. We don't have the three-tier state here. That opens up the door for all these small breweries to get their stuff out.

> **"I think that's one of the hallmarks about Ballast Point in general: we do make a very wide variety of beers."**

Nick: How do you feel about all these new guys opening up breweries?

Yuseff: There are definitely some guys out there who are coming from other breweries who are opening up their own places. I think those are the guys that are really coming to it with an A game. They've got an idea. And then there are some folks, I think, that are coming from other industries that aren't doing too well. Hopefully they're at least home brewers. But they're experimenting. That's where it gets a little bit scary, because when you come in to the market with an experimental product you could be unleashing that on somebody that's never had craft brew before, and they try something that's just not all quite right, and it turns them off. So you're actually doing an injustice to the industry.

I have to say—to be honest—I don't really understand the nanobrewery concept, unless you have another business. If you're trying to make a go at brewing in San Diego as strictly a nanobrewery with nothing else, it's going to be very difficult. Selling three barrels of beer at a time is a pretty hard business to make successful.

Like I say, it's kind of a dream to a lot of home brewers. Almost every home brewer wants to open up a brewery some day. For some reason, now people are deciding to act on that dream a lot more than they did, maybe, five years ago. Depending on who you're talking to in the industry, some people are saying, "Well, in another couple of years there is going to be a big shakedown, and all these little guys will fall."

Nick: So, what do you see in the next 5 years, 10 years?

Yuseff: I think in 5–10 years you will see some people that are disillusioned by turning their hobby into a business because

it's hard. I mean there's the old adage that you hear all the time: the best way to hate your hobby is to make a job out of it. That definitely can come true if it's done in a way where you're struggling nonstop.

And to get distribution, to get your beer handled . . . Not only are there the games that big distributors play and the big brewers play, but there are loyalties that bar owners have to certain distributors and to certain breweries—for good or for bad. I think it's going to be a little bit of a wake-up call for new breweries when they try to get their beer out the market.

Nick: Why do you think so many breweries have started up in San Diego?

Yuseff: I think if you were going to nail down one thing it would be the fact that San Diego has probably one of the richest home brewing traditions of any city, and that would be the number one reason why there are so many breweries here. You've got QUAFF [Quality Ale Fermentation Fraternity], which is the biggest club in San Diego for home brewers. They've actually won the nationals multiple times. If you look at their base of people, you'll find that a lot of our brewers started in QUAFF.

I also think Home Brew Mart did a lot for the home brew community here. Back when I was starting, and went to the original store before Home Brew Mart existed, there wasn't a whole lot of knowledge there. That's why Home Brew Mart was so successful. We had people that actually brewed. Every week, we were brewing, and we were coming up with fresher ingredients, more varied ingredients, new liquid cultures of yeast grown right here in San Diego. Between White Labs, Home Brew Mart, and QUAFF, and just home brewing in general here, I think that would be the hallmark of why San Diego is what it is.

Julian Shrago
Beachwood BBQ and Brewing

Julian Shrago is the brewmaster and co-owner of Beachwood BBQ and Brewing in downtown Long Beach.

Nick: So walk me through your brewing history and tell me how you got started.

Julian: I first started brewing in college. I heard some friends talking about home brewing and I thought it was something that sounded really interesting. I happened to mention it to my parents in conversation when I was home for the holidays one year they said that they knew of a winemaking and beermaking store in Berkley. It was called the Oak Barrel Wine Craft—they took me there and bought me my first home brew kit. I really got into it and I did it on and off for a number of years. When I bought my house in 2004, I was able to take a deeper interest in it, and had space to buy and store equipment. That really marked the beginning of when I got into it pretty intensely. Through good fortune, I was able to make some friendships with professional brewers over the years and that definitely helped me step into professional brewing. I received invitations to come brew some of my brews on a commercial scale before I even got a chance to open this place and that was a tremendous opportunity—a huge honor. Places like Pizza Port, Port Brewing, Tustin Brewing, Triple Rock. So I was able to get some good experiences.

> **"To me, the thought processes in engineering (my old job) and brewing are really pretty similar. I've always felt that engineering was a marriage of art of science."**

It was probably in 2006 that I become a little discontented with my day job as an engineer and I started thinking about opening a production brewery and making a go at this on my own. Right about the time I was getting serious about rolling out that plan, Gabe and Lena Gordon were getting ready to do a Beachwood restaurant enterprise. We decided to join forces in 2009. It seemed like a really natural evolution based on Beachwood BBQ's history as a draft beer orientated business. To me, the thought processes in engineering (my old job) and brewing are really pretty similar. I've always felt that engineering was a marriage of art of science. I think architecture is the same way. I think a lot of cooking is the same way. It's a marriage of art and science and, for me, brewing is just and extension of that. So I think it's no coincidence that a lot of people in the craft brewing industry are ex-engineers. I think it's a logical transition and I think the skill sets kind of translate between both professions.

Nick: Once you started brewing here, what that kind of things opened up to you?

Julian: One of the things that I love about having this place is total creative freedom. We do have a lot of beers that we keep on regularly here, like our Foam Top cream ale, Knucklehead Red (American red ale), and Breaker pale ale, which is a fairly hoppy American pale ale. But we've got tons of room to experiment, so we're constantly doing new types of beer and new styles. We'll do twists on old styles by using special ingredients and we're always trying to be innovative and creative. And we're not really bound by the expectations that somebody might have in a production brewery.

> **"I put every bit of effort into every beer that we make."**

Nick: Do you have any favorites right now?

Julian: It's like asking somebody who their favorite child is. You're not going to get an honest answer. I really enjoy everything that we make here and I put every bit of effort into every beer that we make. So they really all do hold a special place in my heart. And some days I'm in the mood for one thing, other days I'm not. But each beer I enjoy for different reasons.

Nick: Do you remember the first beer you ever home brewed? Do you remember how that turned out?

Julian: I do. It was an extract beer. It was an American wheat beer and it turned out fine. It was clean and that's kind of what gave me the hope to continue home brewing. I think if it had come out disastrously I might not have—my interests might not have piqued the same way.

Nick: So now, many years of brewing later, do you have any overriding principles or philosophies when you're thinking of a new beer to brew?

Julian: I think of flavor first and foremost. When I think about a beer that I'm going to brew, I think of what flavors I want to taste in that beer and how to go about creating those flavors. From there, I might think: well, if I have flavors A, B, C in a beer, what am I going to need to support that beer in terms of carbonation, in terms of body, in terms of alcohol percentage. So every ingredient and every parameter of the beer has a purpose. There's definitely an artistic aspect to everything we do here, but there is also a decent amount of science that goes into it. You have to make sure you have an engineered outcome and you have a process that's repeatable here.

"Every ingredient and every parameter of the beer has a purpose."

If I was brewing, for example, an IPA, and I wanted a hoppy IPA, I wouldn't just throw hops in there for the sake of throwing hops in there. I would want to pick varieties that are complementary to each other or maybe contrasting in a non-offensive way. I would want there to be enough alcohol to carry the aromatics of those hops and the dry hopping properly. I would want the beer to be dry so it's fairly drinkable, but I wouldn't want the body to be so thin that it seems watery. So those are the kinds of things I think about while creating that type of beer. I start with flavor and then I think of what other things it would take to support those flavors.

Nick: I know a lot of people have different ways for naming their beers. Do you guys have a method?

Julian: Sometimes it comes from one person, other times it's a decision by committee. Whenever inspiration strikes, our general rule here is if you can come up with something clever, let's start with that, otherwise we put it through a vote. Sometimes somebody will come up with a name just on its own, before a beer has even been created. Gabe called me once and said, "I got a great name for a beer, Hoppa Smurf."

Nick: No one has done that one?

Julian: That's an awesome name, but we didn't have a beer for that. It was a good name that we kept on the back burner. I thought about it for a little while and then I realized that Smurfs are Belgian. So it made sense to me that we would take that name and brew a Belgian IPA.

Nick: As a professional brewer, do you have any advice for all the aspiring home brewers out there?

Julian: Yeah, I think there's a lot of really good information out there now. I think the general quality of home brews is going way up from when I started brewing. Home brewers have access to all the same ingredients the commercial brewers do.

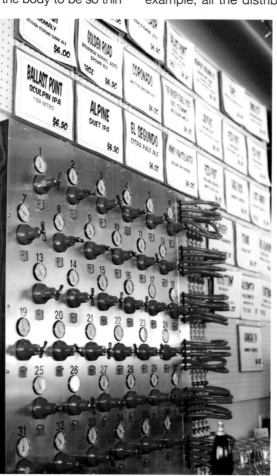

There are a lot of great recipes and books out there. I would say just try and keep your process as clean as possible and enter competitions so you can get objective feedback. If you invite your buddies over every Sunday and watch football and drink beer, I think people are pretty happy no matter what you put in front of them. But, if you really want to improve, you need to get objective feedback.

Nick: What do you think of this recent craft beer explosion and how do you think it's going to play out?

Julian: I don't think that anybody knows exactly how it's going to play out, but I think one of the things that is different from what's happening now versus the explosion that happened in the 90s is the distribution network and the distribution methods are much bigger and much more supportive than they were before. If you went back in the mid-90s for example, all the distributors were really run by big corporations. These were people who might not have been terribly familiar with the craft products they were pushing. Now you have companies, for example, like Stone. Stone has a huge distribution portion of their business and they're focused entirely on craft beers for that distribution portion. And they know all the beers that they sell very intimately and they promote those all very well. So that's something that's really different. And there are certainly a lot of breweries opening up now. It used to be that I could count the number of people I knew on one hand that were opening a brewery. Now it's difficult to keep track of them. But the energy is fantastic and I think American consumers are a lot more educated on craft beer and good beer than they ever have been in the past. The demand is there. The demand is continuing to increase.

One of my favorite things has always been being tied in locally. Where you live, where you brew—that's why we chose to open a pub. For us, it was best to be rooted in the community and have everything contained locally. While we do distribute outside the pub to a degree, we like keeping it local. And so that may be something that you continually see an increase in, too. There are a lot more people spending time in tasting rooms. That's a super integral part of craft brewing now. It used to be in the past that people had packaging breweries. They'd brew beer. They'd keg it. They'd bottle it. And visiting a brewery was kind of a rare thing. Now you have to have a tasting room, they are big money makers, and they are places that people really want to visit. So I think that aspect has changed, too.

Nick: Do you see this whole craft beer boom sustaining itself?

Julian: Gee, I sure hope so. Yeah, at some point it may equilibrate. This is also a business that is heavily based on natural ingredients, and some of those are fairly scarce commodities, like hops. Granted, certain craft oriented varieties are being planted with a lot more acreage than they were in the past, but as long as the ingredients don't become scarce, as long as people run clean businesses, then, yeah, it will continue to grow. It may reach a plateau at some point where it's a good healthy sustained level. There's still plenty of room . . . I mean, if you look

> **"One of my favorite things has always been being tied in locally. Where you live, where you brew—that's why we chose to open a pub. For us, it was best to be rooted in the community and have everything contained kind of locally."**

at craft beer as a total, take all the craft breweries—everybody from a small nano brewery up to Sam Adams, which is considered the largest craft brewery—I think that still represents well under 10% of the total beer market in the United States. So there's still plenty of room for growth.

Nick: What are your near-term and long-term plans for Beachwood?

Julian: Our immediate plan is to increase production here at the pub and service more offsite accounts. We have a decent amount of craft accounts, but we'd like more capacity here at the brewery to make more draft beer for offsite accounts. So that's our immediate focus. Beyond that, we'll see where this place maxes out. We have room to add more tanks, if we want. We can start doing bottling at some point down the road. But if all goes really well, then a packaging brewery is something that's in the future.

Nick: What is it about brewing that really inspires you to keep going?

Julian: I think the thing that people probably look for most in dream jobs is creative freedom and autonomy and the ability to demonstrate mastery. I think the fact that I have autonomy back here and I can do whatever I want whenever I want is—it's almost like not having any boundaries. I have responsibilities here, for sure. Production has to stay up. The quality of the beer has to be perfect. We've got to give everything our all each time. It doesn't matter what we're brewing. It gets the same effort, the same treatment every time. I think the autonomy is remarkably satisfying and when you get to do something creative like that and you get to share it with people and they enjoy it, that's awesome. One thing that a lot of brewers probably enjoy, too is kind of demonstrating mastery, or at least attempting to. It's like, "hey, this is my best effort at doing something. I hope you enjoy it." And if you get positive feedback, then it completes that circle.

Richard Norgrove
Bear Republic Brewing Company

Richard Norgrove is the brewmaster at Bear Republic and also one of the founders of the company, which he started with his wife, mother, and father more than 18 years ago.

Nick: Can you explain your humble beginnings in the world of beer? And how you got to where you are today?

Richard: I'm one of the older brewers in California, I started out as a home brewer, originally. For a while, I was production manager for a wheel quick-release that we called "the flip off." This is bike history, going 20 years back, when the mountain bike industry was first starting. I went to school for graphic design, but, in an effort to be part of the shop where all the fun was and all the guys were having a good time, the owner would let me practice welding after hours. I was never good enough to weld bikes, though one of the things I could make was a home brew kit. So, one day, Mark Carpenter comes into the shop to buy custom parts for his Motto Guzzi. He was the assistant brewmaster at Anchor Steam at the time, now he's the brewmaster. Well, he saw one of the home brew kits that I was building—I had like three of them erected—and he says, "What are you doing kid?" "Well, I'm looking to get into the beer industry some day." Mark said, "Well, I know this guy, Paddy Giffin." Well, I had met Paddy through the home brew shop, so between Mark and Paddy, there was kind of a formalization of the dream, "I thought hey, maybe I should become an apprentice brewer."

My boss, Ross, at the shop let me take Fridays off to moonlight as a brewer's apprentice. I'd go down and brew with Paddy at Marin Brewing Co. and then, when Moylan's finally opened, I officially got a job working for Brendan at Moylan's. It was about seven months later that we started Bear Republic. He knew that I was trying to develop my own brewery at the time and he was nice enough and gracious enough to allow me to work with Paddy, gaining practical experience.

Nick: You're a pretty accomplished guy: army veteran, firefighter, racecar driver. Have these experiences helped you or influenced how you run this business?

Richard: What I'll say is this. I don't know how or why, but I'm always trying to expand my own horizons in some way, shape, or form. As a kid, I was 10 years old when I had open-heart surgery. I think that was probably one of the key events in my personal life that shaped my ability to feel like, "I'm running on a rebuild." A sense of urgency and intensity was formed.

You wonder that you only have so much time on earth and that you better make sure you enjoy it and make the most of it. My grandfather, Richard Bradley Norgrove, he pretty much lived his life the way he wanted to. Very much a bohemian in

what he wanted and chose to do. When you have those kind of influences, it affects the way you treat your life and what you want to do. I've always tried to push myself, because if you're not moving forward, then you're standing still. Mario Andretti once said, "If things are under control, you're going too slow." I love that quote.

Originally, I was the only brewer, now I have a team. I wasn't trying to design beers or make beers that were going to be mainstream. Actually, we were one of the first breweries where our motto was "bigger is better." There wasn't anybody doing that at the time. Look at our flagship. It's a 7% alcohol beer. In 1995, we were making big beers before everybody was, before there was a whole Southern California, San Diego brewing scene. There's a good rivalry between us and Southern California. In Southern California, all the breweries are so close geographically. They're all kind of feeding off of each other in a frenzy. We're up here in Northern California, spread out and we're kind of all on our own little islands. When we finally decide to do something, it stems from within and it's not so influenced by what the market bears, or what our neighbors are doing.

> **"I don't know how or why, but I'm always trying to expand my own horizons in some way, shape, or form."**

Nick: So you're not into following the "trends"?

Richard: No. Take Racer 5. Years ago, it was one of the hoppiest IPA's out there. Now, it's being referred to as one of the balanced ones, go figure. . . . That's just that whole shift. To be honest, I think people have caught up to where we are. With that respect, we're being pushed at times to make other beers to catch up. We make a beer called, "Apex." Apex is my IPA that I'm allowed to change. If you think about Apex in terms of racing, the only constant in a race is the apex. It's ever-changing, because, as the tires wear, as the driver becomes fatigued, as the car heats up, all those dynamics change. Apex is a beer like that. We do a series of beers at the pub called, "Rebellion," which are single-hop varietal beers. Those are there to educate us, first and foremost, about what new hops can do, what flavors they are. You take a base pale ale, you hop it like an IPA and you change the hops to 100%. Whether it's a German hop, a Czechoslovakian hop, or a new numbered hop that hasn't been brought into the industry, we get to try it in its raw form and then we integrate it into something new.

Nick: Are there elements or characteristics that you try to incorporate into all of your beers?

Richard: It's really about balance. It's trying to have the flavors of the yeast, the grain, and the hops all work in conjunction. So when you're done drinking one of our beers, you've had an

experience. And you think, "God, I want to have another one." Or you think what is that characteristic that I can't pick out? It's trying to make it exciting. There is too much, I think, of a shift right now, where it's all about the hops. If you drink a beer and it's just about the bitterness, it's too much citrus in your face. It's all nose, and you have to have the body in the beer to balance it.

We also make real ale. We don't filter our product. That in itself, is going to give you a completely different mouth feel and flavor characteristic than somebody who's run it through a plate-and-frame filter, because anytime you run something through a filter, you strip something out. By making a real ale, you're adding more time to your process. I know some of my competitors can make a perfectly good pale ale in seven days. Well, I won't. I'll make it in 19–21 days. That's the difference. You're going to pay a premium. There is a certain level of exclusivity to our product at times, because it's not everywhere. That's just kind of the philosophy, but it works well for us.

Nick: Speaking of your brewing philosophy, can you describe your new recipe development process? Does it start with an end product in mind or is it more ingredients based?

Richard: That's a great question. There are two ways that we choose to make recipes. One of the best stories I tell people is about "the recovery." Here I am, a young pub brewer, and I developed this recipe over the years—multiple steps with Red Rocket hops, trying to get it to where I wanted it to taste. It was a blending of a Scottish ale with an American IPA. Well, in 1992, what was my IPA experience? Well, there wasn't scope—there weren't all these really great IPAs like today to try to model them after.

I was drinking Anchor Liberty. That was a huge beer for me. Rogue was making IPAs back then also. So, here I am—I'm a pub brewer. I'm working in my restaurant. I'm the owner. People are coming up and asking me questions about where the toilet paper is, and so on. I had this hop profile that was in my head and, at the time, I wasn't taking such good notes.

I was making the pale ale recipe that day, but I had the Red Rocket recipe in my head because I had been making Rocket the day before, and I was going to make Rocket again the next day. I had Rocket on the brain. . . .

I weighed out the hops and threw it in the kettle at the wrong time. I thought, "Oh my god. What did I just do?" I had to recover from that, and recovering from that was to basically formulate a new IPA style of beer. I had this pale ale that was at six percent alcohol, but was now hopped wrong, overly hopped. In 1997, I decided I can't call it house pale ale anymore, because it's not. It's a hybrid. It's Red Rocket hops and the pale ale recipe. I wanted to call it Springtime Strong Ale, SSA. Then my father reminded me of the Third Reich and the horrors of the feared SS officers. I was thinking Chevy SS—tough, loud, strong and didn't make that connection. I had to come up with a new name and always thought Racer would be a great name for a beer. Springtime Strong Ale morphed into what is now Racer 5. It took another three to four recipe iterations and "Here it is!" We started with Racer, and then there was Racer number two, three, and so on. Then there was Racer 5 and we got it. The balance was struck. That shows you the recovery portion of how a recipe can be developed, it's all about the recovery . . .

Sometimes, there is, literally, the "brew by committee," method, where we'll all get in a room and we'll say, "We want to develop something that is new to us." Hop Rod Rye was

> **"I know some of my competitors can make a perfectly good pale ale in seven days. Well, I won't. I'll make it in 19–21. That's the difference."**

developed that way. As the story goes, Racer was selling well in southern California, but Stone was our distributor and they saw Red Rocket as direct competition with Arrogant Bastard, because they both reflect that style of American red ale.

We as a team said, "We've got to do something different." I was so in love with rye malt at the time. I had been experimenting with rye pale ales, and this was the first time we designed a beer to go into a market. Hop Rod Rye was developed and it was basically the first rye IPA. It had a little bit of a different color than an American Red, was made with a high proportion of rye, highly hopped, and would not compete with Arrogant Bastard. Rye malts and new hop profiles all of a sudden took off. That's a good example of how we decided to make a specific style of beer, sometimes it's based upon peer pressures.

Nick: You're also doing funkier styles, too, right?

Richard: Yeah. Tartare is a classic example of where we use spontaneous fermentation. We're not buying bugs. We have so much local flora and fauna. This area has grown grapes, plums, nectarines, peaches—all of the stuff that's in our air. We figured, we better go capture the essence, or terrior, of our valleys, so we did. We started out by capturing all four seasons fermented with the base of Racer 5.

The base of Racer 5 allowed spontaneous fermentation, so we collected it, started a solera system within small barrels, and we built the mother up enough to where we're now producing large batches in wooden "foeder" fermentation vessels down in Healdsburg. That's something new from us. That's an example of brewers getting together and saying, "You know what? We need to get involved with this." It has taken on a life of its own, and we're known for hoppy beers, but we can do this, too."

Nick: It kind of sounds like you're saying that Racer 5 almost started as a—

Richard: Oh, it was a mistake, yeah. It started out as a mistake.

Nick: What do you think about what some people are calling the current "craft beer revolution"? Do you think it's sustainable?

Richard: Our brewery started in the last recession. My fear is that history has a tendency to repeat itself. There was a big fall out during BRBC's early years. Today, we're seeing a new influx of people who are getting into the beer industry because they see double-digit growth or they see growth in a way that you're not seeing in other industries. They have to remind themselves that, at the end of the day, you have to make good beer and you're still manufacturing. We make a product that has to be made consistently every day. I'm hoping that there will always be people who are industry leaders on quality and not totally motivated by sales. I'm 45 years old. I've been brewing commercially for more than 20 years. There are younger guys that are growing up with craft beer that already have an expectation of where the quality should be. It is exciting that we're returning to a time before Prohibition, where your local breweries are going to represent the area, or region.

> ## "We're returning to a time before Prohibition, where your local breweries are going to represent the area."

There will always be people who are going to be fly-by-night birds. You're not going to hear about them in five years. They've got the best marketing and the best look, but then are you going to go back and buy the second one? As a brewer, you have to make a beer where someone's going to want a second one. It's about managing expectations and love of craft.

Nick: What is it about beer and brewing that excites you?

Richard: It's constantly changing and that constant change makes it a challenge. I remember when I was in the service, any place I went, if I wanted to taste what I consider to be a consistency from home, I would have a Budweiser. I never knock Budweiser. To have a beer taste consistent as a brewer is a true measure of success—my hops change every year, my malt changes every year, our water changes seasonally—all those variables make for an interesting job. Every day I come to work, it's not the same thing. It's ever-changing, ever-evolving. I think that's the beauty of beer.

Nick: Last question: What's the one thing you've never been asked that you always wanted to say?

Richard: Because this is a family business, my mother always wants to make sure I'm very humble about this: Bear Republic is a family brewery. Yes, I am the brewmaster, but I don't want to be known as the central figure.

There's too many "cult-of-personality brewers," where it's just one guy and people say, "That guy is the guy." For me, it's about our team. I can't do it every day without surrounding myself with really strong, good people. That goes down to my father who manages the sales, to my mom who'll greet you at the door, and to my wife who is the CFO. It's about our team family here at BRBC, and that's what drives us forward. . . .

Daniel Del Grande
Bison Organic Beers

Daniel Del Grande is the owner and brewer for Bison Organic Beers located in Berkeley, California.

Nick: Can you remember the first time you ever enjoyed a craft beer? How did you get from that point to where we're sitting right now?

Daniel: My first memory of a craft beer is back in 1986 or '87. I had a Red Tail Ale. There weren't that many craft beers back then. I tried that Red Tail Ale and thought, "Oh my goodness. This is so good." It had hops. It had a lot of the yeast character. It was just really a fantastic beer.

We were in college and mostly we drank the crummy keg beer. No one complained about it because we didn't know any better, right? I went down to the home brew shop, Oak Barrel, here in Berkeley. Somebody had told me, "Dude, it's legal to buy all the ingredients to make beer and then you can make your own beer." So I started brewing my own beer. We would use the yeast that we found in a Red Tail Ale bottle because we really liked that character. After college, it was the way all of our friends stayed together. We all went off to start our own careers, but we'd brew beer at my house every Sunday.

Nick: Do you remember how your first batch came out?

Daniel: The first batch came out really great. I can't remember what it was exactly, but I remember my third batch was a beer called Buddha Belly Porter. It was a kit, the malt extract and the hops and everything. It was just terrible. That was my first fermentation gone awry as a home brewer. When the first two batches went fine, I just kept on doing what we were doing, but we weren't paying attention to the science of it at all. We were just going through the process. Then we got infection, and I became curious. "Why did I have infection? What did I do?" I asked the guy at the home brew shop, and he gave me a number of things I did wrong. I realized that beer was a lot more complex and difficult than I had thought.

In the summer of 1997, I went to brewmaster school at the American Brewers Guild. When I finished, I found out Bison was up for sale, and I thought, "Oh my gosh, what great fortune!"

I had a business plan to open up my own place, but all my family and friends were telling me, "You found an existing business. All the pieces are there. Then you can just mold it to your way of doing things." I took their advice and put in a bid. I was the successful bidder, so I've been a professional brewer since the summer of 1997.

Nick: What were some of the major challenges going straight from home brewing to a more industrial scale?

Daniel: First of all, it wasn't my intention to go right into my own thing. I wanted to work with somebody else and make mistakes with somebody else, learn from some other people. This opportunity presented itself and so I jumped into it. I actually learned quite a lot in my brewmaster course work about how to put together recipes.

Budda Belly was one of the first beers I translated from home brew completely to the pro. I think I called it "Graduate Porter" at the time. I tried scaling up my other home brew recipes. Some of them worked and some of them didn't. Usually, the ones that didn't work well were the ones that had a complicated hop bill and a complicated malt bill. They just never really seemed to translate to the big scale.

There's so much more to making beer than just scaling things up. It's about how you're treating the yeast. What I found over the years is one of the most important things is how you feed the yeast when you're creating your wort. How do you manipulate temperatures? How do you filter it? Those are skills that you can't really practice as a home brewer. You don't have the equipment. These days, they sell these mini-fermenters that are glycol cooled and stuff, but back in the 90's, that wasn't available. We were using plastic buckets and carboys.

Nick: Were there other challenges to being a pro brewer as opposed to just home brewing?

Daniel: Well, moving from 10-gallon batches to 10-barrel batches (that's 310 gallons) is . . . well, there's a lot more riding on it. There's a financial escalation that doesn't seem trivial anymore. There are the demands of being on time, not letting your taps run empty because, if you're running a brew pub and everyone expects to have their IPA and their stout and their blonde ale, you can't mess up a batch. Whereas home brewing, if it didn't turn out quite like I wanted it, no big deal. I found the hardest part of being professional is being consistent, trying to get the beer the same every time I brew it. That was the hardest part. Things would change on me.

Nick: Do you have any advice for home brewers who are thinking about going pro?

Daniel: Well, home brewers should hone their craft so that if you send your beer away to a lab once and then you brew it again in a couple of cycles later and send it away again, you should be able to get the same numbers back from the lab.

> **"I tried scaling up my other home brew recipes. Some of them worked and some of them didn't. Usually, the ones that didn't work well were the ones that had a complicated hop bill and a complicated malt bill."**

Short of that, I recommend getting really high quality hydrometers, getting a high quality pH meter, really measuring what you're doing in the brewery and taking notes and watching.

Nick: Are there generally any characteristics that you look for in the beers that you brew?

> **"I found the hardest part of being professional is being consistent, trying to get the beer the same every time I brew it."**

Daniel: Well, one of them is I like my beers to finish dry and crisp on the palate. I don't like big, malty character. I don't like a lot of residual sweetness in the beers. I pay a lot of attention to the yeasts I select to make sure I completely dry the beer out. Dry finish is one of the main things that leads you to wanting to have another pint. I'm not really a hop-head. I'm not into enormous bitterness in beers. I've just never been a fan. You won't find many of my beers having that abrasive hop character.

Nick: Describe your brewing philosophy. When you're coming up with new recipes, what's the process?

Daniel: I would say that I'm mostly ingredient-focused. Take a beer like the Honey Basil Ale. That's made with, guess what? Honey and basil! I take those two components and I think about them. "Well, what color is honey? All right, well, let me adjust the malt profile to produce a color reminiscent of honey in a glass and how best to get this basil character in the beer. How much basil do I want? Do I want it really subtle or is it overwhelming? What style of basil do I want to use?"

I'm working on a Belgian beer made with marmalade right now. That's very creative, but once I kind of get the recipe direction and create it, then it turns into science. Then it's just making sure that it's all the same every time. If I'm making changes in the recipe, which I do occasionally, I only change one thing at a time. I'll change it maybe half the way I think it needs to go. Then I'll taste it and know where I'm going with it and take slow and measured steps. Things don't happen overnight.

Nick: Can you talk about Bison and about what being an organic brewery really means?

Daniel: Essentially, I was brewing these beers at the brewpub in the late 90's and early 2000's and the business was fine. I wasn't questioning anything, but when I saw a malt store offer me organic malt, I was like, "Oh, yeah of course. I go to the farmers' market every weekend and buy all these organic foods for my house. Why am I not reflecting those values in my business?" I started experimenting with the malts and working

them into the beers. Over time, more and more ingredients became available. I was able to convert all of my business to being organic and was certified in 2002. Then in 2003, I had enough ingredients to make the most complex beer (the chocolate stout). That was the hardest to convert because it had so many different malts in it—eight different malts.

Now, we're organic for a number of reasons. One of the reasons is that supporting sustainable agriculture is one of the most ecological things you can do. It reduces the runoff to our rivers and streams. It doesn't kill fish. It doesn't cause pollution in the Gulf of Mexico. It doesn't harm farm workers. All these sustainable agriculture practices are things I believe in, and so I look to reflect that in my business. When you look at something like organic beer production, if you as a consumer decided that you would buy a six-pack a week of organic beer, you would cause a conventional farmer to convert 1,700 square feet of land to grow your malt and hops. That's a huge impact!

My dream is to have everybody using, at least, organic malt. I think that would be really fantastic. We would be able to convert acres and acres of farmland to organic out there in the plains.

Nick: People talk about the craft beer revolution. Are you seeing this on your end?

Daniel: On the brewery side of things, there's a lot of breweries out there that aren't making any money. They're paying people minimum wage. They aren't really being treated as the artists that they are. It's really, really difficult to be in the craft beer business right now, from just a financial standpoint. Why is that? It's because consumers won't pay higher prices for beer. But without consumers, there wouldn't be a revolution, nor would there be such a huge variety of beers out there, so I have to thank them.

I think a lot of young consumers, from 21 to 30, instead of going into the wine culture, they're finding all these craft breweries. Millenials can get world class beers for a fraction of the price of world class wine and spirits. Plus, beer has a great culture in America. You don't sit at home drinking great craft beer all by yourself. You're usually drinking it with friends, Tweeting, etc. That's why these great craft beer bars have popped up. Places like Toronado was a needle in a haystack for many, many years. Now, there's Beer Revolution, City Beer Store, a whole bunch of them that have popped up. It's good. Right now, in the bay area, craft beer has about a forty percent share. Forty percent of the beer sold is craft beer.

Social media has enabled that as well. Now, people can talk on social media about what they're drinking, why they're drinking it.

Nick: Do you see this trend sustaining?

Daniel: Oh yeah, absolutely. Nationwide, I think, eight percent of the beer sold is craft beer and the rest is imports and the mass American lagers or the mass American beer companies.

I think they're going to keep growing, especially in urban areas. I think you'll see a lot more people begin to drink starter beers, more Blue Moon and Fat Tire. Fat Tire is actually not a really super complex beer, but it's very well made and it's very tasty and it's better than all the mass American stuff. People are trading up, but they're not ready to jump right to double IPA's.

Nick: What is it about beer and brewing that keeps you getting up every morning?

Daniel: I think most people, at least entrepreneurs—people that are creating things—want to make a difference. When I'm dead, I want to have made an impact on the beer industry. One of the ways I want to make an impact is encouraging more people to go organic. Once the consumers are demanding it, that will simply roll back to the farmers. That would be a huge impact. I think the brand, Bison, stands for a lot of that and will be rewarded.

There are other things that keep my interests in sustainability. Solar hot water is something I'm actually studying right now. I'm building a solar hot water heater to put on the roof of my garage. I could find other things that interest me and make me want to innovate and come up with cool things.

Nick: What are some of your long-term goals for the brewery?

Daniel: My goal is to build a green urban brewery. I want it to be urban because that's where people are and they can come here and see it. I can touch more people and tell them about the sustainability message. I want to have an urban brewery that's off the grid. A hundred percent off the grid. I'm looking at solar hot water because one of the biggest energy inputs into a brewery is bringing water up from 55 degrees, out of your tap, up to a boil. If you can harness the sun to get your water up near 172 degrees or so, then I just have to use some sort of bio-gas to get it from 172 to boiling. That's a huge energy savings.

Nick: Is there anything you've never been asked in an interview that you've always wanted to say?

Daniel: I mentioned it a little bit, but I think consumers, soon, are going to need to change their tolerance for what they'll pay for beer. You can't have world-class beers and a sustainable industry if people are not being paid living wages. That goes all the way back to the farmer who's growing the hops. About 40% of the cost of a six-pack is labor. I just really think that if you look at the quality of the beers that are being produced today by American craft brewers, that there's no reason that you shouldn't be willing to pay $ 12.99 or $14.99 a six-pack. It's just not fair that craft beer is tied to Bud/Miller kind of price points from these huge factories that are producing so much beer. It's great quality. It's consistent. Every single batch is exactly the same. They've got the science down. They're doing exactly what they want to do. Maybe someday when craft breweries are buying old Budweiser plants and making beer at that level, we'll be able to have those kinds of efficiencies.

> **"When I'm dead, I want to have made an impact on the beer industry. One of the ways I want to make an impact is encouraging more people to go organic."**

Tyler King
The Bruery

Tyler King is the senior director of brewing operations at The Bruery, in Placentia, California.

Nick: How did you get started in brewing?

Tyler: I got a home brewing kit when I was a senior in high school. My art teacher had another one of his classes make root beer. As part of making root beer, they had to design the label for the bottle. In his class, you could see these jugs of root beer fermenting, and I knew instead of making root beer, I could make beer. I got bored one day, went home, ordered kind of the same exact kit that he had, and just started making beer. At the time, I didn't even like it, but, well, actually I didn't drink at all at the time. I was seventeen.

When I went to college, my parents told me I had to get a job. I didn't want to work in the restaurant industry; I didn't really want to do anything at all. I started looking around for jobs in a brewery, because that was kind of what I was into at the time. I interviewed at a few different Orange County breweries, got turned down by most of them, or they said they couldn't pay me. Luckily, BJ's Restaurant and Brewery, out in West Covina, California, hired me on as a cellar man. I was pretty much a keg washer, and I washed kegs for probably about a year and a half. During that year and a half they trained me and then, after that, I just kept moving up in the brewery, until finally I was brewing the beer there.

Nick: At what point did you come here?

Tyler: I worked at BJ's for four years. During my time there, I joined a home brew club called Brew Commune in Orange County. From there, I met the vice president, Patrick Rue. We started talking, and I heard from a mutual friend of ours that he was opening up a brewery. He knew I worked at a professional brewery, so he and I met up a few times and we talked. We went out to lunch one day, and we were talking about his plans for the brewery, and I said, "hey, you really need to hire a brewer. You need to hire someone who knows what they're doing. You can't do it all." He said, "OK, do you want it?" And I thought, Oh yeah! Awesome! When I put in my notice at BJs, I told them what I was going to do. That we're opening a brewery that's going to do all Belgian and experimental-type beers and package it all in 750-milliliter bottles. So, I helped Patrick build The Bruery from the ground up and I never returned to BJ's.

> **"Most beer ideas come up when we're eating some great new dish, or tasting a new spice, or something that we've never had before."**

Nick: Did you major in chemistry, or anything like that?

Tyler: No, advertising because it seemed like the easiest major and the communications building is where I saw all the best-looking girls going.

Nick: Do you guys have any overriding approach to coming up with a new beer? Is there an overriding philosophy that you guys adhere to?

Tyler: I don't think there is a philosophy behind it. Most beer ideas come up when we're eating some great new dish, or tasting a new spice, or something that we've never had before.

Our anniversary beer was thought up by Patrick. He wanted a big beer that could age for a long time, and he also wanted to do a Solera method (adding older beer) to make it special. As The Bruery gets older, the beer is actually getting older as well. There's always 25 percent old beer in the next year's release. It just gets a little more complex as the years go along. It's the same way they make port. We steal a lot of ideas from the wine industry and definitely from the restaurant/food industry. That's our big thing right there. We want to be a very food-friendly beer. We love eating good food. We're inspired by food.

Nick: Do you have a personal philosophy about what should go into making a beer?

Tyler: No. It depends on the time. Talk to me during the summer and I'm going to want to brew something crisp, light, and easy drinking. During the winter, maybe I'll be going for a little bit heavier beer. For us, now, it's about what we lack in our portfolio. What beer do we not have? Or what can we do to kind of push the limit? Can we make a beer with a different flavor that people aren't used to? The fun thing is getting flavors to combine to make a great beer.

Nick: Do you have a favorite beer that you always love to drink?

Tyler: It really depends on the mood, but Sierra Nevada Pale Ale is just standard. No matter what, you'll see me drinking that at any bar.

Nick: What's your take on what's being called the "Craft Beer Revolution?" Do you see it as a big change?

Tyler: Yeah. When we first opened, the craft beer scene was just beginning to explode and we weren't really sure if we could sell our beer at the time. We knew we were making a good product and we knew people would want the product. It was kind of a niche product at the time. Not that many breweries were doing what we were doing. Then, over the past few years this thing has definitely exploded. I think it's a good thing. It happened about seventeen years ago and from that we got breweries like Stone and Ballast Point. These are the big names that you see now. I think that the same thing is happening now. The only scary thing

is the market could potentially become flooded. Right now, all the breweries, we're all friends. We hang out, we help each other, and it's a great industry to be in. At some point, there may come a time where we're starting to fight for shelf or tap space and we're not going to be so friendly toward each other. I would hate for that to happen.

The good thing about craft beer consumers is they want variety. You don't go to the store and buy the same craft brew every time. You're not buying six, twelve-packs of our beer and just pounding them. There's no brand loyalty. I think that helps us stay friends, 'cause you go to the store and you might buy one of our bottles. You go back you're going to buy maybe one of Bootlegger's bottles. Then you might come back and visit one of our new beers or one of our older beers. That's a good thing. The bad thing—since everyone is open-

> ## ❝I think I agree with most people where I don't think the growth is going to slow down any time soon. I think there's a lot more room for more breweries, especially in Orange County and L.A.❞

ing up a brewery—is, if people start putting out bad beer, the consumer might start being afraid to buy craft beer. Once they start becoming afraid of it, they're not buying it. Then we might see a lot of shutdowns or a lot of breweries closing. It happened 16 years ago, it could happen again.

If you talk to most people, they don't think that this is even the peak of the boom. I think, right now, within the craft beer industry, most people think it's still going to go for a few more years before it levels out. I think I agree with most people where I don't think the growth is going to slow down any time soon. I think there's a lot more room for more breweries, especially in Orange County and L.A.

Nick: What do you see for The Bruery in the next five years?

Tyler: For us, we project a very calm growth over the next few years. We focus a lot on our barrel-aged product. About 50–60 percent of our production right now goes straight into oak barrels and sits for 1–3 years. We don't have any major expansions planned after our current one right now and we're going to see where the market takes us. We have a lot of beer in oak barrels that we plan to release in the next few years, and if we see a huge need for our beer in the market, then we'll start considering another expansion. Until we see that huge need, we're probably going to sit back, keep producing our high-end products, our barrel-aged products, and just wait for our space to grow.

Right now, we don't push product, and we don't really want to push our product on anyone. At one point we might have to. If we did expand, if we did open up a bigger brewery,

> **"I'm proud of every beer we put out. Oude Tart is probably the closest one to me. I came up with that beer when I was 17 or 18 years old."**

we would have to sell our beer, we'd have to hire a salesman. Our company does not have a salesman at all. We don't really plan on hiring one anytime soon. That's nice. It would be nice if we could keep it that way and grow at that pace.

Nick: What beer are you most proud of? Can you pick that?

Tyler: I'm proud of every beer we put out. Oude Tart is probably the closest one to me. I came up with that beer when I was 17 or 18 years old. It was the first sour beer The Bruery ever made, and it was also one of the first beers from our company to win a major competition. It's won multiple gold at the World Beer Cup, so we beat Belgians in their own category, and won a gold at the GABF. Just being one of my very earliest recipes, that's pretty awesome.

Nick: What are some of the other accolades that The Bruery's racked up over the years?

Tyler: Oh, man. We've won a fair amount. We've kind of taken a different approach, though. We've won a lot of the local county fairs, like Best of Show in L.A. County. They're good competitions, but the awards that really matter to us are the Great American Beer Festival and the World Beer Cup.

Nick: What do you think makes The Bruery unique among breweries?

Tyler: I think our beer. I mean, that's a pretty lame answer, but we're not out to brew a standard IPA or pale. We want to create an experience with the beer, so we want something different. A beer that you're not going to find at your average bar. Something that is going to go well with food and something that you're going to share with family and friends.

Nick: You guys do a lot of sours. Why so much focus on sour beers?

Tyler: Why not? We love sour beer. I mean, there's only a few breweries who are making good sour beer. And it's what I like to drink. It's what Patrick likes to drink. It's what almost every single person in our brewery likes to drink, so it's pretty much what we do. We brew what we want, or what we like to drink.

Nick: I know you're as obsessed as any brewer with consistency, but with sours, every beer is different. Almost every bottle is different. How obsessed are you, or do you realize that there is a lot of variation?

Tyler: There's always going to be variation when were talking about sour beer. When we're talking about our clean fermented beers, we have a lot of measuring points to make sure the beer is as consistent as possible with the equipment we have. The one thing that does kind of suck about being in a smaller brewery is that, even though we have the capability of blending batches for consistency, they're still pretty small batches. When we talk about consistency, our recipes are almost dead on and I think we do a pretty damned good job for how young and small of a brewery we are. We spend a lot of money and time on making sure our beer is consistent. I'm not saying it always is, but we try our best at it, and I think we're pretty damn good at it.

As far as sour beer goes, that just comes in quantity. I just spent 6–8 hours blending this year's Oude Tart. That's literally me sitting in front of like 10–20 different jars of beer and just blending them together until I think it tastes like how Oude Tart should taste. With that, the quantity of barrels we have, that helps out a lot. 'Cause you might have one batch that tastes really good, might have another one that tastes really bad, you're going to have a few in-between. The hard part is getting all of those blended together to make one consistent product. Then, on top of that, you only release it once a year, so when you try to blend it, you're going off of what you did a year ago. The beer's always a little bit different because the beer's aged for a year. I mean, sour beer, it does what it does. You have to just do your best to blend it together.

And then there's the oak barrels themselves. We brew it, we put in bacteria, we put in brettanomyces, we put in yeast, and we try to get it to ferment in a certain way. But the bacteria is a living organism. It's going to do what it's going to do. You can't tell it to do one thing and make sure it does that. It's just going to do what it wants.

Evan Weinberg
Cismontane Brewing

Evan Weinberg is the head brewer and one of the partners at Cismontane Brewing, in Rancho Santa Margarita.

Nick: How did you get interested in beer? And how did you wind up where you are today?

Evan: I got into beer specifically, when I lived in Napa. A friend and I had a tomato farm up there and, of course, I spent a lot of time in vineyards and wineries. We got to drink a lot of really great wines. I enjoyed it, but you need a good beer every once in a while. At the time, craft beer was very hard to find. So, I took it upon myself to make beer out of sheer necessity. We used what we could find around the winery, went down to the Napa Fermentation Supply and basically bought everything they had in there that had anything to do with making beer. I quickly learned that; not only is beer more scientific in terms of the process—it also has a lot more diversity than wine. I was hooked.

In terms of my history as a worker bee, I did a lot of random jobs, like electrical work, while I was in college. Just before I got out, I started working in oceanography at the Marine Science Institute, Santa Barbara; worked at Scripps in San Diego, and then I worked for NOAA in Hawaii. From there I found myself working for developers in residential and commercial real estate. Needing a change of gears I traveled for a while then ended up in the tomato business. From there I went to software for a while then. . . . Beer!

The land that we grew the tomatoes on belonged to Caymus. If Mr. Wagner didn't decide to grow more Cabernet on the "tomato" property, who knows where I would be today? I ended up taking a job in Orange County for a software company. I brought all my brewing stuff with me and kept brewing. Several of my friends egged me on to build a brewery. One of them actually found the facility we're in today on Craigslist. It was an extract brewery that needed a lot of work to rebuild it and make it a viable brewery. We were just crazy enough to take a crack at it.

We ripped everything out, meanwhile keeping my job so I could feed myself. Then we started to produce and that was the beginning of it all. It was just Ross, the other founder, and myself. We did everything; sales, brewing, accounting, delivery . . . the list goes on. We split up the construction as much as we could, found all the equipment in random places, brought it all in, and installed everything. It was a ton of work and it still is.

Nick: Do you remember the first home brew that you tried? Do you remember learning anything from that first experience?

Evan: You know, I don't even remember the first home brew I tried. I know I tried some when I was younger but nothing really that impacted me. I always preferred craft beers. The mass

produced American lagers never did it for me. Old Scratch and the SLO beers were some of my favorites early on.

For me, the excitement of brewing was an amalgamation of all the stuff I learned and all the things I enjoy—they all happened to fall in the right place at the right time. Just the creativity you get to have when you're brewing; the science behind it, the social aspect, the construction and engineering component of building all the stuff. The added benefit of having a good community surrounding you—people that support a product that's tangible, is made with integrity, and has intrinsic value. It's like the whole package.

Nick: How do you go about developing a new recipe? Do you start with a style and then try other beers in that style, or do you just go for creativity and see what happens?

Evan: There's a lot of different ways we come up with beers. Generally, when I want to brew a beer, I come up with something that has the general characteristics of a particular style but shows what we want to represent with that beer. We just try to make a really balanced product no matter what we do.

As for all the one-offs and stuff, it could be anything. It could be like, "Damn, this sounds really good. Wouldn't it be good if we had a nice clean lager with some good dry hop character or something?" When it comes to barrel age stuff we are a bit more adventurous.

One of our flagships, The Citizen, is a steam beer. We did some research on the style and found that there were over 20 breweries in CA brewing this style before Prohibition. The range of beers was quite a bit bigger than what is described in the style guidelines. So we fermented the same way, but made it hoppier, lighter in color and on the stronger end of the spectrum. We don't carbonate the beer the old way, which is called krausening, which essentially makes a cask beer. It just doesn't make logistical sense to do this for The Citizen based on how the market is set up today. People say it's not to style, well what is the style really? Just because there's one big brewery that survived Prohibition making steam beer one way, should everyone else's look and taste like that? History says no.

"I quickly learned that—not only is beer more scientific in terms of the process—it also has a lot more diversity."

Nick: Is it more what we call a common?

Evan: Yeah, we can call it California Common or California Lager. Anchor Steam Brewing trademarked the term "Steam Beer" so people came up with these alternative names for the style.

Nick: Can you talk about how science and creativity play off each other to create what it is you create?

Evan: I think we can all agree we prefer drinking good beer. In the effort to make quality beer over thousands of years people have developed all kinds of equipment, techniques, and processes. To do this we have literally created new materials, fields of science, power sources. You name it, it has been made for beer! Let's take Luis Pasteur for instance. He was one of the most influential microbiologists ever. Everything he did was to make beer better. He laid the ground work for the taxonomy and understanding of yeast we have today. Because of science I can make any yeast-dependent style of beer in the world in my own facility! We can even create new yeast strains to do want we want.

Brewers are all total geeks. We collect tons of data. The data allows us to make informed decisions to make our beers the way we want to. It's that simple.

Nick: You guys are growing your own hops now?

Evan: Yeah we do. We don't grow a lot, there's maybe ten vines out there, something like that. We get enough to throw them into casks and do some stuff like that. I did a cream ale recently that came out nice and mellow, super drinkable. We filled a couple of firkins just as the hops were starting to ripen. Fresh hops right off the vines gave the firkins a beautiful, bright aroma.

"For me, brewing was an amalgamation of all the stuff I learned and all the things I enjoy— they all happened to fall in the right place at the right time."

Nick: Have you seen a big explosion in the popularity of craft beer? What do you attribute that to?

Evan: Yeah, I think it's great. It's exploding in a lot of ways; people all over are opening up craft beer bars, gastro pubs, and little breweries here and there. I think it's a good thing. This isn't the first time it's happened, though. This happened in the late 80's, early 90's and then the entire market imploded. So everybody thinks that this thing is sustainable and will last forever. Maybe that's true, but it also may not be true.

Nick: And what about Cismontane? Can you tell me a little bit about the direction you guys see yourselves heading and where you see yourself in that market as well?

Evan: We definitely have a lot more room for growth, but with little capital it's going to be tough. Even though we're small and we're undercapitalized, we own most everything we have. If the shit hits the fan, we're not going anywhere, so that's a good thing. At the same time, in order to get to a point where we can actually get a paycheck and be a little more comfortable, we need to find a cheaper way to operate while increasing sales. Life's great mystery. . . . So it's going to be a balancing act for a little while to figure out how to do that.

We fit in a strange place between the regional craft brewery and a brewpub. This means higher cost and lower revenue. What an amazing business model . . . Ha!

Nick: Where does the name Cismontane come from?

Evan: It means coastal Southern California. It's a term from the old days. It's a term that describes the geographic region from Santa Barbara to Baja. It means, "this side of the mountains." So "Cis" is like the down side of the mountains, "transmontane" would be the other side of the mountains. It originally comes from the Alps, the French Alps. When people moved to this region of California they started using that term to describe Southern California. In the 1800's, if you lived in coastal Southern California and someone asked you where you were from, you would say Cismontane, California. Today, the scientific community uses it to describe the area.

Nick: What would you say is the source of your inspiration and drive? What motivates you to get up every morning and come in here to brew?

Evan: I wish I could tell you. I think it's just built-in. It's just who I am. Everything I've ever done I've worked really, really hard at. When I come in the brewery and some big project has been finished you walk in, look at it and think "That feels pretty good, we put the tile on the floor, we built these walls, poured the epoxy on the floor, cut the concrete drains. We laid all that shit by hand. We sold the beer, and we brewed the beer, and we delivered it for a year and a half or longer, almost two years. We did it all. We built the company, every little piece of it."

Having that sense of accomplishment, by doing it is the benefit. I'm not doing this to prove a point, I'm not doing it to get some accolades, I'm not doing it so people come in here and say, "Dude you're fucking out of your mind. What are you doing to yourself? But, by the way, this is awesome." That's not why we do it. We do it because we love it. The work is intrinsically motivating.

Mark Jilg
Craftsman Brewing Company

Mark Jilg is the owner/founder of Craftsman Brewing Company in Pasadena, California.

Nick: What exactly is your beer history? How did you first get involved in brewing?

Mark: I went to high school in Northern Virginia, and no one wanted to have their graduation ceremonies at the high school. They wanted to do it some place else. So our class president got elected and decided, "Okay, we got to start raising money." As we all know, the easiest way to raise money is to sell alcohol, so we had keg parties.

Actually, I look back on it and I think it's a shame that we live in a country where the drinking age is 21, because most people have access to alcohol now when they're not around family or people that really love and care for them. They learn about beer when they're off at college or after they've moved out of their family's house. I can remember drinking Anchor products when they were first becoming available on the East Coast in the late 70's. I moved back to California in the early 80's, and was around for the early L.A. beer scene; Wolfgang Puck's, Eureka.

Anyway, I didn't really get into beer until around 1990. My wife bought me a home brew kit and I went off the deep end. I did one extract batch of beer and then I had to do it as authentic and correct as possible, so I got involved in all grain-brewing really quickly. I was fortunate to be here in Los Angeles at that time, there was a really active home-brewing community, so I could learn from other people and do a lot of shared tastings. I learned a bunch about the diversity of beer, subtleties in beer style, subtleties in technique, and beer flaws. At that point, I was working at NASA JPL and had a really interesting job that only required me to work 40 hours a week, so I had lots of time on my hands. I got the home-brewing bug big, and people were really liking the beers I was making. I thought, "You know, this job at JPL isn't going to be around forever."

Desktop computers were finally starting to be powerful enough so that everybody could handle lots of photographic data easily, and I saw my job going away, so I started the brewery part-time. I did the brewery for about two years, trying to sell beer after hours, but it was tough. Most restaurant people want to meet with you in the early afternoon, so I quit my job and started running the brewery full-time. We've pretty much taken a slow, organic, evolutionary approach to the business. We started really small and we're still really small, but we're a lot bigger than we were 17 or 18 years ago when we started.

Nick: What's your process for coming up with a new beer? Is it more style driven or ingredient driven?

Mark: I would have to say, by far, it's ingredient driven. I think we do three distinct beers: We do beers that pay homage to tradition. We do beers that use unique ingredients, because I'm a contrarian by nature—I want to do stuff that other people aren't doing. Then we do beers where we're trying to get people to think about stuff that really doesn't have to do with the beer itself, or it doesn't have to do with the ingredients that are in the beer. For example, back in 2007 we brewed Point 5 as one of the "soapbox beers" where we're trying to get people to think about stuff. IPA, I think, is a beer style that's gotten completely hijacked by these double and triple versions, which are syrupy sweet big beers. They're not dry, spicy, thirst-quenchers like IPAs of old. So we tried to do this beer called Point 5 to try to say, "Hey look, if you can make a double version, you should be able to make a half version."

That was a really fulfilling beer because the people who got the joke really got the joke and they thought it was really funny and they really enjoyed the beer. As a commercial product, though, it was a real challenge because it's just not the American thing to want to have half of anything. If it's the American thing, it's got to be at least a double or a triple thing. It's always got to be super colossal. It can't be normal.

So we do beers that are driven by tradition, beers that are driven by ingredients, and then beers that are driven by my desire to stand on my soapbox and yell at people—and I do that a lot.

Nick: What do you say to the brewers who are making these doubles and triples who say, "We're California. We pioneer the style."

Mark: I think California really is sort of fashion-and-fad driven. Unfortunately, it's a horrible truth, but it really is. Americans, in general, really are about the new and the exciting and about the new experience. Americans and Californians aren't really about subtlety and refinements and connoisseurship. It's about being brash and it's about having a new experience.

It's a real challenge, because once you get on this path that you really like having new experiences all the time, you're always going to be chasing that. There's nothing necessarily wrong with that. It's just that there's the other side of beer appreciation, which has to do with subtlety and nuance and really deeply understanding something.

> **"So we do beers that are driven by tradition, beers that are driven by ingredients, and then beers that are driven by my desire to stand on my soapbox and yell at people—and I do that a lot."**

It's impossible for you to have a fully understood, deep appreciation of something if you don't repeatedly have that experience. It's tough. I love making specialty beers. We only do 3 beers year round, and we probably do another 20 to 25 specialty beers throughout the year. We're feeding the monster. We're making these new beers all the time. But every time we make a new specialty beer, it's not an extreme beer, for the most part. Usually there's some little thing I find intriguing about a beer style or a particular ingredient that I want to play with and a new beer is the result.

So, I don't know. I'm struggling with this trying to figure out whether I'm part of the problem or whether I'm part of the solution. I'd like to think I'm part of the solution, but there are times I look back and I think we really should be doing half as many releases and spending a little bit more time interacting with the people. We should interact with people who drink our beer in a way that they can appreciate the beers the way we appreciate the beers, which is trying to figure out little quirks or special little nuggets that are buried in the beer.

> **"It's impossible for you to have a fully understood, deep appreciation of something if you don't repeatedly have that experience."**

Nick: It sounds like the concept of Craftsman plays to all of that, that attention to detail and really trying to create something that will last. Can you talk a little bit about the philosophy of Craftsman and tell me what that is?

Mark: If you read the traditional arts and crafts stuff from the turn of the last century, you know, 1890 to 1915 is sort of the "Arts and Crafts" period, the "Craftsman Era." The core of that philosophy was rage against industrialization because handcrafted stuff was disappearing and everything was being made by machines. If I could reinvent that, I would reinvent it for the turn of the 20th century, or the 21st century, to be a rage against corporatization, because it's essentially the same thing, but it's even more pervasive.

It's not just physical objects, it's how people view the world and the products that they consume. I'm over 50 now and so now I'm like the crotchety old man who's always yelling at people to turn their music down and not go so fast. But I really think that is an important deal. If everybody would just slow down, so many of the problems that exist in our world would disappear.

We'd have the opportunity to really appreciate the subtlety of a well-made, simple beer. It doesn't have to be super alcoholic, super assertive, it can be really subtle and you can just slow down and enjoy it.

There's a lot of philosophical inspiration from the original Arts and Crafts Movement—it'd be cool if we could get people to slow down and have a relaxing beer and not have beer be this source of entertainment sucking the air out of the room. Beer should just sort of exist there with the furniture and the friendship and the conversation and all the other cool stuff that usually happens when there's beer around.

Nick: Are there core characteristics or elements you look to put into all the beers you create?

Mark: That's tough, because I really spend way too much time thinking about this stuff. But I really do like this idea we have, this core trio of beers. If I could say anything, I would like to think that all of our beers are thoughtful in some way,

that there's an underlying motivation for doing the beers, and it would be cool if, from my point of view, all of the beers had that. From the consumer's point of view, I hope they just have a good experience by drinking them.

When you really get down to the core motivation for why we do what we do, we're not doing this to make lots of money. If we wanted to do that, the path we would've taken would have been quite different. I feel fortunate that I haven't had the financial pressures to make a bunch of money. We started with a very pared down, handmade by me, brewing system and we've evolved by adding to that and making some fairly dramatic steps from one system to another. But we've never been in debt. We've never had investors. As long as there's money in the checking account, we're pretty happy.

Nick: Do you feel that Los Angeles is the right place for your brewery?

Mark: We're in a huge population. We have, within a 100 miles of our brewery, about 12 million people. One of the beautiful things about Los Angeles is it's such a megalopolis, you can pretty much do what you want and you should be able to find a niche easily.

When I first started, there was very little craft beer here. Most of the craft beer that was here came from somewhere else. So I took this very seriously. It was really hard to get other people to take it seriously, so I've kind of internalized the motivations for doing the beer. If I'm going to put all this effort and all this time into making the beer—if no one else is going to be blown away by it, at least I should be.

Nick: What's your take on this notion of a current "revolution" in craft beer in America?

Mark: The explosion in craft beers is really driving me nuts, because I cut my teeth when, for beer appreciation, you had to make your own beer. If you wanted a certain beer style, Los Angeles didn't really have much, so you had to make it yourself.

That being said, L.A. is a huge place. There's a lot of cool beer knowledge here. There's been a lot of really good beer here for a long time. I think it's always hilarious whenever you see people interviewed about the L.A. beer scene. They think that it's only happened in the last 3 or 5 years. But I think, honestly, if you objectively went back and looked at the L.A. beer scene in 2000 or even 1995 and you compared that with places that supposedly have great beer culture, we had it. We just had it on a much smaller scale. That's when my sense of beer culture was set. So, to see craft beer everywhere now is a little strange for me, because I think, somehow access changes your appreciation of things. If you can have this world-class beer experience everyday, it sort of loses its world-class affect on you.

Nick: So, is the "revolution" a good thing or a bad thing?

Mark: I think, in the long run, it's a good thing. My sense is that I would be perfectly happy with a world where 10% of the beer that people consumed was what is considered "craft." When I say "craft," I mean that the experience you have is really a considered one. It's one where you really show reverence for that experience.

It is just nuts how fast the craft beer industry's moving, and I think it's making tons of mistakes right now. Everybody's putting all of this effort into adding value to their product, but they're not doing a very good job of adding value. They're not getting the consumer to really understand that added value, and that's what worries me; craft beer isn't really paying attention to the trajectory of what the consumer experience is going to be like five years from now.

If you are always pandering to the geeks, making huge, big, super expressive, new experiences every time, is that sustainable? I don't really think so. A lot of those beers are not particularly drinkable, and if you had to drink that beer everyday, you would get tired of it in less than a week. But if you could only drink it once a month, then it's still really cool. It's really special. It's really exciting. It does all of that.

So there's this weird contradictory thing going on. There are all these breweries who think that craft beer should be 25% or 30% of total beer sold. That's true, but what's the product mix going to be like? It's not going to be Russian imperial, double, quadruple, whatever. It's going to be some real beautiful nuanced session beer that is food friendly, drinkable.

Nick: Has the term "craft," when it comes to beer, become one of those words like "organic" that's sort of lost its meaning?

Mark: Oh yeah, to a very large degree. Read press releases from breweries and you could just take the word *craft* and *beer* out and replace it with any commodity product and you wouldn't know the difference.

Nick: What does "craft" mean to you?

Mark: "Craft" means that the producers have a real honest commitment to making a well-made experience first rate product. The idea that they're going to be "the next big thing" really shouldn't play a role in craft products. Craft products really are these small-scale, heartfelt, and heart-made products, and I think the industry's getting taken over by people who want to be millionaires more than they want to make great beer.

John Gillooly
Drake's Brewing Company

John Gillooly is the brewmaster at Drake's Brewing Company in San Leandro, California.

Nick: What were your earliest experiences with brewing and how did you wind up where you are today?

John: I started home brewing in 1990, literally at home—kitchen-sink style—until about '93. Then I moved up to all-grain home brewing and really started nerding out on it. In 1994, UC Davis opened up a side program called the American Brewers Guild. I was working in a warehouse at the time, and I decided that I wanted to take a class there. That class had an internship element to it. I got sent up to Redhook in Seattle, where, after the program was done, I got hired. So my first two years in the industry were with Redhook up at the big Woodinville plant.

I liked Redhook. We were brewing around the clock, it was busy, but there wasn't really much advancement potential there. So we moved back to the Bay Area. I took a job as the lead cellarman at Golden Pacific Brewing Company, a defunct local brewery that did a lot of contract brewing. It was kind of interesting; we made so many different brands for so many different people. You learn a lot about ingredients, a lot about process. We made hefes and we made lagers. We made all sorts of different kinds of ales. Ultimately, that place was not financially stable—when your paychecks are bouncing, you start looking for another job.

I landed at a brewpub in downtown Sonoma called Sienna Red Brewing Company. They also no longer exist. I was the only brewer there, it was very cool. I was writing my own recipes and basically home brewing for a small restaurant/bar, which was great. I still pull things out of that recipe book every so often.

When they closed down, I was able to go to Mendocino Brewing Company, where I was the lead brewer for exactly one year before I took the brewmaster job at Dogfish Head in Delaware. I was at Dogfish from 2002 to 2004, when they were really just starting to make that big push. We went from like 3,500 barrels to almost 8,000 barrels to 14,000 barrels my last year, and they've continued that growth curve. That was a really good place to be and it was really exciting because, when you're doubling your volume every year, you've got to figure out your job differently every week.

Eventually, I took a brewer job at Trumer, which is funny because Trumer is where Golden Pacific was. I just walked right in there, I was like, "Yeah I've brewed on this brew house before." I spent a couple of years there—Trumer is a great place, but you're only making one beer. After that, I took a job at Speakeasy, where I was the head brewer for a year.

I got brought into Drake's on kind of a contractor basis. My original primary job was to help out Head Brewer Brian Thorson, who had cut his hand badly and I was to (literally) be his right hand. Originally, most of the work I did was assisting the barrel program, though I was quickly given full time duties in all aspects of production. A year later, some people above me were moving on, and I got put in charge of Drake's Brewing Company, which is kind of awesome. I was super stoked to be here. It's a really dynamic place to work, we're growing really fast. This is very Dogfish-esque: the nature of our growth and just having to figure out new ways to get more beer out and all that kind of stuff, which is fun.

Nick: Dogfish has played a huge role in the industry and you seemed to have been right there on the cusp of it. What was that experience like?

John: Working for Sam Calagione for two years was a pretty awesome experience. That guy is not only a great marketer, he's really got one of the biggest brains in the industry. Plus, the way he approaches beer is a way more people should approach it. Sam really approaches beer as a beverage that should be respected.

When I was there he was doing that whole, "He Said, She Said" thing, where they would do these dinners and a sommelier would come and pair with wine, and Sam would match with beer. The marketing there didn't denigrate your intelligence like some . . . I mean, you've seen some ads out there, we've all seen some of the stupid ads out there. Sam was very into trying to elevate the role of beer and the perception of beer in the industry, which I think is a great thing.

Nick: At the time, that must have been a pretty uphill battle.

John: Oh yeah, it still is. You got to a beer fest and you see the bro contingent, "I'm gonna get hammered!" It's like,

"Ugh." That's one of the things I love about this place, we do that Session Ale Fest in May, no beer over 5%. I think that's a great trend in the industry and I'm glad that we're really on the edge of promoting that one, too.

Looping back to Dogfish: not only did I appreciate the way they were trying to sell beer there but, there was wide open experimentation. 20+ percent beers. Beers with weird ingredients. When I ordered, I ordered grain and hops, but I also got a food truck in because I had to bring in licorice root and chicory and raisins, which we boiled and pureed and chucked in kettles.

There was also a lot of technical stuff—a lot of, "figure out how to make this beer, how to make that beer." Plus they were cutting edge on the hops. 90-minute IPA was a real cult thing when I got there and we launched 60-minute IPA when I was there. For 2003, launching a Simcoe-Amarillo beer was really cutting edge.

Nick: What's really interesting to me is, you went from that to Trumer, where you were making one beer. There, it's really about perfecting that one beer.

John: Making it exactly the same every time, it's all process. You go there and you think in a different way. You're just thinking about, "How can I make this exactly the same every time?" You're trying to cut out variance.

Nick: A lot of brewers will describe the brewing process as a perfect marriage of science and creativity. Do you find yourself on one side or the other as a brewer?

John: No, I like to think we marry them really well here. We make a lot of one-offs, a lot of specials, but we're very process-driven here. We have extensive notes, we have a lot of paperwork. We can break our beers down a lot of different ways. You want something to be reproducible. I've done some consulting gigs at pubs where those guys barely take notes. I'm like, "How are you going to make it again?" They say, "Ah who cares man, it's my pale, I make it however I want to every

time." That's great, but take notes anyway. If this one came out real well maybe you'll want to brew it again.

Nick: Do you have any overriding philosophies or guidelines regarding how you brew?

John: I like really clean, well-delineated flavors in the beer. The beer should be about something and you should be able to focus on it. I've got a beer in front of me right now: Clean, light, dry body. The Simcoe-Amarillo dry hop is what pops out at you, the malt is like barely a whisper. That's what this beer is. Other beers, like the amber, are focused on the malt quality. When I got here we were in the process of switching our English specialty malts, and that was a real thing because that drives that beer. Getting that dialed in just right is important.

In general, when I'm putting a beer together, I like it to be bright, well-focused. I don't like a lot of muddy flavors in the beer. If you've got 16 things going on at once, you actually don't have anything going on.

> **"If you've got 16 things going on at once, you actually don't have anything going on."**

Nick: Drake's has a really great lineage of great brewers. Can you talk a little bit about what it means to be a part of that?

John: It's a great tradition of brewers here, man. A lot of really good guys popped out of this place. You're always building on what the last guy did. It's fun, I get to look at old recipes from way back in the day. I looked at some old Rodger Davis recipes. Those were always fun.

Nick: Is there a shortage of supplies because of how many breweries are opening up? If so, how are you guys handling that?

John: We're pretty well contracted on supplies over the next few years. You're always guesstimating on growth, so hopefully we're well contracted. I would hate to be the anchor if this thing really starts going. I think my scaling is good. It's the little guys who are in trouble, man.

If you're just opening up. . . . We have, actually, a brewer here named Collin McDonnell, who opened up Henhouse Brewing Company. While he was opening that place he was brewing here. He told me flat out, "We don't do IPAs because I can't get any hops," so he's doing Belgian-styles and oyster stout. At least he thought about it, because otherwise it's tough. I think it's tough for a lot of the guys opening up.

Nick: You've seen tremendous growth in the industry lately. Do you view that positively?

John: I do feel like there's a bit of a mid-90s feel out there. There are people who are getting into brewing who don't

know anything about brewing, they just think it's the next cash train. That's what happened in the mid-90s, there was a shakeout. There's going to be a shakeout. There are some guys who, they're just in it for the money. There are some guys who, they're home brewers with extra money. Maybe they'll stay alive, but just as a small thing.

For the serious players I think there's a lot of growth potential out there. I think the segment in general could continue to get bigger. People looked at Budweiser and Coors with Shock Top and Blue Moon and they were like, "Oh, that's terrible for craft." I think it's the opposite. I think it moves people closer to craft. Once you've made that step off macro lager to Blue Moon, you're now requesting beer with more flavor. Maybe not everybody goes from Blue Moon to something else, but some of those people do. They're getting filtered our way. We're more than happy to receive them and offer them something. God knows I've got 20-odd taps up there, there's probably something for anyone.

Nick: What do you love most about being at Drake's?

John: I would say the great thing about being here is that we have a mandate from our ownership to always make the best beer that we can. That means sometimes a new ingredient comes in that you want to play with, and we get to play with it. The door is not shut on us. Nobody says, "Well this is the recipe, it goes back 10 years. You can only brew this exact recipe."

If a new maltery opened up somewhere and they had some product, I'd play with it, I'd do a little one-off batch. If it's worth working into our recipe we'll work it into our recipes. New hop varieties, the same thing. I've bought a couple hop varieties this year that don't have names, bought them on spec. We're probably going to build up an entire skew around some of them because they're so interesting.

We've been doing this experimental IPA series. Maybe we constantly just have an experimental IPA on tap, which is great. Our staff loves it, it's always something different to drink, always something different to do. We are a small brewhouse so, you know, we have big tanks and we'll fill the big tanks up with IPA and 1500 and Denog, but those little tanks? We do these little one-offs.

We can just blow it out in our own tasting rooms. When I have a little bit of time on the schedule I just let the brew-

ers brew what they want. Here, it's a really fun, somewhat challenging blend of being experimental, being able to fool around with things, but still drilling down on consistency. 1500 needs to be 1500. If you're going to buy one, it's got to taste like 1500 every time.

It's fun and I have a very young staff. A lot of them don't have a lot of experience. For quite a few of them, this is their first brewery. I'm in year 20, I feel like my job is to sprinkle them all with fairy dust experience from my back pocket, kind of move this place up.

Nick: Would you say that there's kind of a new school and an old school to brewers?

John: I will say there's a new school and an old school to flavors. I think drier, cutting edge beers are like the dry, hoppy ones, not necessarily strong. I don't know if session ale is really going to take off, but it's a niche that's getting bigger and bigger.

Nick: I hope so. Is bigger necessarily better these days? It will get you noticed . . .

John: It will get you noticed.

Nick: Where do you fall on that?

John: I don't know if bigger is necessarily better. Some beers are made to be big. That booziness is part of the style. If somebody tells me to re-create a style, I'm going to do it spot on, regardless of what it is. I'm not impressed by big beers. I think they're a place where a lot of brewers can hide. If you're a mediocre technical brewer you can always knock out a double IPA. You can always hide behind the booze and the hops, but you can't knock out a good session beer if you're not a technical brewer.

Nick: What is it about beer that you love so much? What's kept you in the industry for 20 years?

John: Well, it's my favorite thing to drink. Before I started working here, I was a 1500 fan for years. Just coming in here and being able to carry that torch, I feel like I'm a backup guitarist in Lou Reed's band.

> **"I feel like I'm a backup guitarist in Lou Reed's band."**

It's like, "I get to play Sweet Jane," you know. It's like, "Shit I get to play this for real. I'm not covering it, this is actually happening."

We have all these specials, the Hopocalypse just happened. Those recipes are different every year, so I'd like to see if we can advance that ball a little bit further down. Keep it current, keep it good. I think the market is moving more to cleaner and well-delineated beers. Since that is my direction too, we're all meeting in the middle on that one.

Jeremy Raub
Eagle Rock Brewery

Jeremy Raub is the brewmaster and one of the owners at Eagle Rock Brewery in Los Angeles.

Nick: Let's start at the beginning. How did you first get into craft beer and brewing?

Jeremy: I guess my first beer was just a sip of my dad's or my uncle's Milwaukee's Best, or something like that. I remember just not really thinking much of it. Near the end of high school, when I was getting ready to go off to college, my dad had just started getting into home brewing. This was around the mid-90s.

So I tried some of the home brews that he had finished and thought they were pretty good, pretty interesting. We brewed a couple batches together. Had a lot of fun. Our beer turned out okay. We gave it to friends and neighbors. About six months later, we were at our neighbor's house, and they still had the beer in their fridge. They never drank it. They said, "Well, you can have it back if you want." So we thought, "Okay. Cool." We took it back and opened it up. It was amazing. It was the best thing we'd ever tasted. It was really chocolatey, and had this really nice body to it, and this nutty character. We just looked at each other and went, "Holy shit. This is great."

That got us excited about brewing. We brewed a couple more times before I went off to college. In college I sort of forgot about home brewing. I went to school and learned about the technical side of post-production audio. I decided to move out to L.A. with friends from school so we could get into the film industry and pursue our careers.

When I had moved to L.A., my roommate and I would go out to Vendome Liquors and just look at the beer selection they had. It wasn't much at the time, but they had maybe 15 or 20 different beers. We would sit there and look at the labels, take home the cool-looking ones, and then taste them. That's when I really started getting into appreciating flavors in beer and the diversity in beer. I remember the one that I would always go back to again and again was Rogue Dead Guy Ale.

About eight . . . I don't know, maybe six, or seven, or eight years later . . . I met Ting, and she had come to appreciate really good craft beers when she was going to school in Atlanta. As we started getting our relationship going, we would always go out and try new things, new wines, new beers. I hadn't really thought much about home brewing again, but, after Ting and I bought a house, it was right around that time my parents moved out from upstate New York to California. They had moved to the L.A. area, and so I thought, "Wow. This is cool. We just bought a house, so we have space, and we can brew again. I said to my dad, "Hey, do you still have any of your old home brew stuff?" So he brought it out with him, and we found a local home brew shop, and we just got back into it.

We were brewing in the kitchen. We were starting to make more of a mess. Ting wasn't happy about that. So we set up in my garage and started making bigger batches. At that point we went from extract brewing to all-grain brewing and started learning how to write our own recipes.

As I was working in the film industry at the time, I was able to take time in between projects to work on a business plan for a brewery, and I was able to start getting the actual planning of the business together. It took probably close to two years to get all the planning together. Then it took us about two years once we found this building to get all the permitting and licensing. Since we were one of the first new microbreweries to open up in the city of L.A. in decades, it was quite a process. The health department, for instance, they treated us like a wholesale food processing facility. Because of that, they made us do a lot of specifications in our build-out that I've never seen in other breweries in California. We had to fight back and forth, but we were finally able to get open.

Nick: What year did you officially open?

Jeremy: We brewed our first batch here at Eagle Rock Brewery in November 2009. That first batch was Solidarity, which is our black mild. We had really focused on the home brewing side, and I think we did nine different revisions of the recipe, until we found something we were happy with. Each one of those revisions we brewed half a dozen times.

Nick: Talk a little bit about how you would revise a recipe over and over again. Do you think that revision process is important, to start with one recipe and continue on that until you get it right?

Jeremy: Yeah. On the home brewing side, we were doing a lot of one-off recipes. It was sort of whatever we thought sounded interesting. At some point, I think a lot of home brewers realize, "Hey, I'm getting pretty good at this, and I can brew these styles well." Developing consistency, though—I think that's something that brewers, whether they're home brewers or professional brewers, something they strive for.

We tried brewing the same exact recipe and getting it as close to the previous version as possible. Then, when we felt comfortable with that—that we could get consistent results—then we started tweaking the recipe, so that we really understood what those changes were doing to the finished beer. If you don't have consistency, you could make a change and then not really understand how that change affects the finished beer, because there are too many variables going on.

Nick: Tell me a little bit about your process. I want to know if, generally across the board, there are certain general aspects that you like to have in your beer.

Jeremy: Generally speaking, I like—and I think all of us agree—we like our beers to finish clean, more on the dry side, and to have a really good balance. That's an overarching, very non-specific set of guidelines.

Balance is important, but balance is also very subjective. An IPA, in the general sense, is out of balance, because it's more weighted toward hops and accentuating a profile of hops. But, within that little world of IPAs, you can have balance, or extremes where the bitterness is way out of balance with the malt, and on your palate you're only experiencing that bitter aspect. Balance may be an overused word, or maybe it's just a word with a very broad meaning. I believe balance is the sense of having lots of palate sensations involved and lots of sensory harmony. It's not that every beer has to have an even bitterness to gravity ratio to be balanced. No.

Nick: What is the process like for you to create a new recipe?

Jeremy: Usually it starts with an idea. It could be a flavor component. It could be a color. For instance, the beer that we're brewing today, this Prickly Pear Berliner Rye, was a totally new creation. We all got together, got some prickly pear fruit, and tasted it together. Knowing what we know about beer, we all said, "What would capture the essence of this fruit?" So, one of the first things that came to mind for all of us was, "Okay. It's a very light-flavored fruit, so we probably don't want to go too heavy on the malt side. We don't want to use crystal malts that are going to mask and cover up the subtle nuances of the fruit." A lot of us leaned toward something that was tart, because tartness can help bring out the fruit character, and there's some acidity in fruit anyway.

An idea, a lot of times, will start with just a picture—a mental picture, of the beer, or a flavor picture of the beer. Then we just build it from there. Once we have that initial recipe, we can evaluate it and see how close we came to that vision in our head, and then make adjustments. That's something that, for me, I think is pretty important. You can't be so dogmatic that it's like, "This is it. This is the recipe. It has to stay pure. There's no changing it." Beer is a living thing; it changes. From batch to batch, we try to get consistency, but, for me going from home brewing these beers and having them on a small scale to brewing them on a larger scale and sharing them with a whole city, that changes the beer. In a sense, people's perception, my perception of it in other people's hands, and seeing people interact with the beer, it becomes its own thing.

> **"If you don't have consistency, you could make a change and then not really understand how that change affects the finished beer, because there are too many variables going on."**

You have to, I think, get to know the beer and not just say, "Well, this is what it's going to be," and force it into a certain set of restrictions. You have your idea of how this beer is, but then having the finished product in your hands and tasting it changes that image a little bit. You have to be able to change and be open to the fact that beer can be what it is. It's kind of its own living thing.

Nick: Tell me a little bit about the philosophy of Eagle Rock and also about the collaborative aspects.

Jeremy: It really evolved from the idea that when we were thinking of opening up, L.A. was this black hole, in a sense. There were a few good breweries here making good beers, like, for instance, Craftsman, up in Pasadena. They've been making really good beers for 17 years. The idea that San Diego—you mention San Diego and everyone's like, "Oh, yeah. They've got Stone and Ballast Point and Ale-Smith and Green Flash, and Port and all these great breweries." San Francisco. You mention San Francisco and people think of Russian River and Bear Republic and Lagunitas, the 21st Amendment, and Magnolia, and Speak-easy, and all those guys. But then L.A. It's like, "Okay, well, there's Craftsman and . . ."

I guess the idea was, "Hey, why don't we have a better beer city?" That was one of the real motivating factors for us starting Eagle Rock Brewery in the first place.

Nick: Why didn't L.A. ever embrace beer like some of these other areas?

Jeremy: I don't know. That's a tough question. It could be because of the unfriendly nature of the city of L.A. to small businesses. During the mid-90s there was a whole craft beer boom around the country. It was starting to happen in L.A. There were a lot of brewpubs that popped up. But people that I've talked to that were in the industry at the time point to the fact that those brewpubs were opening for the wrong reasons. It was just like they saw this as an opportunity to make a quick buck, which it's clearly not. I guess because of the failure rate of a lot of those, it maybe scared people off, or the consumers thought, "Oh, these microbreweries that opened in the mid-90s made crappy beer," so people thought, "Well, I don't want that." That could be a reason. I think there's a lot of factors, but, whatever the case may be, L.A. is about ten years behind most of the country as far as craft beer goes. I think right now we have a pretty good foothold, and we're starting to catch up.

Nick: What about the aspects of collaboration you guys have here?

Jeremy: That also plays into working as a team here, because all of our full-time employees started off as home brewers. They came to us, offering to volunteer, just because they loved brewing. They were excited about the fact that a brewery was opening up in L.A. and they wanted to be be part of the beer community and beer culture. Again, it's all tied into that idea of creating that sense of community. That's why we do a lot of collaboration, make a lot of these decisions together.

All of us are beer judges as well. That came out of us being home brewers and wanting to improve our palates and improve our beers, so we all became beer judges. In that training you learn that you always should have somebody to bounce an idea off of. You almost never judge a flight of beers solo, because you could have an off day. You might not be sensitive to certain flavor components that somebody else is more sensitive to. Whenever we're evaluating beers, we always evaluate beers together for that reason.

For me, I feel like it makes us stronger as a brewery to have such good communication and such good teamwork between all of our members. Nobody's afraid to say, "You know what? I taste this off flavor, this defect, in this batch of beer." It's not like the brewmaster is handing down these decrees to people, and then they have to follow those. It's a very open and collaborative process.

When we come up with ideas for new beers, it's open to everybody. Seasonal beers and specialty beers, we let our staff be creative and have that creative outlet and have fun with it. They can brew something on the big scale that they've always wanted to try. Or something that they brewed on the home brew scale that they really liked, they can brew it on the big scale and see people's interactions here in the taproom, and talk to them about it. It just completes that whole circle.

Nick: Is having your family involved an important element for you?

Jeremy: The idea of having a family business was to just be able to spend more time with loved ones and be able to share the process. When I was working in the film industry, my schedule was dictated by forces out of my control. I would work long hours, and then have plans over the weekend to go away with family, or whatnot, or go out dinner with my wife. They would almost always end up getting messed up, because my schedule would change at the last minute.

> ## "Beer is a living thing; it changes."

I also just wanted to have a little bit more ownership over something. Of course, then, there are struggles, ups and downs, with the whole process of working with family members. No one can fight like family, but no one can really get along quite like family either. It's been great, though.

It's been really nice working with family, because, at the end of the day, we're sharing in this together. No matter what struggles we're going through, we're still going to end up together and struggle through it. We made it through so far, and that's pretty rewarding.

Todd Ashman
FiftyFifty Brewing Company

Todd Ashman is the head brewer at FiftyFifty brewing company in Truckee, California.

Nick: So, when did you first get interested in beer? Give us the story right up to today.

Todd: It really starts when I moved from Texas to California and started to go to Santa Rosa Junior College. After the first day of school I went to a place called the English Rose, I had my first Sierra Nevada Pale Ale and that . . . it set me on a path to where I am at today. I discovered hoppy beer, I discovered what was essentially the California benchmark for beer at the time, which would have been 1987. I got involved with the Sonoma County Beerocrats, which is a home brew club, and there were people in that organization that believed that I had brewing talent. They encouraged me to go to brewing school, which I did in 1995.

It went to the American Brewer's Guild/UC Davis extension program—Craft Brewers Apprenticeship program. I ended up doing eight weeks of class and then six weeks of apprenticeship at Bison Brewing Company in Berkeley under Scott Meyer. After I graduated, I ended up with a very short stint at a brewery in New Mexico called Kegs and I was hired out of Kegs to Flossmoor Station Brewing company in Flossmoor, IL in 1996. I was there for eight years, and during that time, I started barrel aging, which is something I continue to do to this day. During my tenure at Flossmoor, I had managed to garner 11 Great American Beer Festival medals, five World Beer Cup awards—most of those for either my barrel-aged beer or my porter.

I left Flossmoor to go to Titletown Brewing Company in Green Bay, Wisconsin. I was only there a short while before I was offered a job at Rahr Malting Company. I took the job at Rahr, which was just outside of Minneapolis. I was basically a desk brewmaster, giving malt customers advice on brewing beer styles, processes, and procedures. During that time, I decided that I wanted to get back into brewing. I bided my time looking for the appropriate situation and the job in Truckee at FiftyFifty came up. So I moved out here in September of 2006 and got the brewery operation started. We opened in May of 2007, and here we are today.

Nick: Can you talk a little bit about the barrel aging process? How did that start for you, and what made you think to do it?

Todd: I became aware of it while brewing in the Chicago area at Flossmoor Station. There was a home brewing tradition that took place on St. Patrick's Day in a community called Beverly. They always had a big parade, it was a big to-do in a Chicago suburb that had a large Irish population. The local home brew store and home brewing club used to get together on that day and brew enough beer to fill a bourbon barrel and used it as the fermentor. Apparently, from what I understand, Greg Hall from Goose Island saw this and took it a step further. He actually used the bourbon barrel as an aging vessel, and thus was born bourbon county (barrel-aged) style.

I arrived in the Chicago area a few years after this had started, but I'd never had Bourbon County stout. I thought it was a brilliant idea. It was a wonderful way to actually get something like an imperial style or a barleywine aging in a bourbon barrel. You let it sit for a while and then bring it out six months later, a year later, two years later and see what that does. It was a wildly successful undertaking and customers loved it. So there was no real reason to stop it. We got into blending different beers and the results of those beers are products that I still continue to make to this day.

The bourbon barrels actually tend to bring the most flavor into the beer and leave the most nuance. At FiftyFifty, we are not just producing a barrel-aged imperial stout, we are produced seven or eight in a given vintage year. This year, I believe we are working with seven different types of barrels and the average age on the beer is 180 days in the wood. If we can go to 225 we will, but on average it's about 180 days in the barrel. From the barrels, we get not only the underlying spirit that was in the barrel prior, but also the oak tannins and their flavors of coconut and vanilla.

Nick: Many people consider you to be one of the pioneers of barrel aging. Is that an appropriate title for you?

Todd: I want to bring new flavors to the craft brewing audience—people that want to drink unique beer. I want to demonstrate what the barrel does to a particular base beer, and I think that—as someone trying to deliver that message—I'll take the title of pioneer, but it's a continual exploration. When you are passionate for something you basically let it envelope you. In Berlin they call me the "Godfather of Barrel Aging."

> **"I want to bring new flavors to the craft brewing audience— people that want to drink unique beer. I want to demonstrate what the barrel does to a particular base beer . . ."**

Nick: A lot of your beers have big flavor, you are known for big flavors, so—generally speaking—are there certain characteristics that you like for the beer that you brew?

Todd: I've always been under the impression that if you were going to ask someone for five or six dollars for a pint of beer that it better be flavor driven. It really needs to be what it says it is; if it's IPA, it needs to have a significant malt backbone with great hop character throughout. If there is one thing that I guess I have been known for, it's that I never make anything that is low alcohol or light, unless it's meant to be.

> **"I tell my brewers, my assistant brewers, we make a beer to tell a story."**

I like using lots of hops, and creating a distinctive malt character based on what that style is. Our porter has molasses in it. It has hand-toasted oak flakes, a nice array of roasted malt, and then a nice hop character as well. We want layered complexity—we're looking to strike a balance with all those ingredients, but at the same time, be unique. I don't want things to seem normal on our bigger beers.

I tell my brewers, my assistant brewers, we make a beer to tell a story. Generally, the beers need to transport the drinker on a little bit of a Belgian, American, or English journey, inspired by Belgian ale or English ale or American styles.

Nick: What is your approach to coming up with a new beer?

Todd: Usually there is an inspiration from my travels. I've been to Belgium 16 times, to Germany 9 times, and you always come away with so much. These days, there are so many quality ingredients coming into the United States that you can pretty much emulate whatever you want.

Nick: How are beers that you lay down, or age, different from those you drink fresh?

Todd: Well, there are lots of variables in the wood. Barrel aging is about letting the organic chemistry run its course—it's the serendipity that goes on in the barrels. There really isn't a reason to rush because time is really the secret ingredient for these beers—the more you just leave them alone and let them do their thing, the better it works.

Letting beer take its time, that's something that you get from Belgium and the lager traditions that go on in Germany. You have to give beer time, because beer is a living product. You have to allow it to do its thing—it will let you know when it's ready. There is no need to rush. You know, IPAs are great when they are fresh—so is wheat beer, Hefeweizen—there are certain

beers that don't want to wait, they demand that you drink them fresh. Our angle right now is, at least with the bigger beers, to let them take their time.

Nick: You have been judging at the GABF for about 16 years. Is judging important to you? Is being a part of the larger craft community important to you?

Todd: I love taking part in the Great American Beer Festival as a judge because, I have traveled the world, they allow you to select beers styles in which you have a strength and background. By applying my knowledge, coupled with the knowledge of other judges, we come to a consensus based on knowledge and expertise. No beer is awarded a medal by less than six judges and there has to be consensus. Sometimes people champion a certain beer over another and there is a deep discussion—there's a lot of heartfelt discussion and a lot of passion that comes up in the judging process when it comes to awarding medals. I do feel that I'm serving the brewing community at large by being a judge, yes.

Nick: What's your take on the explosion of growth in craft beer industry?

Todd: Never before have we seen the kind of growth that we are seeing in the craft industry today. There are upwards of 2,000 breweries in planning and there are over 2,000 breweries in existence. It's incredible. Is it sustainable? I'm going to go out on limb here and say no. I don't see it, because there is going to be a point—probably in 2014 when we see the new Sierra Nevada brewery, the new New Belgium brewery, the new Lagunitas brewery, the new Oskar Blues beer all go online— there has to be some attrition. Somebody is going to lose some market share.

Nick: What have you never been asked in an interview before that you have always wanted to say?

Todd: Oh god, I don't know. That is a good one. I don't want to say anything cheesy, but it would be something like, "Who is the future Mrs. Ashman?" or something like that. I would love to have my significant other be someone that would be really into beer and totally be supportive. That would be it I guess.

I think, because I was never really good in school and I only focused on stuff that I enjoyed, it took me a long time to realize that I wasn't going to be taught anything unless I wanted to know it. It was all of the book reading, I got a hold of every brewing book and magazine and piece of literature I could get a hold of, and read it backwards and forwards until—literally—I memorized it. And I talked to my assistants, and they want to know, "How is it that you know this stuff right off the top of your head?" and it's

like, when you are passionate for something you basically let it envelope you.

Nick: I guess here is my last question then, I haven't asked you this yet. Why do you love beer?

Todd: For me it's something that people enjoy and it's always nice to hear, "Hey, you've made a great beer!" and "This is a great beer that you are creating, by making it from raw materials." It's working with those raw ingredients, putting those things together and making something that is not only consumable but enjoyable. Then, if you take that to the Nth degree, you get accolades, you know that your peers recognize you and that this is a great beer. I work with great people, like my assistant brewer Alyssa Shook. My colleagues and all

the folks I have worked for make up such a great community.

All of those things come together in a way that just makes it all quite amazing. It's like being a chef or a baker. We are making something out of agricultural products and working with yeast and coming up with a finished product. And it's what we do with that in our work that is essentially our signature. It's ours, we put it out there for people to judge, to enjoy or to not enjoy, be that as it may. It's an interesting process, but brewing is different than cooking. Brewing is done over a several week process, it's like a cheesemaker or a similar pursuit. Do you really know when you're putting all that milk together, do you really know what's going to happen in the end?

Ten years down the road, if you are aging it that long, it's an interesting journey. Until you've done it, it's got to seem somewhat like alchemy. To the uninformed, it's got to almost seem like magic. It's a lot of hard work and I don't even understand all of the organic chemistry and the reactions that go on from the time we mill and mash and brew and ferment and then age until we enjoy. There's a lot different things going on and it's quite interesting, but fun. If it wasn't fun, or if it was really hard, I don't think a whole lot of people would do it, but I enjoy it! I can't imagine doing anything else!

> **"When you are passionate for something you basically let it envelope you."**

Matt Brynildson
Firestone Walker
Brewing Company

Matt Brynildson is the brewmaster at the Firestone
Walker Brewing Company in Paso Robles, California.

**Nick: What's your earliest memory of enjoying craft beer?
And how did you first start brewing?**

Matt: I was born and raised in Litchfield, Minnesota. Minnesota
is, of course, more of a beer state. California, where I am now, is
more of a wine state. I remember my first beer experience—my
grandfather cracking a can and handing it to me, thinking it was
a joke, that I wouldn't like it. Of course, I did like it.

I did my college years in Kalamazoo, Michigan, which was
fortuitous because Larry Bell of the Bell's Brewing Company
was already making craft beer there. So he was one of the pioneers, if not the pioneer, in the Midwest. My first craft beer
epiphany was tasting a Bell's porter and realizing that there was
something more to beer than just fizzy yellow water.

course under my belt. That was in 1995, the year that Goose Island was building their first production facility.

While I was at Siebel, there were quite a few job offers out there. The light bulb just went on. I thought to myself, "Man, I could be doing this professionally. I don't want to be a lab rat anymore. I can go on and be a brewer." So I went home and resigned from the Kalamazoo Spice Extraction Company and took an entry-level cellar position at Goose Island Beer Company.

That very first year, we went from being a brewpub to doing 25,000 barrels of production brewing, so it was just trial by fire. Pretty much the entire staff were Siebel graduates, but we had very little experience in big league production craft-brewing. We were all basically home brewers, and all of a sudden we're turning 200-barrel fermenters over as fast as we possibly could and trying to learn how to bottle and trying to learn how to keg, so I think that the learning curve was highly accelerated.

Again, it was just this fortuitous coming together of sorts, because Goose Island was right there in the same town as Siebel, so every time we ran ourselves into a wall or into a corner, we could go across town and ask our instructors at Siebel the questions.

I stayed there until 2000. I actually got a call from a headhunter asking me if I was interested in coming out to the West Coast and applying for a job with SLO Brewing Company. Being young and dumb, and not really doing my homework, and coming from such a solid company, I thought I could do anything. So I quit a perfectly good job and moved to what I thought was the big leagues of craft brewing here in California in January of 2000.

SLO Brewing at the time was in an upward crawl, trying to go from being a brewpub to a production brewery at this very site. A year and a half later, the production facility was purchased by Firestone Walker, and in July 2001, Firestone took ownership of the brewery and asked me to stay on as their brewmaster. I've been here ever since.

> **"My first craft beer epiphany was tasting a Bell's porter and realizing that there was something more to beer than just fizzy yellow water."**

Nick: What is it that you bring to a brewery that makes it successful?

Matt: Oh, I don't know. It's a combination of things. I'm super-passionate about quality and making beer. And I have a little bit of a lab background, so that works well in a production setting. I think the majority of my success has been able to piece together really good teams and hold the teams together.

I've said it before, but I always say that production brewing and being a brewmaster or a head brewer at a production brewery is like being a coach of a sports team. My job is to put

I spent a good deal of time in Europe during my college years, I had exposure to Larry Bell and craft beer made in the U.S., and I picked up home brewing at some point during college. I was also studying organic chemistry, so all these dots started connecting.

I wound up working at Kalamazoo Spice Extraction Company (KALSEC), which is actually quite well-known in the hops world. So I was home brewing as a hobby and doing hop chemistry as a job. I was biding my time because I thought I was going to go to medical school. My company sent me to the Siebel Institute of Brewing Technology and I got my first short together the best team I possibly can, keep the communication alive, and keep these guys happy. I want to keep them doing what they're best at, which is making beer. That's how I see my position.

Nick: Talk a little bit about your brewing style and your brewing philosophies. Are there general characteristics that you're trying to incorporate in every beer?

Matt: Yeah. You've probably heard it a million times; I think that beer is about balance and drinkability. Those are at the nucleus of everything that any brewer needs to be in touch with. Now, that's relative, because there are really hoppy beers that still possess balance and drinkability, and super sour beers possess that, too . . . but there is that balancing point you always have to keep in mind.

Our philosophy is actually pretty straightforward and I really adhere to the 101 of brewing science that I learned at Siebel—and I apply that to everything. We try not to overthink anything. We're really trying to keep things as simple as possible, to keep quality up, and we really center around quality.

> **"That's why I love the brewing industry. We're not saving lives, we're making beer. We're having a good time and we're bringing happiness to people in a very simple way with liquid bread."**

As the brewery grows, we have to think more and more about what the beer is really tasting like in New York, what the beer is really tasting like in a pint glass in Kansas City. . . . It's really easy for brewers to blow sunshine up each other's asses inside these four walls if we are drinking right off of the swickle and we're drinking the freshest beer possible.

We spend an exhaustive amount of time keeping beer in warm libraries, tasting it at 30 days, 60 days, 90 days and 120 days, and it's brutal. It's really not necessarily fun to taste your beers after forcing them in warm storage, but it's the only way to learn as a brewer.

You know what, though? I could have gone into medicine. I could have been sitting in a hospital ER stressing my balls off in a life-or-death situation. That's why I love the brewing industry. We're not saving lives, we're making beer. We're having a good time and we're bringing happiness to people in a very simple way with liquid bread. I think you can get too serious about it, but at the end of the day, we're just making beer, right?

When it gets so big that we lose touch with what's fun about it and the flavors that we're trying to create, well, then it's time to call it quits. I haven't gotten there yet. I'm still pretty stoked about it all.

Nick: What's your process for coming up with a new recipe? Is it ingredient based? Style based?

Matt: That's a good question. Our brewing philosophy as a company has always been to do a few beers really well.

We chose pale ale as the medium by which we were going to build the company—starting with English Pale Ale, Double-Barrel Ale, and moving on to American Pale Ale in the form of Pale 31, and later Union Jack. If you look at our portfolio—the nuts and bolts—the pale ales in the middle are pretty simple beers. Tried and true. . . . Breweries have been doing them for 150 years. We're not inventing any styles or doing anything like that, but we are putting our own twist on them.

I would say I'm not an artist, but if you talk about beer like art, then you've got to know the classics and you've got to be able to do a stick figure before you can paint the Mona Lisa.

I think that, way back when I was a home brewer, and still today, somebody burnt in my brain: "What is the perfect pale ale?" It has something to do with a little lighter body than what is considered the classic, something that's maybe a little more like a pilsner in body and drinkability that then allows the hops to really pop off of it. We've used dry hopping in pale ale to try to really express hops across it.

The other thing Firestone's done is brought the fifth element, which is wood, to the program. There's a lot of comfort in being able to say there's something unique about your process that sets you apart from other brewers, and at Firestone that's oak. That wasn't something that I brought to the table. That was something that I had to adapt to as a brewer and really get comfortable with because a non-negotiable part of brewing for Firestone Walker is that oak will be incorporated.

Nick: What's your best advice to a home brewer who is thinking about taking it to the next level?

Matt: I always say keep it simple. When I was home brewing, I must have brewed 25 pale ales in a row trying to figure out how to make them as professional-quality as possible. I guess it was in my head as a home brewer that someday I wanted to get paid to be a professional brewer. I think that a lot of brewers, especially when you first get into it, are looking for that magic bullet or that fairy dust—that thing that separates your beer, "Oh, he uses Caramel 60 from such and such supplier.

That must be what's setting his beers apart." But it isn't. It's an adherence to the 101s—remembering the simplest stuff and just making sure that you're nailing the basics—and don't overthink it.

Nick: I hear about the sour program that's going on. Can you talk about that?

Matt: We started the barrel aging program for our 10th anniversary. That helps get us a little more credibility, I guess, with the beer geek world, so to speak. That has led us to embark on the Barrelworks Wild Ale Project in Buellton.

Nick: It seems like sours are one of those trends within the brewing community.

> **"... If you just concentrate on attention to detail and making sure that everything is perfect at all times possible, you'll make the best possible beer."**

Matt: Like sour is the new hoppy?

Nick: Is that the case?

Matt: Well, I don't really know. I'm probably not the one to ask. I guess I think about it in terms that we're all developing as a craft brew community and we're pushing each other, and sour is one of those outer limit type areas that is hard to perfect. It's not practical to do it in a normal brewery because it requires barrels and a lot of time.

Now that breweries are a little more developed and have some more resources at their disposal, or at least maybe some have more expendable time to work on these things, there's some great sour breweries coming out of the craft brew community. What's after that? What's next? I have no idea. I've been trying to pace myself.

Nick: What's the best piece of advice that you've received when it comes to brewing?

Matt: Well, the one I remember the most was a brewmaster by the name of Rudy Held, who was one of the brewmasters at Stroh's. He went on to become one of the lead guys at Kalamazoo Spice Extract when I was there. He was a seasoned German brewmaster, and I would ask him home brew questions. When he found out I was going to get a job as a brewer, he just gave me one piece of advice. He said, "Attention to detail in everything," and he repeated himself.

I think about that a lot because you can allow yourself to get a little loose and sloppy out there, but if you just concentrate on attention to detail and making sure that everything is perfect at all times possible, you'll make the best possible beer.

Nick: Tell me about the festival, which is an invitational. Why did you guys choose to do it in that format, and what do you hope for the future?

Matt: I think my favorite part of going to a beer fest is to commune with other brewers, so the invitational concept was in part to make sure that we got the brewers themselves to come.

We had to have some ground rules, and the ground rules were we don't want a ton of beers, we want sessional beer, we want one of your experimental beers or something you're proud of, and you need to come and pour your own beer. It's not a dig against the distributors or the sales team or the marketing team or anything like that, but I wanted it to be a true brewers' event for brewers.

In an invitational format, we could control the number of people so we could really show them a good time and make sure that we could be hospitable and accommodating for everybody. And we could make sure that we kept the quality up. We needed to make sure that whatever we were doing was special, unique, and that we're in charge and in control of it all.

Nick: Last question: What's the one thing you've never been asked in an interview that you've always wanted to be able to say?

Matt: Well, it just came to me. I didn't get a chance to say this and I don't know that I've said it in an interview before, but one thing I believe strongly is that we should all be sharing all information. I think that's important for the craft brew industry. I think when we start becoming like the bigger brewers and hiding our secret recipes and suing each other over proprietary processes and things like that, then the business of craft beer will go sour.

I've gone on record before, but I'll do it again: I think that all information—any research we do, anything we discover as a craft brewery in our lab or on the floor, whatever—we want to share with everybody. That's always been our policy. If we can say, "Hey, there were certain brewers here in California or certain groups that had a positive influence on the future of brewing. That's money in the bank for me. That's where I want to be. I want to be educating other brewers to make better beer, keeping craft beer on the upswing, and keeping good beer in people's pint glasses. That's what I'm here for. That's why I'm in this business.

Jesse Houck
Golden Road Brewing

Jesse Houck is the brewmaster at Golden
Road Brewing in Los Angeles, California.

Nick: Can you recount your brewing history, from your early influences through to today?

Jesse: After I finished at UC Davis' Master Brewers Program, I landed a job in San Francisco, at a brewpub out there. From there, I wound up working at almost half the breweries in San Francisco, somewhat consecutively. I worked as an assistant brewer, then a journeyman brewer, all the while trying to learn from all the brewmasters that were out there at the time.

Nick: Can you name some of them?

Jesse: Shaun O'Sullivan at 21st Amendment, Brenden Dobel at ThirstyBear, Andy French at Speakeasy, John Tucci at Gordon Biersch—just all really good guys and great brewers. Learning different dogmas behind brewing and how there's a thousand different ways to do everything. I really felt fortunate to be able to work with so many people and have that kind of experience to really help develop and create my own style of brewing.

I wound up getting most closely aligned with 21st Amendment and Shaun and his style of brewing. I wound up staying on there for a little over five years. I became the head brewer at the 21st Amendment Brewpub down on 2nd Street and really was able to create a lot of great beers and start them out there; Bitter American, a nice session IPA, Back in Black, a black IPA, and a bunch of other fun stuff. It was a great place to really learn and be a part of the brewing community.

From there, I went across to the East Bay to work at Drake's Brewing Company where I was the production manager/head brewer there for two years. I really got a good taste of production brewing growth, managing all that. Two years into that, I got a phone call from Meg and Tony, whom I'd known for years. They asked me to come down here and be a part of Golden Road. They wanted me to help them build the beers that they really wanted to make. They knew those were the beers I wanted to make as well.

Nick: What is that partnership like?

Jesse: I met Meg when I was at 21st Amendment. She was working for Oskar Blues at the time, launching cans on the West Coast. We had just bought a two-head canning machine at 21st Amendment, so we did a lot of symbiotic can promotion events in the city. That was a lot of fun.

I met Tony on my last day at 21st Amendment, actually. I was walking out the door, I'd given my notice ahead of time, but it was my last day there. It was kind of a sad day. I was drinking a little bit and I got a phone call from Meg saying, "Hey you've got to stick around, there's this really cool guy. He's opening this crazy beer bar in L.A." She's like, "Will you stick around the brewery and show them around?" I said, "Sure, whatever, it's my last day." So I just grabbed another beer and waited.

I met Tony and his manager. I showed them around and I was a little skeptical about the beer scene in L.A. I didn't believe that L.A. was really waiting for craft beer.

Through a couple of craft beer bars, Tony was able to launch into building a brewery. I think the craft beer bars helped pave the way, but L.A. at the time didn't have much brewing happening in the city. There was Craftsman, and Eagle Rock had just opened, but other than that, there wasn't too much craft beer going on. Tony and Meg are big dreamers, they think big. They decided to build an amazing production facility and asked me to come down to help run it.

Nick: You said that they had an idea of what kind of beers they wanted to make and that matched the type of beers that you wanted to make? What were those beers?

Jesse: Symbiosis and that kind of relationship is always great when you find the right fit. As a brewer, I always feel it's my job to make whatever beer I'm supposed to be making as best I can. That's the scientific part of it, but when the artisan side is aligned, it will shine through in the beer.

I like clean, hop-forward, drier beers. I really enjoy the experimentation with new varieties and being on the leading edge of what craft beer is doing and where we're going. They have the same dream, the same vision and it feels great to be a part of that.

Nick: Golden Road seems to focus on beers that are a little bit lighter, with easy drinkability, but still full of flavor. Is that what you mean when you say like you guys share a vision of that type of beer?

Jesse: Definitely. I think we're trying to not only speak to what we enjoy drinking, but also to the L.A. market in general. We want to be relevant in the market. We want to be L.A.'s craft brewery and thought of in that way. L.A. being what it is, it aligns itself with the more sessionable beers. We have at least two seasons here, sometimes, three. We get to make summertime beers almost all year round, which is great.

I think it's a lot of fun to keep a nice lager at 4.8%—our IPA runs at 5.9%, which is still pretty sessionable for an IPA. Some people might look at it like an overly hopped pale ale, but I don't care how you look at it. It's the beer that we want to drink, so hopefully that speaks to the market as well.

Nick: You said you were initially skeptical about the L.A. beer scene. What has it been like brewing in this particular city?

Jesse: It's pretty amazing to be a part of what's going on down here right now. Coming from San Francisco and having been born up there and lived up there for the last couple years, San Francisco has probably the longest craft beer history of any city in the country. Anchor was the founding father of the American IPA.

Being part of that, and having such a rich heritage of bars, restaurants, and breweries in San Francisco, I felt a little bit foreign when I first came down to L.A., where it was such a young market. It was only probably five or six years ago that a lot of the craft beer bars started popping up. Three or four years ago

breweries finally started opening in the area. There is definitely a demand across the board for craft beer down here.

Once the beer bars opened and they started feeding people what they wanted, there was the need for breweries to do creative beers and to make them available locally. L.A. has a great history of bringing in beers from Northern California. A lot of beers come from San Diego—being able to be part of the growing L.A. beer scene—it's pretty amazing.

Nick: Where do you see that going?

Jesse: I see it becoming fully saturated, and by that I mean I believe there is a place for a craft beer—whether it be ours or somebody else's—in almost every establishment and every home in L.A. And that's a lot of homes.

Nick: That's a big market. So, what's next for you guys? What are you guys excited about?

Jesse: I'm still excited about our flagship IPA, Point the Way. It's still one of my favorite beers to drink, and I go back to it constantly. It's great to see it grow and continuously get more dialed in; It's on its way to becoming a perfect beer. With that, we always keep things fresh with our rotating Custom IPA Series. That's been a lot of fun to be able to create those beers.

We did Heal The Bay last summer, which is a 6.8% all pale malt IPA with a lot of Nelson, Centennial, Citra, and a little bit El Dorado in there—just a great summertime IPA. We just launched our 2020 IPA, which is raising awareness for the Greenway 2020 project that is going to connect 50 miles of the L.A. River with bike and walking paths.

It's great to be able to have an IPA that is a great beer itself, but also speaks to a bigger cause and raises awareness for that. Those IPAs have been a lot of fun to develop and kind of give back to the community. By somebody raising a pint, they're raising awareness and really just putting a message on the can, the box, everything just to get it out there.

We're getting ready to launch our first lager. 329 Days of Sun Lager. It's a Helles-style lager that we think is really going to be approachable and exciting for the L.A. market. And with the 329 average days of sun here in Southern California, it's going to be a go-to beer that doesn't have to just be a seasonal. I'm really looking forward to that one.

Nick: How did the recipe development process work for 329 Days of Sun?

Jesse: When we decided to launch the lager project, we wanted to bring something relevant to the market, something fresh, new, and exciting. We started looking at different lager strains that might not be a traditional German strain or

> **"We get to make summertime beers almost all year round, which is great."**

a Czech strain that's been around for hundreds of years. We played with a couple of different things.

We brewed a 50-barrel batch and split it into three 15-barrel tanks that we still had from our old system. We pitched three different yeasts, all different fermentation temperatures according to whatever strain we're using. We filtered all those beers a couple of weeks later and had a great tasting panel. We brought in our distributors, outside tasters, our entire staff, and everybody filled out surveys just trying to find the best yeast for that beer.

Nick: Is that a practice you guys are going to be interested in continuing?

Jesse: It's a little bit outside the norm. We generally know which direction we want to go. This was really fun to actually have the challenge of being in a place where we knew what direction we wanted to go, but we didn't know exactly which yeast strain was going to take us there.

We play around with hops. I'm always trying to get experimental hops and stuff that isn't in large production yet. I want to see what's new, what's going to be the next greatest hop out there in the market. Point the Way is brewed with an experimental hop, HBC 342. It's a hop I used at Drake's. I'm really fond of it. It gives you great tropical notes that are backed up with a little bit of pine.

Nick: Is that Drake 1500?

Jesse: No. It's a different hop. 1500 was Simcoe and Amarillo when I was there. The HBC 342 was used a little bit in Hopocalypse Black Label and one or two other places, just trying it out. We went to selection harvest last year up in Yakima, Washington. We met the grower, Jason Perrault and talked with him about how that hop is doing and let him know that we've got a huge interest in continuing to buy the hop.

Nick: Does that bring everything full circle for you? Going up and seeing the ingredients fresh?

Jesse: It's everything. It's extremely important for brewers to connect with both their maltsters and their hop growers. The relationship has to be there to get exactly what we want. You can buy off the shelf, but it's much better to go up and pre-select

and have that relationship to make sure that they're on board with the same things you are.

Nick: What are some of the beer-related things you're passionate about? What's your soapbox right now?

Jesse: I don't know, I don't always like standing on the soapbox, but I think simplicity in beer would be a good one. The craft beer industry sometimes gets a little away from itself and sometimes the best beer is just a very simple one. Most of my favorite beers are just very simple and straightforward, not a lot of extraneous ingredients. I'm not saying that these are wrong or bad, we even make some that fall into that category. I think simplicity is really where the beer is at.

Nick: Let's talk about cans. Do cans give you anything in the way of quality, or is it just a packaging thing?

Jesse: I believe that cans are a high-quality package. I'm not going to stand on that soapbox, I want to tell the consumer that it is a package, it's a delivery system. We think it's a much better delivery system than a bottle. But, at the end of the day, it's about the beer inside.

> **"The craft beer industry sometimes gets a little away from itself and sometimes the best beer is just a very simple one."**

Nick: Does the beer hold up better in cans?

Jesse: The quality of the equipment is going to determine that more than the actual package itself. Beyond that, cans do have advantages. They cost less to ship because they are lighter and more can fit on a pallet, they have no light penetration, and they're more often recycled. You can take them places bottles can't go. I love them for that reason. I think they fit with both our company ethos and also with the L.A. market a lot better than bottles.

Nick: On purely an emotional level, what is it about beer that keeps you coming into work everyday?

Jesse: I think beer is a beverage that really ties communities together. It ties friends together. It's a simple beverage. It's almost the working man's beverage in a way, and I think that's one of its most amazing attributes. It really brings people together—from the British pubs to the American bars—and it unites people that might not be otherwise having conversations. Especially when it's craft beer, it gives you something to talk about, something to relate to. I think the challenges of brewing excellent beer keep me coming back to work, trying to always make the best beer possible. I love trying to perfect everything and to be able to continuously give that back to the people is a lot of fun.

Dan Gordon
Gordon Biersch Brewing Company

Dan Gordon is the co-founder and head of brewing for Gordon Biersch Brewing Company. Their production facility is located in San Jose, California.

Nick: Let's start at the beginning. What are the first memories you have of getting into beer? And how did you wind up where you are now?

Dan: My parents took me to Germany when I was 15. I came from a very liberal consumption background, so I was drinking beer all day long during the trip. I loved the flavor of beer at an early age, especially German-style beers, and that was what straightened out my taste buds and aligned them into what I was going to do career-wise. I went to Berkeley as an undergrad, spent my junior year abroad.

I was in Göttingen flipping through a catalog of all the different fields of study at the various universities in Germany, I saw a course that focused on brewing science and beverage technology, and I said, "Bingo. That's what I was put on earth to do."

I love manufacturing, and I figured combining manufacturing with brewing would be the ideal future for me. In my senior year at Cal, I applied for the graduate program in brewing engineering at the technical university in Munich. I was accepted and went there for four-and-a-half years. I worked at some breweries getting hands-on experience and then wrote the business plan for Gordon Biersch while I was in grad school. I ended up meeting Dean Biersch, and we combined forces.

So I wound up graduating from this very technical university in Munich. It is the ultimate—it's the MIT of engineering programs for breweries around the world. I was actually the only American in about forty years to graduate from the program, so it was highly competitive—made Cal look like a breeze. I was very fortunate to get through it. I bought some brewing machinery while I was still in school—kind of set it in stone that I was going to actually enter the industry on my own, be independent, and get going in brewing on a commercial basis for the rest of my life.

Nick: So, you got a classic German beer education but you're not just "a German beer company" in California. Can you can talk a little bit about where the German influences end and the California influences begin?

Dan: Back when we first started off, there wasn't a crazy over-hopped beer syndrome that's going on now. That just kind of took off. It was all about balance and flavor profiles, being true to style. So that was my niche; doing authentic German-style beers. No one else was doing it, and that was, to me, a great void. Most of the brewers in the craft industry had home-brewing backgrounds, but none of them had industrial backgrounds. They had never worked in a German brewery before and that's why I felt that we would fit in. There was a big void in that area and we jumped into it.

Nick: What's your recipe development process like? Do you have certain overriding principles and philosophies you rely on?

Dan: To me, I'm trying to make something that's incredibly delicious—that's drinkable. I'm not out there to make a statement saying, "I can use more hops that anybody else. I can throw more wood in a tank of beer." I want to make beer that's incredibly good and, to me, there's a basic subjective differentiation between good and bad beer. There's some beers out there that I think are just trying to make a statement. You don't want to have a curry that is so spicy that you can't taste the meat in it. You want to have some balance to it.

That's my philosophy in brewing. Make sure that there is balance and it's got some layers to it that are perceptible to your taste buds and are not one big shock to the system. I think that's one of the things that's been going on right now. I'm a traditionalist in the sense that I think there's a reason certain things are done well over time and why they taste great and there's no need to improve upon it. Though there are always areas that you can improve upon—like brewing techniques and making sure that you have yeast that isn't dying—that's vital. I mean, we put an enormous amount of effort into using our yeast just one time. We're the only brewery in the world that does that. From the quality differentiation standpoint, there's nobody out there. It's like saying I'm not going to use a single piece of fruit unless I've personally gone into that tree and verify that it's absolutely perfectly ripe. That's my philosophy on how we approach all of our raw materials.

Yeast is our number one teammate. That's the most volatile element in the entire brewing process because it's a living organism—you have to nurture it, cultivate it, and treat it with respect. So, creating a perfect environment for it to flourish is going to enable our beers to taste consistently great. That's first and foremost. Then you get into the raw materials like the malt and barley. I'm not settling for anything that isn't absolutely the best, so I'm buying, a lot of our specialty malts from Bamberg, Germany because I know they are the only ones that are able to produce these caramelized malts, signature flavors, and the perfect element. You cannot get this from any domestic malt supplier and, if you look where a lot of these guys are sourcing their specialty malts, they're just buying the cheapest crap out there. We're going out and making sure we have low protein, which is very difficult to source, and we're spending about 25% more per pound to get low-protein malt

that is consistently in the area of what we want for brewing authentic German-style beers. We apply that to every brew we make.

Nick: When you come up with a new recipe do you have an end result in mind? A style? Or, do you think, "This is the type of hops and malt I want to use. Let's see how that recipe organically evolves?"

Dan: No, I'm not really experimenting in that regard. I've thought it all through and I know exactly where we're heading. It's like when you're doing a composition in music. A good composer knows what it's going to sound like when he's thinking it up because he hears it first. We don't do a test brew on it. I know exactly the formulation of malt we want to have. I know exactly the original gravity that we're going to target. The process is locked in.

Nick: What's the Gordon Biersch story as a company?

Dan: We started in 1988 as a brewery restaurant in Palo Alto, California. Our focus—our concept—was to create authentic German-style beers in a casual, but semi-upscale atmosphere. Executing on the food side, putting focus on having a great chef involved with us from day one was something different back then. Today, you have a lot of brewpubs as opposed to brewery restaurants. I think we're really the first to do an actual brewery restaurant. We put as much emphasis on the food as we did on the beer. Then, we added great service; it was not the, "stand-behind-the-bar and go self-serve and we'll see if we care about you type thing." Dean Biersch was a professional restauranteur. I had training as a chef in the early years, and also, the brewing expertise. We approached it from a professional standpoint. That's what differentiated us. That's what enabled us to succeed and grow. We went to San Jose and then to San Francisco, then Pasadena and then Honolulu, which was not a grand slam. Then we built a draft beer production facility in Emeryville to test

the waters and see if we could go commercial, so to speak, and do distribution. We maxed out our brewery at about 10,000 barrels a year in the first year. Actually, in a six-month time frame, we had maxed out our capacity. Then we said, "Okay, let's raise money to go larger," and that's why we built this location in San Jose. We did around 44,000 barrels in our first year and then, we grew it. Right now, we're doing around 110,000 barrels. Subsequently, the brewery restaurant count is 35.

Nick: Back in the early days, did you ever think that you were going to get to this point? Do you ever think it was going to get this big?

Dan: Well, Dean and I originally wrote the business plan to do five brewery restaurants, so we pretty much executed exactly what we said we're going to do in the first six years. We did five brewery restaurants in six years and that was a goal. We didn't originally plan on doing a draft beer production facility or going to bottling. That dream evolved in '93–'94, when the craft beer revolution was just going crazy. That's when we made the decision to raise more money to expand the company.

Nick: Are you guys seeing the continued growth in the craft beer revolution? What do you attribute that to? Why now? Why are people getting back into craft beer?

Dan: I don't think it ever stopped. If you look at the growth rate starting back in 1984 until now, there was never a lull.

> **"I'm trying to make something that's incredibly delicious—that's drinkable. I'm not out there to make a statement . . ."**

If you look at the stats and growth, I think you're going to find it's been double-digit growth for a long, long time. It's not sudden. The only thing you're finding is that there's double-digit growth in the total amount of beer being produced in the craft sector. Then you have this ridiculous exponential growth in the number of entrants to the industry because, I think, it's a situation where everybody thinks they know how to brew beer. The craze is on super-high-hopped beers that really don't take a lot of finesse to brew, honestly. You're finding that they can cover up their flavor flaws and mistakes simply by tossing in a ton of hops, so you really can't tell the difference between a good IPA and bad IPA. But it's the aura and panache that they're selling. They're selling an image as opposed to the actual beer that it's in the bottle.

That's a little frustrating from my perspective, but at the same time, I'm staying true to what I do. I'm not going to change a lot. We're going to introduce some beers that are taking the German school of brewing and applying some of the American creativity—doing some styles that don't really exist over there, and that's where our next limited release beers are. The IPB is something you can't find in Germany; a pilsner that's 6.5% alcohol and 50 bitterness units—that doesn't exist over there. It was interpretive and it tastes great and it's not overpowering, although the amount of hops per barrel is probably higher than a lot of the IPAs that you find out in the marketplace. That's primarily because we're using Hallertau aroma hops and Tettnang, which have very low levels of alpha acid concentration, so you have to use a lot more to get the bitterness out of it. But we're still maintaining the German Purity Law application of not dry hopping. And we're naturally carbonating all the beers, aged for six weeks, which is longer than any other craft brewery out there. You hear about some of the craft brewers that are supposed to be ultra crafty and you find out that their brew cycles are 12, 14 days. To me, that's like not following the applied science. It impacts flavor.

Nick: A lot of brewers feel that being a brewer is kind of like being a mad scientist in a way. It's kind of a mixture of creativity and science. Do you put emphasis on one over the other?

"To me, it's not about being creative. It's about making something that tastes great. I think a lot of these guys are enamored with sensationalism and creativity and they're not worried about what it tastes like."

Dan: To me, it's not about being creative. It's about making something that tastes great. I think a lot of these guys are enamored with sensationalism and creativity and they're not worried about what it tastes like. To me, all I care about is: how does it taste? Is it really great? I want people to say, "This tastes incredible." I don't want them coming back and saying, "Wow, that's the spiciest thing I've ever had in my life." I don't want that, or, "That's the most bitter beer I've ever had." I'm not going in for those extremes. I want to have balance and I want it to taste incredible—so that's my philosophy. I don't want to grind up 5,000 pounds of wood chips and have it soaking in my beer.

Nick: Is there anything that you've never been asked in an interview that you've always wanted to say?

Dan: I'm kind of hitting it right now because the craze is going on with a number of new brewers and I just don't know if a lot of them have that much to add. Again, it reminds me of music. All of the notes have already been played before. It's just how many different ways can you play it? I play jazz, and that's why I relate to music in a lot of stuff. When I was in Germany as an exchange student back in 1980, the Germans were just getting into music education. They didn't have much of it. None of it in schools, it's all private and outside. The jazz groups I got invited to play in were two extremes: Either really old-time jazz—Dixie stuff—things that are super easy and simple to play, or free jazz where you couldn't tell whether you're playing it right or not because there was no right or wrong and it wasn't very melodic. But finding guys that could play bebop and make it sound great was really tough, and I equate that to what's going on in brewing. As you go into these breweries and see what's going on in there, "Is it a place you can eat off the floor? Are they really putting attention and detail into the getting the very best malt and hops that they can, or is it just a matter of throwing it all in the kitchen sink and see what comes out? The fundamentals have to be reinforced.

Nick: Do you find the market too saturated now?

Dan: I think it's very bacterial. I think there are just so many small breweries going for the local approach that it is getting cluttered out there.

Chuck Silva
Green Flash Brewing Company

Chuck Silva is the brewmaster at Green Flash Brewing Company. He's been a brewer for more than 20 years, and has been with Green Flash for 10 years.

Nick: How did you get started in brewing and how did you wind up where you are today?

Chuck: The real catalyst was actually my home brewing hobby that started in 1994. I had a friend in Northern Virginia turn me on to his home brew, I distinctly remember his Pilsner, and I loved it. Shortly after that I went all in finding a home brew shop and purchased everything I needed to make my own beer including a book by Charlie Papazian, *The New Complete Joy of Homebrewing.* Funny thing is I remember sometime in the early 80's, my dad ended up with a home brew kit—a beer in a bag kind of thing, where the hops and other ingredients came through the mail with the bare necessities to make the brew. He never used it but I was seriously intrigued. It was the science geek in me that was thrilled. I thought, "Really? You can make your own beer?" Well I finally got my chance over 15 years later.

> **"My dad actually drove for Coors back in the day. So, that's when I got my first taste of beer that I can remember, Coors Banquet Beer."**

Looking back even further I was introduced to beer at a younger age, probably the mid 70's. My dad actually drove for Coors back in the day. So, that's when I got my first taste of beer that I can remember, Coors Banquet Beer.

The thing that got me where I am today was a leap of faith—quitting my day job to pursue more brewing knowledge. I signed up for the American Brewers Guild Intensive Brewing Sciences course and graduated in April 1998 after an apprenticeship at Hops Bistro & Brewery in San Diego. There's been no looking back, except maybe in moments like this to reflect on how my brewing career has progressed.

Nick: What was your job at that time?

Chuck: I had a good paying job in the defense industry still supporting the United States Navy after my 6 years of service. Initially I was a field technician, then a writer for mainte-nance schedules and eventually I took a position as a project manager for a logistics division in a top secret electronics program.

After 5 years in the defense industry, I had an opportunity to relocate to my home state of California, which was very appealing to me. So I quit my day job and started preparing myself to move to San Diego. Of course, I needed to find a new job, and as I was looking for work, I began to seriously consider pursuing work in brewing beer. By the time I was ready to move I had decided to give a brewing career a shot. Since I had discovered the American Brewers Guild, I figured this was my best chance to break into the industry. I enrolled and began brewing school in February 1998.

After completing brewing school, I landed my first brewing job as an assistant brewer working for Paul Segura at Hang Ten Brewing Company (he's now the brewmaster at Karl Strauss Brewing Co.) Almost a year and a half later, a position opened up at Hops Bistro & Brewery where I had apprenticed during brewing school. I jumped at that opportunity and landed the job as head brewer. I had a great time during my 4.5 year stint at Hops. I brewed numerous beer styles, orchestrated monthly beer dinners, and actually received my first medals at the World Beer Cup and the Great American Beer Festival. Unfortunately, the lease ended and Hops closed in 1993, so I called on my buddy Paul Segura over at Karl Strauss and he put me to work brewing again. This is where I gained some exposure to production brewing.

Nick: What do you remember about your first awards?

Chuck: My first award at Hops was a gold medal for Kolsch at the World Beer Cup in 2000, I actually traveled to New York to the awards ceremony and received the gold medal in person. That was awesome! Then, in 2002 I won a bronze for Altbier and the next year a bronze for IPA at the GABF. Those are fun beers to win awards with.

Nick: Well, especially a Kolsch at the World Beer Cup.

Chuck: Yeah, a delicate German-style blond beer.

Nick: A dude from San Diego.

Chuck: Yeah. Times were different then. There was a different focus in craft beer and people still really liked their fizzy yellow beer quite a bit, so we embraced it instead of just saying, "Oh, well, here's my blond ale that I have to make," and not giving it its due. I embraced it as my number one selling beer, and I made it as best I could. Then, landing a gold medal, imagine how great that made me feel.

> **"There's a lot of romance to brewpub brewing, but then also, there is a romantic side to production brewing where you see your beer reach a lot more people and go farther away than imagined."**

Nick: Do you enjoy the production side more than the brewpub side?

Chuck: Well, with brewpubs you get anonymity. Often it's a one-man show, so you're definitely the guy that's creating all the beers, and you usually have the opportunity to create more. You're not really stuck to a set brand, depending on the brewpub. There's a lot of romance to brewpub brewing, but then also, there is a romantic side to production brewing where you see your beer reach a lot more people and go farther away than imagined. I have enjoyed both brewpub and production brewing for their own unique experience. While production brewing seems like more of a grind, it also continues to present new opportunities with new projects and challenges as the company grows.

Nick: Is that one of the coolest factors for you, now, where you are? Are there factors like that that give you that same kind of jolt?

Chuck: It certainly is super cool to see and hear how much people enjoy our beer, especially in other countries. Now, I have to say that I'm energized by new projects like building a barrel house where we can produce barrel-aged beers in sufficient quantities to package and ship around the country.

Nick: How would you define your brewing style? Do you have any sort of approach when you're coming up with a new recipe?

Chuck: My inspirations come from a lot of different sources—books, other brewers, new and traditional ingredients—but mainly I think you have to tap into your creativity so as to not recreate what has already been brewed. Part of what makes me successful is the early experimenting with home brews

using a broad base of different ingredients, as well as all the time I've spent working in the brewpubs using different yeasts, hops, and malt to produce a wide variety of beer styles. Tasting ingredients in their raw form as well as tasting brews at different stages during the fermentations will give you more insight into what raw ingredients taste like in a finished beer. Beyond all of this, I really enjoying taking a traditional beer style and turning it on its head, giving the brew a new twist. I like very flavorful beers but they need to have drinkability and finesse.

It certainly seems like one path I've been going down is in using more hops and learning about which hops are brighter and more citrusy or more pungent, and what is delivering the most awesome hop nose and big, but satisfying flavor in an IPA.

Nick: Yeah, you brew some pretty big-flavored hoppy beers. So, robustness versus refinement: Are the two mutually exclusive?

Chuck: Well they can be, but I take the approach that there needs to be finesse in all the beers I make. I don't want to make something that's robust and just in your face just to make it big and strong. It needs to have qualities that are refined with an eye toward drinkability as well. I don't want to have a big malty-ness or sweetness in a beer that's under-attenuated and leaves your mouth coated with dextrin, so chewy and sweet that it's not refreshing. I think beer, by and large, is a refreshing beverage—even though there are so many directions you can go with flavor.

Nick: Can you use any beer that you've made, as an example for that? Is there one beer that you think is kind of a good example?

Chuck: Well we can look at our West Coast IPA. The West Coast IPA is a good example of how we wanted to deliver something different even though there was a lot of IPA available. We released that beer in 2005. We set out to create a new benchmark for IPA, and thus, we called it West Coast IPA. Its

name is almost generic in a sense, but also brilliant in a way that it's self-defining. It tells it's own story.

West Coast IPA is brewed with Pacific Northwest hops in such an extravagant way that it's very pronounced. I accomplished that with a beer that has 95 IBUs and almost 7.5% ABV, so it's kind of pushing the limits on IPA as a style. I layered West Coast IPA with Simcoe, Columbus and Cascade, and additions of Citra and Centennial in the dry hop. I wanted to include all of the traits that are in IPAs: floral, pine, citrus, even tropical fruity notes. So I layered all these hops in throughout the brew and got this menagerie of extravagant hop character. I created something new.

Nick: You mentioned that you feel beers and beer names tell a story. Can you elaborate on that?

Chuck: Absolutely, I think that learning about world history through researching about beer styles and where they come from has been much more fun than when I was sitting in a classroom. Interestingly enough, beer is a cultural beverage and it bridges socioeconomic barriers. The common workingman can get a beer, and if the beer is a wonderfully fine beverage, then the banker is going to have a pint as well. I think that because beer has an appeal for a broad audience, entire cultures embrace their local brew. These are often proudly named after their localities and the people who created it.

Nick: What's next for you guys? What's exciting you right now in brewing, and what new flavors are you interested in tackling?

Chuck: Great question, especially in an environment where there are a lot of new upstart breweries. The number of craft breweries that are opening is staggering. What are they going to be brewing? What are they going to be bringing to the table that's unique? Are they going to be riding our coattails?

We continue to create new brews, as we are a continuously evolving company. Also, we are reintroducing beers we have created in small batches in the past to a broader audience. For instance, we re-brewed the first nine of our anniversary beers as we celebrated ten years while we also created a new

> **"Part of what makes me successful is the early experimenting with home brews using a broad base of different ingredients, as well as all the time I've spent working in the brewpubs, using different yeasts, hops, and malt to produce a wide variety of beer styles."**

beer named Flanders Drive Sour Red Ale. More recently, we rolled out a new series to embrace a variety of hop-centric beers that we have in our arsenal, Hop Odyssey. A new hoppy beer is released every other month.

Nick: What do you think makes you unique from other brewers?

Chuck: Oh, that's a tough question. I've certainly taken inspiration from other brewers' traditional brewing styles, techniques, and even current trends—like with the West Coast IPA. I guess it's what I've done with all of it that makes me different. My interpretation of beer styles and what I am doing with the raw ingredients, the quantities, the layering, and the whole composition that makes my juice different.

Nick: Do you have a rigorous recipe development process?

Chuck: Of course I do. I start with whatever my inspiration is and then model it out in a spreadsheet in a scientific way. I come up with a grist and then figure out what the IBUs are going to be. I always go back and study what I've put down on paper and ponder adjustments using my intuition to determine if the right levels of malt and hop character are in the right place. I like to hit a home run and I don't want to do a bunch of experimental batches that need a lot of changing and tweaking. I really want to figure it all out so I achieve what my vision is for the new beer. When I'm done with creating a recipe I want it to be the recipe that we will use again and again if the beer is well received.

Ben Cook
Hangar 24 Craft Brewery

Ben Cook is the owner and brewmaster at Hangar 24 Craft Brewery in Redlands, California.

Nick: Let's start at the beginning. What first sparked your interest in brewing and how did you wind up where you are today?

Ben: My very first experience, like a lot of people, was drinking a lot of pale ale. My brother went to Sonoma State to play baseball and they were playing Chico State. I had my first sample of a craft beer there and really appreciated it. It wasn't like a life-changing moment, by any stretch, but I was like, "Oh, that's pretty good." When I was 21, my girlfriend at the time and I were bored and she actually found "home brewing" in the phone book. I thought that sounded cool. I was kind of a science geek, as well, getting my degree in biology at Cal State.

We drove down to San Diego, and I believe I bought my first kit from Home Brew Mart. It was like a red ale or something like that. Made it, extract only, and it turned out pretty good. Then I really started getting into it. I moved to all-grain pretty quickly and fell in love with—not just the process—I loved the process of brewing, but also the fun of having friends over and seeing their faces when they tried it. It was exciting.

It was after a flag football game in Orange County, my brother's best friend's dad (who is a "higher-up" at Anheuser-Busch) tasted my beer and said, "Wow, This beer is really good. You ever thought about brewing for a living?"

I said, "No, I haven't."

Then he said, "Well, I could introduce you to the general manager down at the Van Nuys plant. It's one of the biggest breweries in the country." That sounded like fun, so I did it.

I got a job as a quality assurance manager. My love for craft beer was getting pretty intense at that point. I was also getting to know a lot of the breweries down here, a lot of the guys in San Diego were real open with me about what it's like to own and operate a brewery.

My parents are both entrepreneurs and have owned their own businesses since they were fairly young, so I've always been around people starting their own business and running a business. So I went to my parents and said, "Hey, what does it take to start a company?"

> **"... a 'higher-up' at Anheuser-Busch tasted my beer and said, 'Wow, this beer is really good. You ever thought about brewing for a living?'"**

They said, "Well, the first thing is you have to write a business plan." There's the Economic Development Agency, I believe it is, and the Small Business Association. I contacted them, went and met with one of their counselors, bought some business planning software, and worked with them. I spent about three years developing a business plan. During that time I was also refining recipes. I brewed for about seven years before I opened the brewery on a home-brew scale. Eventually, I felt like I needed to know more than just home

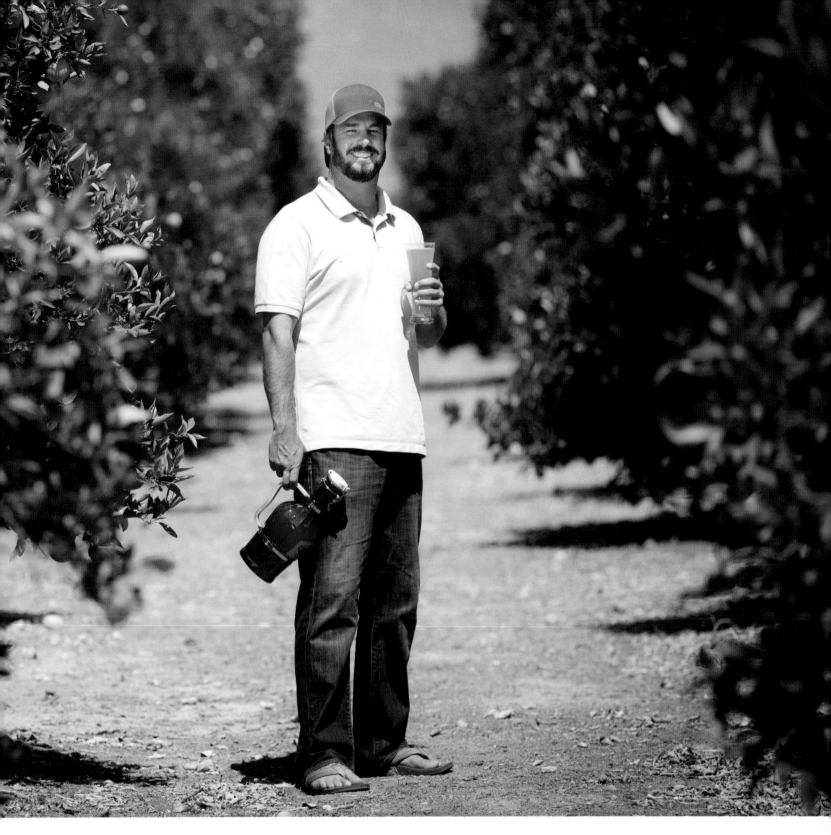

brewing. So I went up to UC Davis and graduated from the Master Brewers' program up there. Towards the end of that program I was traveling all over the country and looking at systems. I had all my financing lined up already. I was ready to rock and roll, and I found the system that I liked at Monte Carlo Casino in Las Vegas.

I brought the system back here, and my dad and I did at least 90% of the work ourselves. We had friends and family help, but budget concerns meant we did almost every-

thing—pretty much everything but the electrical. We had a lot of friends from the airport that build all their own airplanes, they came over and built. So it was fun to get the help from the community, getting started, and it's kind of fun that now we're able to give a lot back to the community.

Nick: What is your approach to creating recipes? Do you have specific principles or philosophies that you always follow?

Ben: It depends on what we're trying to do. With a special release beer, like our Russian Imperial Stout, we brewed it because we all wanted to drink a Russian Imperial Stout. And we knew we're going to brew relatively close to the guidelines if not within them. A lot of times, we'll have at least three brewers come up with a recipe, we'll pilot batch each, and we'll all taste each. Then we'll usually combine the best aspects of each recipe. Then we'll pilot the new recipe, and if it tastes great, we brew a big one. If it doesn't quite meet our standards, we'll continue to pilot it until we hit it.

We've hit a beer that we wanted to brew on the first try, but we also had one, I think it's Palmero, that took us about 15 pilot batches. It's a very hard beer to brew.

Nick: You obviously had something in your head then?

Ben: Absolutely. We have our different series of beers, and we have our year-round beers, the fairly standard ones: a wheat, pale ale, IPA, double IPA, our porter, and our lager. When coming up with those recipes, I thought, "We're in Southern California, we have to brew an IPA, right?" We came up with a few recipes, we brainstormed together, and we created a recipe. And that one, I think that was a single pilot batch. We loved it. We used 100% Columbus hops.

Then we wanted a series of beers that really represented us and our area. What's to say that our pale ale is any better than a pale ale brewed in Florida or brewed in Chico, or brewed somewhere else? They're all pale ales, they're all great. What sets one apart from the other? I don't know. I wanted to come up with a series of beers that represented this area because a brewery in Maine, for example, couldn't brew Orange Wheat and be authentic. They'd have to import oranges from somewhere. Our orange wheat is "us." That's Redlands. It represents this area, and sure, you can copy it, but it's not going to be authentic. The authenticity is one thing that makes that beer special.

We expanded on that beer. We created an entire series of beers called the Local Fields Series that utilizes one local ingredient and showcases that ingredient. The beer I was speaking of before, Palmero, uses dates from the Palm Springs area, the Coachella Valley.

Essence? That was a Double IPA with blood oranges, navel oranges, and grapefruit, all from this local area. So we kind of caught the essence of the area, that's where the name comes from. We do a beer that uses grapes and oak from Temecula. We actually get those from a winemaker down there. The pumpkins are coming from a local source. So it's an interesting series of beers.

Once we came up with the idea to do beers that represented the area using local ingredients, the first thing we did was

to go and talk to all the local farmers that we already have relationships with. We said, "What can you grow for us?" They gave us a giant list of things and I thought, "All right, well, which one of those would make a good a beer?" So I said to my brewers, "Alright, anyone who comes up with a recipe, we're going to brew it."

> **"Our Orange Wheat is 'us.' That's Redlands. It represents this area, and sure, you can copy it, but it's not going to be authentic. The authenticity is one thing that makes that beer special."**

Nick: Representing the area and staying local seems important to you and Hangar 24.

Ben: Absolutely. Being a part of the community is part of our culture, part of who we are. And I think one of the driving reasons for our success is that we're not just a leech on society trying to be money mongers. We're really a part of this community, we're involved in a ton of community events, and we donate a lot.

Nick: Do you feel a vast difference working for your small family-owned company now as opposed to when you were working for Anheuser-Busch?

Ben: Oh, yeah. See now, when I worked for Anheuser-Busch, I worked for Anheuser-Busch, not InBev. That whole company flipped upside down when InBev took over. Anheuser-Busch as a company was actually an amazing company to work for. They treated their employees well. And they took really good care of their facilities. One of my duties was to

walk around and look at ceiling tiles, to see if there were any chips or discoloration, so I could report and maintenance could come and fix. That attention to detail is probably the biggest thing that I learned, and I had a pretty hard-core boss. Her attention to detail was just insane. I appreciate the way they did business. The way they make beer is as good or better than anyone else in the world, and I'll always say that. I think any brewer that knows their stuff will also say that.

Nick: Can you talk about what you guys are doing with promoting and supporting home brewing?

Ben: At the core, it's a home brew competition. I think every brewer that's here, except for one, was a home brewer before they became a commercial brewer. I think that resonates through the entire industry. We were all home brewers at one point before we became commercial brewers. It's a cool way to give back to all those people.

Nick: Can you tell me about your annual home brew competition?

Ben: Yeah, we have an annual home brew competition here at the brewery, and we hand out first, second, and third for every category and then we give a first, second, and third best of show. The person who gets best of show for the entire home brew competition, is invited to the brewery and we let them brew their beer on our system. Then together we enter that into the Pro-Am Competition at the Great American Beer Festival. We also put it on tap here at the brewery. We give them lots of credit on our website. It's a lot of fun.

Nick: So what's the story behind the actual name of the brewery?

Ben: Before the brewery opened, and up until about when the brewery opened, we'd meet every Thursday at Hangar 24 after work. A lot of us had small planes, we're all hobby pilots, and we'd bring friends, family, whoever wanted to show up, we'd all hop in all the planes and we'd follow each other around. We'd just kind of cruise around the area, go over friend's houses, they'd come out and wave, just enjoying aviation and introducing people to aviation. Then we would come back and we'd meet at the actual Hangar 24, at Redlands Airport, right across the street. You can see it from the patio. That's where I would bring my home brew, and we'd barbeque. We had a lot of friends who are good musicians and they would sit and play guitar and sing. Generally, we'd just enjoy handcrafted things, and enjoy each other's company. You'd always meet interesting people, we'd sit in lawn chairs and just hang out. I was like, man, this is what we want to embody here. We want people to meet each other and be social.

Nick: What would you say you love most about your business? And what do you hate most?

Ben: What I love is easy: It's the same thing that I loved with home brewing—even though I haven't brewed in a long time. I actually do miss that, there's something tangible in your hands. I love sharing beer with people. I love the social aspect of it. I like hearing what people think of our beers, that's cool. The entrepreneur side of me loves the growth, the business side, and the complexities behind that. It's all extremely exciting.

What don't I like about it? The stress, obviously. I'm sure it resonates for a lot of us. We have a lot of money out there, a lot of debt. Will it all keep going? I hope so, because we invested so much, and we're planning on it. But there are a lot of unknowns, and I would say that the stress is the only thing that I don't personally like. I cannot complain at all—and I won't—but if I had to pick something, that's what I would say.

> **"I was like, man, this is what we want to embody here. We want people to meet each other and be social."**

Paul Segura
Karl Strauss Brewing Company

Paul Segura is the brewmaster at Karl Strauss Brewing Company in Pacific Beach, California.

Nick: So, how did you get into this whole industry? What was your path from beginning interest all the way to where you're at now?

Paul: I got into this industry when I was attending San Diego State, getting my undergrad back in the early 90's. I started home brewing in '89 or '90 while at San Diego State because I had a day job working at a boat yard and a lot of the guys working there were home brewers. These were guys that were old sailors who had been around the world and everything. They'd bring home brews and we'd sit around after work and drink some of these great beers. I said "Wow, you guys made this? I'd like to make this. How do I do this?"

At that time, there was a home brew shop in La Mesa called Beer and Wine Crafts. They sold all the supplies and everything. I took a class there and it was three hours long. It kind of taught me how to make home brew. It got me hooked. I started home brewing a lot after that. Then I graduated San Diego State in early '94 and the whole craft brewing revolution was just starting to take off. I had learned through an issue of *The Celebrator* that UC Davis was going to start this extension program. The lead instructor, Dr. Lewis, was going to found his own private educational facility up there called The American Brewers Guild. He was going to actually teach courses.

The reason he wanted to do it separate from the university was because the university wouldn't actually let him put in a small brewery. The U.C. system didn't allow it, and he wanted to have a full lab there and a small brewery and everything else. When I learned about that I immediately sent off an application, because I had all my sciences at San Diego State out of the way, all the chemistry and microbiology, biochemistry, all that stuff. The program was 10 weeks long—classes 9:00 to 5:00 every day—intensive brewing science. I graduated in late '94, part of the first graduating class.

I came back to San Diego looking for a brewing job and, at that time, I think there were three breweries in San Diego. It was Karl Strauss, San Diego Brewing Company, and The Hops in UTC, which was opening up a brand new brewery out in Phoenix. They needed a brewer for that location and the UTC general manager sent my resume out to Phoenix. They flew me out for a working interview one weekend and I brewed a batch with James Salter, who recommended to them that they hire me.

I brewed in Phoenix from '94 to '96 or so, at that time Hops did a leverage buyout of the old RJ's Riptide Brewery, which was in downtown San Diego. They knew I was from San Diego and that I wanted to come back, so they allowed me to open up that new brewery downtown and renovate that whole place. The place remained open as Hops Bistro and Brewery for about a year and a half.

Hops was looking to offload it really quick because they needed the money to reopen their flagship location in Phoenix. The San Diego location was bought by a local restaurant magnate named David Cohn. He owns half the restaurants in San Diego at this point. He bought the brewery, renamed it Hang Ten, and asked if I could stay and work for him. I brewed there for a couple years and made a little bit of a name for myself before the convention center closed for expansion and they shut down 5th Avenue to rebuild the ballpark downtown. All that construction killed the lunch business right off the bat.

David had just bought the Prado at Balboa Park, so he was looking to offload the brewery. Fortunately, he called Chris Cramer the day he was closing the brewery and the day he told me we were closing the brewery. Chris Cramer is Karl Strauss's nephew, and is the founder and CEO of Karl Strauss Brewing Company. Chris said "Have Paul come here on Monday." Literally, I stopped working for Hang Ten on a Friday and started for Karl Strauss on Monday and have been here ever since. It's been almost 15 years now. I think it started in just before 2000. That's my story.

Nick: Do you remember the first home brew you ever made?

Paul: My first home brew was a batch of brown ale and it was all extract out of a can. It was so rudimentary it was ridiculous. I just took the can, took the label off, put it in a pot of boiling water to get it to flow out of the can easily, and mixed that with water. I think it was hop extract, too. I didn't even have to add

hops to it. I just boiled that for like an hour and put it into a plastic bucket with a packet of yeast and let it sit in the bathtub for a week or so. It bubbled away and I drank it and went "Wow. I can do this. This is fun." It wasn't the best tasting I'd had, but it was a real source of pride that I'd made it. And it was pretty cheap to make and I drank it.

> **"The whole thing progressed out of curiosity, passion for beer, and being a nerd."**

That little piece of early success got me excited, got me fired up to learn more. How was that extract made? What went into that? Obviously somebody took some malted barely and did that whole thing. I started reading up on it, doing a lot of independent research. I found myself becoming a nerd about it. I bought a book called *The Complete Joy of Homebrewing* by Charlie Papazian, one of the earlier editions. I started learning a little bit more about the science. Then I bought another book. I just started buying these books, reading more and more and more.

As I said, I was going to San Diego State and I was taking a lot of science classes, so the books weren't too far out there for me. I understood them. The whole thing progressed out of curiosity, passion for beer, and being a nerd.

Nick: So now, many years later, as you think about creating recipes, are there overriding philosophies or principles that you use?

Paul: For us, as a brewing company, we've always been about drinkability. At the end of the day, somebody's got to drink this beer and you want that to be a pleasing experience for people. I think that sometimes differs from the approach of other people who are maybe going for the shock and awe factor, or something. We want our beers to be drinkable and approachable. If we can get some edginess in there too, if we can do some things that other people aren't doing, or use ingredients that other people aren't doing, that's awesome. That's a bonus for us. There are still a lot of things that we can do that we haven't done yet. That's been our thing: edgy, but approachable.

As time goes on, given the market that we're in, we find ourselves being pushed more and more to the edgy side, but even as we go there we still hear back from people saying "This beer is extremely drinkable. This is delicious and I could drink a lot of this." Even with double IPAs that are 95 BU, guys are still going "No, this is really drinkable. This is awesome." That's the thing we go for.

Nick: What do you think about the guys that are pushing the envelope, getting really creative, but maybe sacrificing drinkability to be experimental?

Paul: I dig that whole thing. I think I'm a person that enjoys a wide variety of beers. I've had people come up and say "I don't like beer." I just say "No, that can't be. You just haven't had the right beer for you yet." The industry, from what I see, is diversifying. There are breweries now that are specializing in what used to be really esoteric styles of beer like sours. Like The Bruery for instance, they're doing a great job with their beers.

I witnessed the startup of Stone Brewing Co. here in San Diego. When they started up it was nothing but great big, huge, in your face beer—high alcohol beers. They went after that part of the market and that's been their niche and they're successful at it. Other breweries like us kind of do a little bit of everything if we can. We do sour beers, double IPAs, we do session beers, we do just about everything. It's difficult to say where the market's going right now because I see people coming back around to session-able beers. I saw the market going off on a pissing contest for a while there—who can make the biggest double IPA? Who can make the nastiest, in your face, most aggressive beer? Now people are coming back to beers that have flavor, that are distinctive and really cool, hoppy, whatever else. These are beers you could drink more than one of, and still have your mental faculties.

Nick: Do you think there's a craft beer revolution going on right now?

Paul: When I got into craft brewing, commercial craft brewing in '94, the industry was just starting to go through double-digit growth. I don't think I've ever seen it stop. I hear people now go, "Craft beer is really blowing up." Now? I'm like, as opposed to what? It's been blowing up since I've been in it—since '94. At least since I've been associated with it and been doing it. I don't think there was a year since then where it hasn't gone through double-digit growth. We still have a lot of work to do. A lot of people that are still drinking Bud, Coors, and Miller.

When you combine all the craft brewers in America, we're still just a small percentage of the market, you know about 10%, which is crazy because you don't see people eating white bread anymore, and you don't see all these people drinking Folgers coffee anymore, or drinking white zinfandel. All these things that didn't have flavor are getting pushed to the side. There's always going to be a place for the lighter stepping stone type beers, but for craft beer to still be 10% of the market, that tells me we still have a lot of work to do. We've got to turn people on to some flavors that they're going to like.

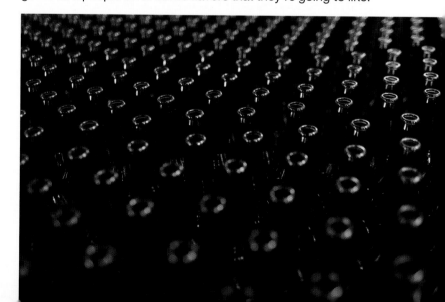

Nick: If you had to come up with a game plan on how to do that, how would you do that?

Paul: I'd stick to what we're doing, man. We're reaching a lot of people. As I said, we do a lot of different beers for a lot of different people. Many of the beers that we do, other breweries wouldn't even think about doing, like a session-able Irish red, a Vienna lager type beer, and Pilsner type beers. We do beers across the spectrum and we sell a lot of those beers that are on the lighter end—a ton. We turn people on to craft beer through those. They taste those, they see how solid they taste and then they kind of go "Oh, I'm going to try the next beer up. I'm going to try this Pintail Pale Ale or this Fullsuit Belgian Brown," or whatever.

When I started out there were beers out there like Samuel Adams, Sierra Nevada, Pete's Wicked Ale. My hat goes off to those guys. I'll give those guys the nod. They introduced a lot of people to craft brewing. We're the Southern California version, I guess, of those guys, but we are also now doing great big huge beers. Double IPAs, black rye, we're doing a lot of great beers that are also stoking up people who are a little more savvy and knowledgeable—people that have been drinking for a while.

Nick: Can you tell me a little bit about what Karl was like?

Paul: He was my boss for six or seven years when I started working here and he was a good dude. He was extremely passionate about beer and brewing. He could tell you a little bit about just about every brewery in the country. He helped half of them start up. He was a consultant on a lot of different breweries. People would approach him and hire him to layout the brewery or help design the equipment or whatever it was, rudimentary recipes and things like that, including some of the biggies that I mentioned earlier; Sierra Nevada, Samuel Adams, and Pete's Wicked Ale. I know for a fact that he helped a lot of those guys get off the ground. For us, as his namesake brewery, he gave us a little more scrutiny. I think it was knowing this beer was going out the door with his name on it.

When he was around, it was like a white glove inspection. He'd walk through the brewery and he was pretty sharp. He had a good attention to detail. He'd say "Why is that like this?" or "What's going on here? You need to fix that. You need to clean this." Just walking through the brewery with him, you needed to have a notepad with you because he'd start naming stuff off. That was even after we knew he was coming and we had the brewery all dialed in. We had everything cleaned.

> **"We do beers across the spectrum and we sell a lot of those beers that are on the lighter end—a ton. We turn people on to craft beer through those."**

He was a very polite man, a very discerning man. He was a very generous teacher to me. I feel extremely fortunate to have worked with him.

Nick: Is there anything that you've never been asked in an interview that you've always wanted to say?

Paul: Hell, I've been asked just about everything. I often get asked by people what my favorite beer is, but I don't think I've ever had somebody in a formal interview ask me that before.

Nick: Do you have an answer for that? Usually, if I ask someone that they say, "whatever beer is in my hand at the time."

Paul: There's a Flanders Brown Ale called Liefmans Goudenband. That's always been my favorite beer.

Nick: Your absolute favorite.

Paul: Since as early as I started drinking.

Kyle Smith
Kern River Brewing Company

Kyle Smith is the founder and brewmaster of the Kern River Brewing Company, which opened in June of 2006.

Nick: What was your first beer "a-ha" moment? And how did that moment lead you to where you are today?

Kyle: In terms of craft beer, I would say the very first time I enjoyed craft beer was in San Francisco. I would have to say it was 1990, and it was Anchor Steam. Shortly after that, it was Sierra Nevada Pale Ale. Those were my first times actually enjoying true craft beer. Before that, it was your mega-swill beers; Bud, Coors—that type of stuff. But the first time I had Anchor I was hooked.

In 1995, I started home brewing. At first, I started off on the stove in my kitchen with kits. I bought two kits and then I went right into all-grain brewing. Eventually it got moved into a garage with the three-tier system

Home brewing was basically my only hobby outside of mountain biking. I was home brewing every weekend; ten-gallon batches. Anything from IPA's to Hefeweizens to triple IPA's—I don't even think triple IPA was a category then.

Before we opened up here, I was up to about six-hundred-twenty-five batches of beer. I did a lot of home brewing for sure. Obviously, as a home brewer, you always want to go to that next level. Maybe not for everyone, but I was a firefighter at the time looking for another avenue to support myself, and I knew that Kernville could use a small brewpub. Then I met my partners, Eric and Rebecca, and it just progressed a little bit more. We purchased our brewing equipment from AleSmith, it was a seven-barrel system. It took us four years from the time we started talking about the project until we opened the doors.

Nick: How did your home brewing experiences influence what you're doing now? Are any of the recipes that are currently your staples from home brewing?

Kyle: I was hoping you were going to ask that, because that's what I'm really happy about. Our four main beers were the four main beers that I brewed at home. There have been a few tweaks to some of them—definitely the IPA has been tweaked a little bit, but not too much. The Sequoia Red is a home brew recipe, the blond, the stout, and the IPA are all also my homebrew recipes.

Nick: You mentioned you were a firefighter. Did anything from that experience translate to brewing?

Kyle: Yeah. I think the biggest thing that translated over to brewing was the work ethic. When you're fighting wildland fires, you're up at four o'clock in the morning, and you work long hours. So working long hours has never been a problem.

Nick: How has being in a small town influenced what you guys have done?

Kyle: We focus on giving back to the community, because it's such a small town. When we were trying to open up, we were on a really tight budget like everybody—I don't really want to get into numbers, but it was extremely small. So we literally had folks from the community coming out, they wanted to see a brewpub here; so they were coming out and volunteering. We had a lot of folks doing all kinds of jobs. People were painting, we had folks digging ditches; whatever their trade was. So, we had a lot of the community coming out just to get us open. We've always felt, in a community this small, you really need to give back to the locals, so we've always been really local-oriented. Friday night is usually our locals night, the place is packed with locals, and their kids are running around having a great time. You can walk anywhere in Kernville, so most people just walk up, bring their families, have a few beers, eat some dinner, hang out and listen to some music. In a town of 1,800 people, for us to still be up and running, you know, it's great.

> **"Before we opened up here, I was up to about six-hundred-twenty-five batches of beer. I did a lot of home brewing for sure."**

Nick: You're such a small brewery, but you've been invited to big events like the Firestone Walker Brewers Invitational, for example. Is that validation for you guys?

Kyle: It's just the way the craft beer community works. It's great. Once you establish yourself and you're making good beer, it gets noticed by some of the other breweries. But, I mean, we're very humble, we try to give back to the craft beer community, we feel very fortunate to be in a great industry.

Nick: Can you describe your recipe creation process? Are there any overriding principles or philosophies that you always use?

Kyle: Let me just pick a beer. I'll tell a story about when we did the Citra for the first time. A lot of times what I'll do is research new hops and new hop varieties that are coming out, and I'll go to some of the small hop growers, or hop providers, and just get a small amount of hops to try.

Anyway, with the Citra, we got Citra hops; I had never even heard of them. They weren't readily available, and the first time I opened that bag and smelled them, I thought, "This is amazing." I formulated a double IPA recipe and what I wanted to do was showcase the hops themselves, but balanced in some way. That's our signature here at Kern River; we have really hoppy beers, but they are also balanced. Most of our hops come in later additions so you get more aroma out of

them. Most of our beers are more on the aroma side than bitter. So, in formulating a beer, I just come up with a good base malt recipe that'll be balanced. The one thing we don't really have in most of our IPA's is a real caramel malt flavor, because it just gets in the way of the hops.

We try to leave out caramel malts, use a little bit of honey malts to balance things out. Then, we're low on the first additions of our bittering hops, because we don't really want an "in-your-face" bittering punch. We add a lot more on the five minute editions, fifteen minute editions, and then a lot of dry hops; so you get a lot of aroma. Our thing here is, once we start dry-hopping for the first beer, it's all about tasting out of the fermenter. So we do several dry-hop additions. A lot of breweries will just add all the hops in one dry-hop addition and then two, three days later they're carbonating it. For us, we do several dry hop editions and taste it along the way. That

is the way we do it here at Kern River. You have to know what kind of flavor profile you're looking for out of your final beer. The Citra has four dry-hop editions, all three days apart; so it ties up the tank for a long time. That's why we brew this beer only two to three times a year.

Nick: So, would you say you more often build a beer off of the ingredients that you find, or do you sometimes start with an end product in mind?

Kyle: A little bit of both, actually. I know what I'm looking for end-product wise. It's hard to explain. I know what I'm looking for at the end, and then you build it as you go. Like I said, that's probably why some of our bigger IPA's take a little bit longer. You add a little bit of spice, taste it, it's the same philosophy, at least, for us.

Nick: A lot of brewers say that it's all a mix of science and art. Do you agree with that?

Kyle: I definitely see myself more on the creativity side than the science, but you've got to put the two together. The science has to fall in place, which, to me, is always more of a challenge than the creative side of things. You just have so many variables on the science side of things: Of course, they're going to blend together, but I would definitely say I enjoy the creative side of things much more than the scientific side. It's always a work in progress.

Nick: What is your vision for Kern River Brewing Company?

Kyle: Kern River Brewing Company to us is—we all love the outdoors, we all love the environment that we live in, and we love the community. We don't want to leave this community and go somewhere else and call ourselves Kern River Brewing Company. So that's us, that's what we're all about. It's nice to be able to finish your day at five o'clock and go for a hike or go down to the river or go fishing or go kayaking . . . whatever your outdoor passion is.

> **"People have discovered craft beer— maybe they got tired of somebody telling them what they're supposed to drink, you know?"**

Nick: Do you see evidence of the craft beer revolution from here in Kernville?

Kyle: Yes, I definitely see it. Just being at the Craft Brewers Conference this year, you see a lot of new faces and a lot of new folks coming on board. The other thing is, unfortunately you're also seeing a huge shortage in ingredients and supplies because there's so many new breweries on board.

Luckily we're locked in with our hops, we have hop contracts. And then there's equipment: your lead time for equipment used to be three months. This was three years ago when we got our fifteen-barrel tanks. It was three months by the time they got delivered. Now you're looking at nine months to a year because there's so many breweries coming on board.

So my take on that is it's just like anything else; there's going to be a lot of breweries that just don't make it. You're going to have people, just like in the mid-90's, that are getting on board for the money and there's not much passion there.

> **"You find a lot more people that are seeking out craft breweries and they're taking vacations specifically for that reason."**

The cool thing is, just in the seven years that we've been open, I've seen a huge change from the folks who used to come in and wonder where the Bud Light was, or whatever beer it was. So people, really in just the past four or five years, they know exactly what they want, and they want a craft beer. People have discovered craft beer—maybe they got tired of somebody telling them what they're supposed to drink, you know?

But it's pretty cool. I think it's awesome. Especially now, because there's so many breweries. You can find them all over the place. You find a lot more people that are seeking out craft breweries and they're taking vacations specifically for that reason. "Okay, let's go see the north coast of Califor-

nia. We're going to hit this brewery, hit this brewery, hit this brewery; but in between, we're going to do: this, this, and this." And you see that a lot now.

Nick: What keeps you going day after day? What is it about making beer that gets you up every day to do this?

Kyle: It probably goes back to what I was just talking about. I just really enjoy when somebody comes to the brewery and is very excited to be here to drink some of our beers and hang out at the pub; especially with the seasonals that we do. And when you go to the festivals it's rewarding when people are just digging your beer. And the camaraderie, that's a big thing, too, in the craft beer industry that I just love.

Nick: Is there anything that you've never been asked in an interview before that you've always wanted to say?

Kyle: I could just go on and on about how much I really enjoy the industry. It's just such a good group of folks. It's not cut-throat. Everyone's out to help each other. Before we started here, Lengthwise Brewing down in Bakersfield helped us out a lot. I transferred beer, cleaned kegs—I did a little bit of everything just to try to get the experience on a professional level. That's just the way it goes. . . . Nowadays, it's a lot different because there are so many folks coming on board. The amount of emails I get from people who want to come work at the brewery to get experience can be overwhelming.

Tony Magee
Lagunitas Brewing Company

Tony Magee is the founder and former brewmaster at Lagunitas Brewing Company in Petaluma, California.

Nick: When you first remember enjoying craft beer? And how did that bring you to where you are today?

Tony: I grew up in Chicago in the 70's and 80's, and the stuff we drank back then was Old Milwaukee and Old Style. Budweiser was like a newcomer, MGD was a sexy one—and there is nothing to these beers except liquid and a little bit of alcohol. You had to drink them fast if you're going to get drunk on them, but I didn't care much for it.

I started selling commercial printing in San Francisco for a company out of Los Angeles, and after a little while I just knew I didn't want to be doing this for the rest of my life. But it was a golden ball and chain, I was making a lot of money—more money than I needed to live on, for sure. I was working 80 hours a week, I got married and almost divorced, and, at that point, my little brother bought me a home brewing kit for Christmas. I brewed it in January 1993 and drank it in February '93 and that was it. That was all I needed to know. I brewed two batches immediately and said I'm starting a brewery. The first mash was December of that year. I started the brewery with about $35,000 in cash, a seven-barrel brewhouse, and it was great. I made all the deliveries myself, all over west Marin, in the back of this old Ranger pickup truck. Then we killed the septic system and the county told me I had to leave, so we moved to Petaluma. As soon as we moved to Petaluma, we had to start growing—all my costs went up, my rent went up, and I had to hire an assistant. I was still selling printing, so I had to hire a brewer, then I had to hire a guy that kegged beer, then I had to hire a guy to clean for everybody. Every time you hire a guy, you have to sell more beer to pay for him. I spent the next 13 years working away before I finally got profitable . . . that's how I came to be.

Nick: You've said that you work hard to put "personalities" into each of your recipes. Can you explain a little bit about what that means and why that's important to you?

Tony: You know, I'm a musician. So you do a composition, maybe a long form of symphony—that's the brand—but within that, there's all sorts of movements and different sections. Each bottle's its own song, it's a composition beginning to end. You commune with it and you experience it and it changes your point of view. The beer gets into your stomach and goes into your blood and goes to your brain, making it do tricks—there is a complete communion with a bottle of beer.

I think of each brand or each flavor of beer as a song, it is its own thing. When Jeremy, my head brewer, and I write a recipe, we write it very carefully. We arrange it like instruments and then we hand out the pieces to each of the musicians who are the artisans or the brewers. There are the filtration guys, the people above the line, that's my orchestra, and they turn it into this thing that could be reproduced into infinity—it's a composition.

Nick: You guys aren't really confined by "styles" of beer, is that fair to say?

Tony: Styles are for home brewers, and home brewers are good at that. They're like the keepers of the history of craft brewing, or of small brewing in the world, but our job is to do something new. Kind of like the Rolling Stones, you know? They're heavily influenced by Muddy Waters and all of these Delta and Texas blues men, but the truth is when they started playing, they didn't sound anything like that. We have a responsibility to bring something to it, it's not enough to copy.

> **"I think of each brand or each flavor of beer as a song, it is its own thing."**

It's funny though, the first generation of brewers in the United States—everyone from Full Sail and Sam Adams, they brew to traditional styles. Sierra Nevada took the pale ale to a place they hadn't been before, but it started from what had gone before. Then, as that second generation of breweries came along, we needed to find a way to differentiate ourselves. We did it by saying, "Well, where do you go from here, where do we take this?

Nick: What does craft beer mean to you?

Tony: I think craft brewing is like pornography, you know it when you see it. The Supreme Court separates pornography from beautiful photographs of naked people—it's like they know it when they see it. So if somebody sees Boston Beer, or any of the others, and loves the beer and feels something about the company and see's themselves in the beer when they think about it, more power to them.

Nick: With your expansion, can you still label yourself craft?

Tony: I started out by saying it's like you know it when you see it. To an individual, craft is what they see. As for the industry having a definition of craft—it doesn't mean anything anymore. It doesn't mean anything anymore than "organic" means anything anymore. It's like yeah, great, that's Nestle and it's organic chocolate, great. I don't even know what that means. When the word *organic* belonged to people, everyone knew what organic meant. It belongs to the government now, it's nothing. Unlike almost anything else, craft brewing is owned by the people that drink the beer.

Nick: As long as you guys keep putting out beer like you do, it doesn't matter how big you are, folks will want to keep drinking it.

Tony: I don't know if this is a weird thing to say, but, if 15 years from now our IPA was regarded as Budweiser is today, I'd be thrilled to make a million barrels a year. We'd do the IPA, but we'd also make Hairy Eyeball and the bourbon-barrel this or barrel that. To me, that would be the best of both worlds. So we'll never stop doing those little things. This isn't for bragging rights, but we were really the first brewery to establish this paradigm of having seasonals that are extraordinary and big—you might love it, you might hate it, but you have to have an opinion about it. You may never drink it again, but you're going to remember it.

Nick: Are you at all worried that you can't be in two places at once? Are you at all worried about quality with opening up in Chicago?

Tony: I spent my whole life worrying. I live in the future, I never look down at what's in front of my feet. I'm looking out 20 feet ahead and I just hope that nothing changes between when I saw it and when I get there. I just hired a guy a little

while ago—he had made Mike's Hard Lemonade, but he'd also worked for Genesee for 10 years. He just wanted back in the craft brewing so badly. He lives in Chicago and he oversaw five plants for Mike's Hard Lemonade, which actually is a beer; it's brewed like a beer. He was responsible for product consistency across all platforms, even though they brew at different breweries, and even though they're brewing on different equipment by different people who don't know each

> **"I spent my whole life worrying. I live in the future, I never look down at what's in front of my feet. I'm looking out 20 feet ahead and I just hope that nothing changes between when I saw it and when I get there."**

other. We hired him and he's working here right now learning everything about what we do and how we do it here.

Nick: Are you worried at all about consistency?

Tony: Every day.

Nick: Are the ingredients that you guys are using bountiful enough that you can increase production so much?

Tony: The ingredients will come from the same supplier, our hops will come from the same farmers, not through the same deal, but through the same farmers. The malt will come from the same malter, and we'll be buying, as we are now, our barley from the same farmers. Unlike a lot of breweries, we don't buy just malt from a malter, we're actually contracting now from barley in the field to be delivered to the malter. It's going to come from the same land it came from before. The brewhouse itself that we're going to put in Chicago is identical to the one we just finished commissioning here. We're going to take our bottling line from here and move it to Chicago, so much of the plant—mechanically how the beer actually gets produced—will be the same.

You know, it's hard to make the same product in two locations, but it's not impossible. It takes work and it takes insight and you have to recognize it as a huge problem. Then you just address it like that. It's hard, it's a problem and you make it work.

Nick: Do you think the term "Craft Beer Revolution" is apt for what we're seeing today?

Tony: See, it's not a revolution and we're not an army changing people's tastes. People's taste change and they're pulling beer from us. This goes back to the idea that brewers don't drive the market, consumers pull the beer out of the market. There are brewers who talk about how much they are promoting craft beer. They're preaching to the choir: The choir wishes they'd just sit down, stop talking, and make more beer. Make more, better, interesting beers—that's what they want from them. It's called a "revolution," but it's a people's revolution and what they're fighting for is the freedom to choose between lots of different beers.

Nick: What is the one thing you've never been asked in an interview that you've always wanted to say?

Tony: Boxers or briefs?

Nick: And?

Tony: I'm not going to answer that. I don't know, what's the one thing I never been asked? Is it harder than it looks? This is a hard, hard business, especially when you want to live up to those people who are telling you they'll love you even if you fuck this up—when you want to live up to the opportunities the world gives you, to the world of beer lovers you know. It's like being chased down the street by a pack of wild dogs. That's really something, how crazy it is, but at the same time, it's the most exciting thing in the world.

You don't even know what your world is around you, you're just in it. You experience it but you can't really define it because you're one with it. The thing about right now, with craft

brewing, it occurred to me a couple of months ago, is that all the founders are here right now and they're still running their breweries for the most part, There's a couple of companies that changed hands, but for the most part, this would be like being alive in 1775 while George and Ben and Paul and Tom were drinking at the local pub. They were just people in town. If you were around Golden, Colorado, at the turn of the century, you might have been around when Adolf Coors was actually running this fucking company—when Augustus Busch was running a brewery, when somebody named Stroh was at the brewery. There is a time and then they're all gone. Augustus Busch and Adolf Coors, they knew who they were and they were trying to put it out there so people would understand them. I love their beer, and I appreciate their work. That's the way it is right now. It's a weird thing, the founders are all here right now, and I don't want to pretend that I'm in anyway special, but it's a fascinating time. If we don't fuck it up, a lot of these beers will still be made 50 years from now, and they'll be popular American beers, probably ten times the size they are now. And I'll be long dead.

Nick: That's what you hope?

Tony: Yes, that people 50 years from now will tell stories about Tony and Jeremy and Ron. We'll be either dead or like laying prone in a hospital somewhere. That's interesting, for people who are into beer right now, it will be another hundred years

> ## "It's called a "revolution," but it's a people's revolution and what they're fighting for is freedom to choose between lots of different beers."

before it's like this again. This is a crazy time you know? Steve Jobs, he's gone. We all lived in the presence of Steve Jobs. A hundred years from now, Apple products will probably be part of the landscape just like Henry Ford's cars are still driven today. There's nobody today who knows what Henry Ford was really like. It's an interesting thing, this is an exciting time, it will never be like this again for at least a hundred years.

Tomme Arthur
Port Brewing and
The Lost Abbey

Tomme Arthur is the director of brewery operations at Port Brewing and The Lost Abbey in San Marcos. He is also the managing member and one of four owners of the facility.

Nick: Can you remember back to when you first enjoyed craft beer? And how did that experience get you to where you are today?

Tomme: I left San Diego in 1991 when I had graduated high school and moved to Flagstaff, Arizona to attend Northern Arizona University. I had originally signed up to go to school there to become a teacher. I was going to go study English and teach.

I got to college and ran into a new group of friends. They got me started on beer, and I spent the next four years at school drinking and learning as much as I could. I attended my first Great American Beer Festival. I moved back to San Diego in 1995, and spent a few months bumming around looking for work, doing small project stuff.

I managed to find a brewpub in downtown San Diego in 1996. I went to work for them for about nine months as an assistant brewer. I had no real background in brewing—I had home brewed a little bit in college—but I didn't have any true brewing skills.

Nick: What was that brewpub called?

Tomme: It was called Cervecerias La Cruda, in Spanish, the Hangover Brewery. I spent nine months working in that environment—it was a startup, not well put together. It was one of the mid-90's startups in this town that didn't stick. So, about a year after I got into brewing, I went to work for Pizza Port in Solana Beach. I wound up brewing there for about nine years.

In the fall of 2005, we got wind that this facility was going to be available, because Stone was moving out. I put together a business plan with Vince and Gina [Marsaglia], who own the Pizza Ports, as well as a fourth partner named Jim Comstock. We wanted to take some of the things that Pizza Port had done and expand those into Port Brewing, and we wanted to develop a new line of beers under the Lost Abbey name.

We spent basically the fall and the early part 2006 sourcing equipment, getting all the parts, and putting the company together. We opened our doors for business on May 5, 2006. That's how we got here.

Nick: Can you provide the explanation of how Lost Abbey differentiates itself from Port Brewing?

Tomme: We're unique on some levels, in that not a lot of breweries have two pure brands that they produce under one roof. Some do it under contract, but don't own both brands. We own both brands and have, from day one, set out to build this facility with two brands being part of the driver. It's helped us grow this company.

Strategically, Port Brewing represents what we call West Coast or "West Coast-centric" brews. It's not unlike a lot of the brewing that's going on in this town, with breweries like Green Flash, Ballast Point, Stone, Coronado, and Alpine. We're all brewing very hop-forward, hop-driven beers, classically styled double IPA type stuff. We call it "West Coast-centric," in that it's got a bigger alcohol level, a higher level of hop threshold, and aroma and flavor.

The Lost Abbey side has always been where we've looked to push out a real departure, a point of differentiation. Here's where the brand can have a real identity out in the world. Sometimes, the Port brands are more ubiquitous and they're a little less identifiable than other things. The Abbey brand truly has a uniqueness about it and a real resonating story. A lot of our energy for promotional opportunities goes into the Abbey brand.

Nick: Can you talk about Lost Abbey's basic mission and your goal of pushing the limits and developing truly imaginative beers?

Tomme: Part of what drives me as a brewer are the possibilities, imagining what beer can be; what it is and where it might take you. I say that a lot. How beer takes me to places that I never thought possible. It's really a fascinating thing to think of

> **"Part of what drives me as a brewer are the possibilities, imagining what beer can be . . . and where it might take you."**

beer as a vehicle. In order to do that, you have to make that conversation endearing; you have to be endearing. It's easy to be in this seat and to imagine great beers and flavorful things. It's another thing to pull the trigger and spend the money and time, and commit the resources to doing them. I knew that once we established this facility, we'd be able to do so, because I knew that my partners were committed to that kind of brewing. We didn't open our doors chasing volume. We didn't open up with six-packs or beer going out on draught. We went after better beer establishments in the form of, not necessarily funky beer, but definitely not what you would align with being a mainstream beer.

Nick: What inspires you to pursue those avenues?

Tomme: Our job as brewers in this environment, in terms of how we look at structure in the beers, is to deviate from the norm with intent. It means that we have a high probability of success, and at the same time, we're not doing it just to stand up and wave the color flag and to say we're that different. We do it with a specific intensity and a direction, with an end goal in mind.

Nick: What's an example of a beer that follows those kind of philosophies?

Tomme: When you look at our Ten Commandments, that's sort of the one that I always can look at and go, "Wow, that's such an interesting beer." It's a dark farmhouse beer to begin with, which is a little bit different than a pure yellow saison-style beer. It's stronger, which makes it more of a food type beer. In my estimation, it's one of the most amazing beers we make, because I always put it in front of chefs and you can just see the look on their faces. They're going in every direction with it.

It's made with caramelized raisins. We have multiple beers that have raisins in them, but the caramelizing process is very unique. It's got rosemary, honey, and orange peel and then it also gets wild yeast added to it. It's an evolutionary beer, it has a lot of potential to be cellarable and to really change over time. There isn't another brewery that I know of that caramelizes raisins in the way that we've tackled that process. We looked at it and said, "What if we altered the chemical structure of the raisin? What if we transition this to a different texture?" It's like taking an onion and caramelizing it, how you can change a raw white onion into something more sweet. You've taken these raisins, which we use all the time, and you're changing the texture and character of the beer. We're making them very smoky, very different, by caramelizing them.

Nick: Would you say your recipe creation process is mostly ingredient based, or do you develop ideas around styles and ideas and look for ingredients to make that?

Tomme: It's a little of both. I used to challenge myself when I was in the pub environment, when we would produce new beers, to always include at least one new ingredient. It wasn't always that a new malt had come out, or that we were chasing a new hop. It wasn't like we had to add Thai lemon basil to this Hefeweizen just to make the Hefeweizen more interesting. The point was that new beer is always in demand. It gave us an opportunity to try things out.

The catalog that I had, working for nine years at over 100 batches of beer a year, gave me a real scope. It's like putting your time in as a line cook. You really learn to understand what the manipulation of those ingredients would afford you and present you with. Nowadays, a lot of what we do is imagine the specifics of beer and work toward that. Whether we use unique ingredients or not comes into play only if the beer needs a back story; does it need more than classic styling, does it need spin, or does it need a complete right turn? Sometimes a spin is enough to make a great beer. Sometimes it demands a right turn.

Something like Saison Blanc, which we're working on. It's another saison-style beer, but low alcohol, with New Zealand hops. We're basically trying to emulate a lot of the flavor and character you get in Saison Blanc. I love a great crisp white Saison Blanc. We took a Witbier base, hence the blanc part, which is unmalted wheat and all the things that go into Witbiers. Instead of adding the coriander and orange peel, we've packed in green raisins and white pepper and then put forth a really refreshing low alcohol beer. That's a pretty right turn on a blanc mentality. Classic styling, potentially homage-style beers. A little bit of a spin and then a full twist.

But again, the guiding principle is we don't chase what everybody else is doing, and that's huge. I think absolutely around here, it's a mantra that our brewers understand. And we don't do strange just for strange.

Nick: What do you think of the notion of styles? You talk about spinning off a style or taking a complete right turn. Are styles important to you as a base, or having your beers fit in a particular box?

Tomme: No, and I hate the notion of brewing outside the box. I'm not convinced that there ever should have been a box to begin with. I appreciate what styles afford and that is, it's a starting

point. If you want to liken it to a journey, let's say that you're a hiker. You park at the trailhead, and the trailhead takes you off the road: that might be the style. Then you get to the end of the trailhead, and all of a sudden, if people have gotten to that point and made those turns at the end of it, that might be where we have an opportunity to continue the evolution.

Styles are not set in stone, necessarily. They're evolving all the time. I judge at the Great American Beer Festival and the World Beer Cup, and they're constantly rewriting those style guidelines as beers evolve. 30 years ago, there was no such thing as American Pale Ale until Sierra Nevada came along. 15 years ago, that style changed completely. 10 years ago, it changed again. 5 years ago, it probably changed again.

Nick: What's exciting to you as it relates to ingredients, techniques, or kinds of beer?

Tomme: I think there's going to be a lot more Brett production. You're going to see a huge commitment to American sour beer coming down. The guys over at Stone are building a facility. The guys at Firestone have built a side facility. Breweries like ourselves, and Russian River, and The Bruery, and Allagash.

> **"Sometimes a spin is enough to make a great beer. Sometimes it demands a right turn."**

The small European producers can't make enough of these beers to satisfy this market. So what's going to happen is a lot of the bigger breweries, breweries that want to get involved in the sour beer world, are going to have a separate facility to deal with sour beer production. That's pretty cool.

Nick: Wild yeast is one of those things that you helped to pioneer. Obviously, it's seeing huge popularity now. What was your inspiration to start using using wild yeasts?

Tomme: When I was in the pub environment, we were brewing so many different beers every year. Every time we were doing these beers, they were fairly straightforward. You reach a saturation point. You start imagining and you start to think, "God if I only I could use X-Y-Z to do more," and so we did. We started dabbling around with wild yeast.

By the late 90's, that's when we started getting into Brett and some of those souring agents to try to make beers that weren't being produced. Fifteen years ago, there wasn't a tremendous amount of sour beer being produced in this country. The rules were very different.

Nick: Do you have any advice for the novices or home brewers looking to get into the industry?

Tomme: My piece of advice always is you have to be a good technician. If you're not, you have to learn it, because there's no room if you don't. If you are a great technician, there's still

improvement. Every single time I travel and visit friends and bigger breweries, I never stop learning. I don't know of a single brewery on this planet that has reached a level of technical proficiency that they are willing to stop trying. That goes from Budweiser to Sierra Nevada to Firestone Walker; it goes down the list. I think that there's never a level of technical proficiency where you can sit back and say, "We've got it all."

Nick: It seems like you're talking a little bit about mastering the science of brewing?

Tomme: Sure. I think that understanding the science of brewing is important. I don't consider myself to be a brewing scientist necessarily, but if you're going to break the rules by adding carmelized raisins, you better understand what happens when you take a raisin and you hit it with a flamethrower, and what that might do to your beer down the road. There's a lot of stuff that comes out on the fringe of weird ingredients. You can't read about it in the literature. Some of it's a leap of faith and some of it's a guided departure.

Nick: So, let's go down to a bare bones level on this: On an emotional level, what is it about beer that excites you? What inspires you to keep doing it day after day?

Tomme: I referenced it earlier. It might be the ultimate vehicle, right? It opens doors, it takes you places, it creates friendships. I can't think of another situation. . . . Wine could do the same, but there's a level of texture that beer provides that wine can't. Wine's not imaginative. Wine has way more history and way more terroir, but it's also way more boxed, fixated, and stylistically, it almost dead-ends.

I'm so privileged to have a job where I have the opportunity to come to work every day and be creative, where I get to work with people who, at the end of the day, I can share a beer with. Sharing the beer at the end of the day . . . When you get off shift at 4:00 and you're drinking with the customers out front, that's rewarding in and of itself, even if there weren't all the other parts that went into it.

Dave McLean
Magnolia Gastropub and Brewery

Dave McLean is the brewmaster and founder of Magnolia Gastropub and Brewery on Haight Street in San Francisco.

Nick: Take me to your first true moment of enjoying beer, and tell me how that got you here today.

Dave: Sure. Like many of us, my early experiences as an American beer drinker were terrible, drinking American mass-produced lagers that had very little flavor. That's all you really knew that was out there. This is the late 80's that we're talking about—mid to late 80's. Craft beer hadn't really exploded onto the marketplace, although there were pioneers out there. I grew up in Pittsburgh and went to college in Boston. It was Boston where I really discovered beer. This is a story that I've told before, but it continues to be a fun one to tell; the most memorable early moments of drinking flavorful, interesting craft beer—oddly—happened in parking lots of Grateful Dead shows.

> **"The most memorable early moments of actually making a transition to drinking flavorful, interesting craft beer—oddly—happened in parking lots of Grateful Dead shows."**

Somewhere, there's got to be an awesome story—a study in how a cultural phenomena like that, could've actually done a small part to spread the flow of craft beer into places where it hadn't already caught on. The Dead were a product of Northern California. A lot of the early craft beer pioneers are products of Northern California. And, back in the late 80's, when The Dead were traveling around, there were a lot of people that loaded up the bus or van or whatever out here with Sierra Nevada or Anchor or Red Tail Ale. I remember those were all beers that were commonly found in parking lots on the East Coast outside of a Grateful Dead show.

One of the compelling things about seeing these uncommon beers that I hadn't seen elsewhere was that they fit in with the mindset in that time and place. They dovetailed with that idea of something that was independently produced. It was not mainstream. It was alternative. The birth of craft beer is also a study in an alternative product—something that, in its first forays into culture, stemmed from people that were not happy with mass produced products, that didn't have a lot of character. There was a compelling reason to embrace these new things, new products. People were trying to put some of their own personality and even eccentricities into the product that they made. Every [industry] has a version of that story now, but beer had it, too. I distinctly remember drinking imports like Samuel Smith—things that were kind of interesting that were coming over from overseas—and drinking things like Sierra Nevada, Red Seal, and Red Tail and really having my mind blown. I thought, well, isn't it awesome that there's an alternative to the yellow beer that we drink by the suitcaseful. These beers are really great.

Around that same time, there were early craft beer pioneers on the East Coast. Harpoon was around then. There were a few others, too. So, I felt like I was seeing something cool kind of being birthed, and it was really captivating on a number of levels, not the least of which was taste.

Commonwealth Brewing Company, now closed, was one of the first brewpubs I encountered in Boston. It triggered my interest in English-style, cask-conditioned beer. Drinking those session beers, English bitters and milds, back then in the late 80's, is a big part of why we focus so much on English brewing at Magnolia.

Nick: So how did you get from there to being a brewer?

Dave: The circumstances were right. I was finishing up college, not really sure what I wanted to do with my life. I was ready for some kind of cross-country, post-college adventure—and I had the Grateful Dead and live music worked into that story. I went on a 3-month journey from Boston to San Francisco, with a plan to move here at the end of that—but seeing a lot of Grateful Dead shows along the way.

An added bonus was visiting brewpubs and beer bars all along the way—places that were pioneers in serving craft brew beer back then. It became a thing to look for on that trip. Every town that I would visit, there was a reasonable likelihood, even back then, that you could find at least one brew pub, one small pioneering brewery, or a place that at least had a nice selection of beers from that region. I think that dramatically shaped my feelings about beer.

By the time I got to San Francisco, I was convinced that I was going to jump into beer. I'd visited enough breweries to know that I was really curious about how beer was being made, not just how it tasted, and who was doing it. I was ready to delve into it, and I jumped right into home brewing.

One of the first things I did when I got an apartment here was find the local home brew shop. I started brewing in my kitchen, just trying to figure out how to make beer that tasted even remotely like the beers I had fallen in love with. The path from home brewing to planning to becoming a commercial brewer—a professional brewer opening a brewery—was super short. It took a long time to execute, but within about a year of home brewing religiously I was 100% convinced that it was what I wanted to do. So I started researching the next steps.

One of those next steps was going to UC Davis, to the Master Brewers Program. I had a very curious mind about the science behind it, so I felt like I would be best served by going to a 9-month program and learning about that part of it. I came out of the program pretty much armed with what I felt was enough knowledge to open a brewery. I was lacking money, space, and the business knowledge—and sadly lacking any restaurant experience—but I was bitten by the bug. I turned an interest into a hobby into an obsession into a career and then into a business.

Nick: So how did you decide what kinds of beers you would make? And did you develop any overriding principles about brewing?

Dave: Well, it's hard not to be a little bit like a kid in a candy store, wanting to make everything. You try a beer, you like a style of beer, you become curious about it, you want to explore how to make that beer.

So we are all over the map in a lot of ways. We do a lot of one-offs and unusual experimentations and sometimes it's with a bent toward Belgium, sometimes with a bit more German source material to draw from. But, having said that, the heart and soul of Magnolia—it's aesthetic and approach—is balanced session beers, generally lower in gravity, lower in alcohol, often very English influenced. English malts. The flavors come specifically from some of the older heirloom varieties of English barley; Maris Otter being one of my favorite barleys to work with.

Nick: So how do you go about creating a new recipe?

Dave: Coming up with a new beer starts with a vision of a flavor of that beer, or a set of flavors of that beer. I kind of work backwards: What are the parameters of this new, yet-to-be designed beer that we're looking for? What do we want it to taste like? How do we want those ingredients to interact with each other? What is the story that all those ingredients are going to come together to tell? But it's inexplicably linked to the ingredients themselves.

I don't know that I can separate it into ingredient-driven or process-driven, because I feel like the part that's so cool about brewing—and doing it for so long now—is that the more you do it, the more intimate you become with the ingredients. Therefore, the more you can draw from your knowledge of ingredients, the more that initial vision of what a beer is going to taste like comes true.

I feel like I'm a lot better at it now than I was 10 years ago, 15 years ago, probably even 5 years ago and I'd love to know that I'm going to keep getting better at it. It's a constantly growing connection to each one of the ingredients you work with. Sometimes it's fun to experiment and work with new ingredients, to come up with a new beer style that's new to us. But other times the most fun and satisfying part of it all is to coax out a subtlely different set of flavors from very familiar ingredients we work with over and over.

Nick: Would you say brewing is more a creative process or a more scientific process?

Dave: It's an incredible marriage of those two. It's so deeply satisfying because of that. It tickles different parts of your brain. That's one of the things I love about it. You can feel like you're expressing an artistic idea following a muse of some sort and then it takes a pretty deep understanding of science to turn that conversation with your muse into reality, to make it actually execute the way you want it to.

Nick: You're in an extremely unique city and in an extremely unique part of the city. Why did you choose this part of the city and how has it influenced what you do?

> ❝I feel like it's just a lot of really passionate people building this community for a long time, like the Anchors and the Sierras and all the other pioneers in the craft beer world who've been around for 30 or 40 years.❞

Dave: There was a moment in time here when there was a community of alternative seekers trying to come up with a different version of life that could suit them and their artistic expression. This was prior to the Summer of Love when 30,000 people just showed up. But there was a point prior to that where the kind of creative expression and the philosophy that was emerging fueled much of what's come since. That Haight-Ashbury ethos was hatched back then. It comes from The Dead among others. I was inspired by all that. I didn't immediately intend to open a brewery in the Haight, but I looked all around and stumbled into this community. The city and the Bay area are very inspirational. They continue to spark creativity and that idea of a little bit of a restless energy, of, hey, why not try something different.

Nick: It seems that we are experiencing a special time in craft brewing. Do you feel it's a unique period in craft beer history?

Dave: We are seeing an increase in demand, an increase in popularity, and a general sense that craft beer is deeply woven into the story of American culture and life.

I see more people, maybe from a broader demographic, finding their way here, and I see them having the same experiences of falling in love with craft beer. We're just reaching more people. It's that element of discovery, and then the element of embracing it, and getting excited about it, and then turning that person into a regular who is now paying atten-

tion to what you're doing. Someone who wants to know what you're working on next or has a favorite of yours that they want to share with their friends.

A lot of those experiences haven't changed in 15 years. It's just that we're touching more people. So my general hunch about all this is not so much that we've dramatically changed anything in terms of how Americans think about beer as much as we've just slowly been chipping away at the mass-produced beer monoculture and reaching critical mass. The number of people in this country who have been exposed to the world of craft beer and are excited about it is much bigger. I feel like it's just a lot of really passionate people building this community for a long time, like the Anchors and the Sierras and all the other pioneers in the craft beer world who've been around for 30 or 40 years. Now people really get it.

Nick: Is there anything you've never been asked in an interview that you've always wanted to say?

Dave: I feel like none of this is really rocket science. There's not a deep, burning, mysterious aspect to it at all. I just can't stress enough how lucky I feel to be in an industry where people love what they do, and there's an open flow of knowledge and sharing that makes us all better. It's full of community and collaboration, and it's pretty special.

Arne Johnson
Marin Brewing Company

Arne Johnson has been the brewmaster at Marin Brewing Company in Larkspur, Claifornia, for over 18 years.

Nick: Can you recount your brewing history? You have some early roots in your life with brewing, right?

Arne: That's a funny history, my parents actually had their first date in Berkeley in 1958 or '59 and they home brewed together. My mom was a microbiologist, and my dad was just interested in beer. So they went to Safeway and got some Pabst Blue Ribbon malt extract and some Fleischmann's yeast. And they made some beer.

When I was 13, they decided to take up home brewing again. So I'd hang out with them on Saturday mornings and watch them and help them clean stuff and just see what was going on. That spurred my interest, and they got into it for quite a while, so we'd always have home brew around the house, which all my teenage friends thought was pretty cool. My parents were nice about letting us taste it sometimes, so that's where I started. A few years later, when I moved out of the house, I bought all my own equipment and started home brewing for myself. I was pretty actively brewing, about 10–20 times a year, and just rolled with that.

I remember tasting Boont Amber from Anderson Valley and I thought, "Wow, they're making really great beer out there, I want to be a part of that." For a couple of years I worked about 70 hours a week, two jobs, and saved up money to enter the Brewing Science and Engineering program with the American Brewers Guild. I was in the second graduating class. It was taught at a hotel in Sacramento at the time, and their program was run by Doctor Michael Lewis, who was the lead guy for the brewing science department at UC Davis. Their program is quite a bit different now; we were a full lecture for 40 hours a week and now it's pretty much an online course.

After the Brewers Guild program, they set me up with an internship here at Marin Brewing Company. I started with Grant Johnston, who was original brewmaster here. I was pretty ecstatic to be able to get in here because, of the 30 people in our class, 15 of them had Marin Brewing as their first choice for the internship. We had an evening where we met with all the brewers and mentors and got to know each other, and I guess I made an impression with Grant because he picked me and one other guy. I think he liked my mom's microbiology background and the fact that I had done some work with yeast while training as a home brewer.

I was very fortunate to land here. I went through the 5-week apprenticeship and then, soon after, Brendan Moylan, our owner, was preparing to open Moylan's. Grant's assistant, Paddy Giffin, was slated to go and start up Moylan's and be the brewmaster there, so I slid right into his spot maybe a month or two after the apprenticeship.

About six months later, Grant left to start Third Street Aleworks in Santa Rosa. So, six months out of my program, I was running my favorite brewery in the world. I've been going strong ever since.

Nick: What were some of those early breweries that you respected and how did they influence your decision to

become a brewer? Do you remember what those first "a-ha" beers were?

Arne: Living in San Francisco, I liked the Anchor products—Anchor Steam was definitely something that inspired me. I did a series of home brews where I was trying to perfect a certain beer and it was based on the steam beer idea of do-ing an ale at a higher temperature. I was using the Anchor Steam yeast and trying to do a beer that was unique but had the same principle as Anchor Steam.

Nick: You've been involved in home brewing one way or another since your were really young. Is there any core advice you would give to a home brewer that's just starting out?

Arne: I think it's all the same answers you hear from everybody: be clean, meticulous, and detail-oriented. All the most successful home brewers I know do those things. Anyhow, just experiment as much as possible; try different things. That's what makes it interesting.

Nick: Would you say that your parent's home brew influenced how you brew at all?

Arne: My dad's a perfectionist and my mom was a microbiologist, so they were very detailed, very clean about how they did everything, and I'm sure that inspired me in a certain way. I don't think any of the beers I brew are really inspired by beers they were brewing. It was a different landscape; there were different raw materials available and just different sorts of beers were made back then. They weren't so based on particular styles, as they are now.

> **"We see it as—instead of being competitive—we're helping out the good of the whole industry by helping each other. If the next guy makes great beer, it's going to help me."**

Nick: So, what's your process for coming up with new recipes? Would you say it's primarily ingredient-based or is there more of an idea of a beer that you're looking for that you then come up with the ingredients to go with?

Arne: We usually come up with a concept for a beer and the flavors that are going to be in it, and then I figure out how to achieve that. I'll do lots of research and talk to other brewers. We have a great community of brewers here in California, most of us are pretty good friends, and we're pretty open with each other. I think it's a nice thing to have other brewers I can call and say, "Hey, have you ever tried this?" We see it as—instead of being competitive—we're helping out the good of the whole industry by helping each other. If the next guy makes great beer, it's going to help me.

I sit down and write up a recipe by getting on my computer and looking at lots of recipes and thinking about ingredients. Basically, I start with the idea of the flavors I want in my beer and figure out how to get it there.

Nick: Can you use a recent beer as an example and go through that process?

Arne: Sure. We did the 6th anniversary beer for City Beer Store. It was an imperial stout with star anise and brewer's licorice. We also used molasses and Belgian dark candy sugar. I had never done a commercial imperial stout here, but we wanted to be unique and different. The folks at City Beer liked the idea of doing the anisey, licoricy thing. There's been a few brewers to try that the last couple of years.

Like I said, I basically did some of the research. I wanted to use brewer's licorice—

Nick: Yeah, how is that different than regular licorice?

Arne: They used to use it a lot in England to actually color the porters and stouts. It's an old-timey brewing ingredient that was more popular quite a few years ago. In some of the first recipes from here, Grant used brewer's licorice and I'd always been curious about using it. It's basically a hard licorice. It's generally made in Italy and they take the juice from the licorice-group product somehow and they harden it into concentrated licorice stick that you thrown into the kettle during the boil and it dissolves right into the beer.

You don't get super assertive flavors in a dark beer from it, but if you use enough you can. Like I said, they used it mostly for color back making porters, I'm sure they got some flavor from it. I knew I wasn't going to get the full anisey flavor I wanted from it, because it's pretty mild unless you use a whole bunch. So I decided to use some star anise and I thought to make it more complex and maybe a little drier by using the Belgian candy sugar and molasses.

I did a ton of research, wrote down a recipe, and we came in with the City Beer crew and brewed it. It was pretty complex adding all these different ingredients at different times, but it went off really well, we were super happy with that beer.

Nick: What are the general characteristics that you strive to have in all the beers you do?

Arne: I tend to go for pretty assertive flavors. I like to have a balance of the flavors, yet be assertive. I think that's the whole idea with craft beers: be bold and be more interesting than the domestic beers that so many people are familiar with. It doesn't always mean making the biggest, highest alcohol beer, but whatever the style, just really trying to pull as much flavor out of it and still work with all the other elements of the beer.

A lot of people love their dry beers. I'm not always that worried about it, because even though my beer might have more residual sugar, I balance it out with the hops and the other elements. It still comes across as not being sweet, but it's definitely not as dry as a lot of people go with their beers these days. Otherwise, like I said, just trying to get lots of flavor and still have a balanced beer.

Nick: You've been extremely successful in terms of accolades, especially at the Great American Beer Festival and World Beer Cup. What do you attribute your success to? What is it about what you're brewing that gets the judge's nod?

Arne: Again, I think what I was just saying about my style, I think [lots of beers] lack flavor and balance and that's a huge part of it. I can't say why mine stick out sometimes. I'm often amazed myself that they like the beer so much. We're very active in entering the competitions—It's always been part of our culture here. Brendan, our owner, really likes to be a part of that, and so we've always been aggressive at entering a lot of competitions. Maybe just from the idea of doing that, we get dialed in, and become really focused on making sure we're getting great beer out.

> **"I think if you're not trying to make the beer better, it's going to get worse."**

We're a brewpub and we don't have some of the quality controls of some of the bigger breweries. We don't have a lot of the things that big breweries can use to ensure their quality, so we spend a lot of time tasting and evaluating our own beer. I try to get our crew together in the brewery once every week or two and sit down and taste all the beers and talk about it, see where they're going.

I'm always trying to figure out how a beer can do better. I think if you're not trying to make the beer better, it's going to get worse. If you just make the same recipe, it seems to go downhill. That's one of my big philosophies, is that you've got to always be striving to make it better.

Nick: Why do you think this area, or California in general, has been on the front lines of this whole craft beer movement that we're seeing? What is it about where we are?

Arne: I think people are a little more open-minded here than some other parts of the country. Obviously, a lot of the first well-known breweries started here, and I'm not quite sure why that happened. Maybe just . . . creative people going for it. I grew up in San Diego and that's where my parents were. We started homebrewing at a time when there was no craft beer at all. I came up here, got into the industry, and now I go back down there and it's such a hot-bed ... There's so much great beer being made down there. I think a few people got it started and then everybody else was inspired by that. I've always seen that down in San Diego. A lot of people get in, get inspired by what others are doing, and grow in the same way. Up here, it's kind of different—it seems like there's a lot more brewpubs and small micros. We are not quite as focused on growth. There's obviously, here in the Bay Area, quite a foodie scene, so people are willing to try new products and try different flavors.

Nick: What's your model for growth? Do you want to stay mostly local?

Arne: We do about 2,700 barrels a year, that's pretty much our capacity. We've been doing that pretty much the whole 17 years I've been here. We're always pushing it, the tanks are always full. We do about 50% in-house, which is sold right over at the bar and then the rest goes into 22-ounce bottles and kegs. Most of it's in California, but we do send some, just a little bit, to Arizona. And we are starting to send a tiny bit out of the country.

We don't have anywhere to grow. We thought about it, and it doesn't really make any sense to try and grow within this space. There is talk of doing a Marin/Moylan's production brewery, but we'll see if that happens. That's cool. I think we can have a bigger brewery. But like I said, I may stay here at the pub if I have the opportunity. I like being a small brewer and I would like to see more people do that; build more small neighborhood pubs to service your neighborhood and do different stuff rather than just a few really big brands.

Nick: Would you say that's a quality-over-quantity type deal? What is it about a smaller brewpub that you like?

Arne: I just like variety and creativity and I like the feel of a brewpub, the neighborhood pub where you've got your regulars. You have instant feedback from your consumers everyday. It's just more interesting to me.

Nick: So, what else is interesting to you? What's exciting you right now in the brewing world?

Arne: Obviously there's a trend toward the barrel-aged beers and sour beers, and I'm very interested in those. Here, I only have room for about 7 or 8 barrels that we've crammed in the corners here and there. I've been doing the barrel beers for 8 or 10 years now, and I would like to do a much more extensive program that way. More hand-crafted beers. I do one barrel of sour beer every year-and-a-half and we only serve it here at the pub.

We do our barrel-aged barleywine and we do some other experiments. Like I said, if we do open the production plant and I took a role there, I would love to take on a barrel program and do something like that rather than cranking out a million gallons of beer. Definitely, that seems like the more creative, artisanal side of it, and that's where I would like to focus.

Brian Hunt
Moonlight Brewing Company

Brian Hunt is the founder, owner, and brewmaster at Moonlight Brewing Company in Santa Rosa, California.

Nick: What's your earliest memory of enjoying beer? And how did that moment bring you to where you are today?

Brian: First of all, I hated beer. I fermented stuff in high school, as Ken Grossman did. I fermented Hawthorn blossom wine as a high school biology project. . . . Maybe I didn't have an acquired taste for bitterness in beer yet, the way I do now. I remember one New Year's Eve I was up in Plymouth county with my brother and a bunch of friends and he was making homemade pizza. I remember eating the pizza and thinking, "You know, I bet that beer stuff would taste good with this." And, damn. It did. I was 19 at the time. Couldn't stand beer until that moment. After that—yeah, well I kind of liked it more after that.

Nick: Do you remember what it was?

Brian: It was Coors Banquet. Did the job. Tasted good in the moment. I tell people that Budweiser makes better beer than I do. After their initial shock, I explain that, based on taste, which is subjective, that we all like different things. My beer can't satisfy the millions of people that Bud can, so I'm never going to be as "good" as that, to those people. Granted, many people adamantly love my beer more than Bud, but I'm not in any position to tell anyone that their tastes are wrong.

Nick: So what came after that?

Brian: I was studying biochemistry and not really relating to it that much. It was too theoretical and it was what the competitive pre-meds were studying. Their attitude about life was different than mine. I transferred to Davis to study winemaking, because of the practicality and the fact that I love fermentation. I could better relate to the integrated nature of all the sciences. Brewing is a lot more fun and hands-on than it is theoretical.

I started in the winemaking program and ended up by chance working in the brewing lab cleaning glassware and doing other projects with Dr. Lewis. I just really enjoyed beer, so much more than wine. The wine philosophy seemed, let's say, less down to Earth. Beer was just more natural, enjoyable, and drinking beer is a lot more fun than drinking wine. Granted, I drink wine from time to time. Even Margaritas too. My god, though, there's just nothing like beer. I just adore the stuff. When I saw the light, I switched to a brewing major instead and the rest fell into place.

My first brewing job was in 1978 working in that brewing lab. Once I graduated, I was hired at the Schlitz brewery in Milwaukee. The job kind of sucked, but the brewery was fantastic. It was built in 1849, and in the unused buildings were old wooden tanks; brewing history long abandoned. Here was the way they made it back when idea was to make really amazing beer, before they cheapened the holy shit out of it.

After Schlitz closed, I came back to California, and I've been working with small breweries ever since. Starting up breweries was really a tough thing back then. It was '80 when Sierra started. "Microbreweries," as they were called, were just starting to catch on, but sadly, there was a lot of really painful beer being brewed. But it was revolutionary. Retailers didn't know how to sell it, and the consumers were unsure what the fuss was all about.

I worked with a number of start up breweries, but I grew frustrated with putting my all into making beer well and doing it for other people who didn't have the same passion that I had. So, I started Moonlight in '92 and worked by myself for 15 years. I started very small, with seven barrel batches. I started on a used shoestring, and slowly built it up. I'm not looking to be huge. I would rather be known for making good beer than making money. I'm poorly motivated by money. It's nice to have enough of it, but you know how much more I give a damn about good beer? So many breweries that I know worldwide have made great beer, and then just lost the concept when they got too big. It's as if once they found fame, they milked it when the name would sell the beer. Like Schlitz. The experience I had from Schlitz was hugely impactful in so many ways for my brewing career. The biggest was the understanding of what happens when you cheapen the product. They cheapened the product in ways too painful to explain.

Brewing "good" beer is just not enough. Great beer is what I dream of. There are great wines from winemakers who don't cut corners, and so you pay 50 or 100 bucks for a bottle. Unfortunately, so few breweries are willing to do whatever it takes to make the best beer that they can, and not do it just for the stupid money.

Nick: You're obviously renowned enough where, if you wanted to make more beer, you could.

Brian: If that was my dream, yes I could.

Nick: So why are you out here, doing this with two employees? Could you make more and finance more without cheapening the product? If so, why haven't you?

> **"I grew frustrated with putting my all into making beer well and doing it for other people who didn't have the same passion that I had."**

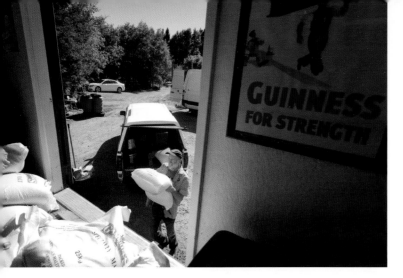

Brian: Stubborn. Yeah, because I'm stubborn. I've learned that lesson of how you can screw up something beautiful. There's no non-human thing that has such beauty as beer, that can be so easily destroyed by an accountant. Accountants are evil. And I'm not big on yachts. I believe in living simply and I love good beer. Why not do what you love? How many people on this planet understand the concept of doing what you love, plus have the ability to do that?

Nick: Can you talk about how you brew? What's your philosophy of brewing?

Brian: First of all, I start with desire, and I don't mean this as a corny answer. This is a very serious answer. I start with the desire to make really good beer. To me, this is art. How many artists do what they do for the money? Pretty much none. Further, I don't believe that I'm totally the driver in being the brewer that I am. I feel like beer picked me. I don't have any explanation of why I have the understandings that I do, why I have the ability to make a recipe, I don't understand.

Nick: Is it ingredient based, or do you come up with an set idea first?

Brian: Both. Death and Taxes. Perfect example—one day I had a particular thirst in my head, perhaps it had been slowly accumulating in the back of my head until it came to critical mass. Eventually it whacked me upside the head and said, "Hey—why isn't there a beer that tastes like this?" I knew there should be, so I made it. I started tasting malts until I had the taste I needed, and made it. I just chose ingredients and procedures that belonged to what I needed this beer to taste I like.

Nick: That was more idea driven, than ingredient driven.

Brian: Yes. Absolutely.

Nick: Are there cases to the contrary?

Brian: Sure. There's a redwood tree right behind us. I'm a huge follower of brewing history, because brewing history is why we do what we do today. For example, the ingredients we use, there's a reason we use hops. It's not just because they taste really good, there are actually political, social, religious, and economic reasons why we use hops today. At the time of Columbus, half the beer in Europe had no hops. People are incredulous when I tell them. Half the beer had zero hops in it. Can you imagine that today? Okay, you go back 100 years before this, probably 80 percent was unhopped.

In the year 1500, hops were banned as unpatriotic and immoral in the England. Why? Because the Catholic church was in control of other brewing herbs. 100 years later, hops became very well embraced. Why? Because the Catholic church had lost control of brewing. When I look at brewing history, and all the styles of beer that have been made over millennia, you know some lost styles tasted really good. Why not explore? If you have, let's say 50 to100 herbs that were used in brewing and today we only use hops, Humulus Lupulus. We have this huge diversity of beers from one lonely species? Imagine what beers we could be playing with those 100! We haven't scratched the surface.

Anyway, I started on a path of trying to understand which characteristics of hops make beer desirable? There's multiple reasons. The aromatics bring delight to our nose. Another characteristic we need form hops is the bitterness to balance the sweetness that malt inherently leaves us. Unless you're a kid, you don't necessarily want that so much anymore, you want that bite. It's refreshing in the same way iced tea is. That bite is astringency. It's not true bitterness—bitterness is perceived on your tongue. Astringency is perceived more in the back of your throat, the back of your mouth. A flavor chemist would talk about bitterness and astringency both as irritants meaning they counter the more pleasant aspects of food tastes. So you have this sweetness with the malt and you have the bitterness and astringency . . . that balancing act is really fun. In the beers that don't have hops, if they have other bitter herbs or astringency—such as what comes from the woody bark when I use redwood or cedar branches—then there is still that same delightful, satisfying balance. Astringency messes with your brain the same way that bitterness does, but we've just forgotten about that as a positive taste component in beer.

Nick: Do you think it's because the industry has chosen to go a certain way and they've limited themselves?

Brian: Over 500 years, hops have taken over. Very few brewers are experimenting with unhopped beer. IPAs are what consumers are demanding, yet maybe that demand is simply as the desire for character, flavor, and uniqueness, not merely that one hop plant? I'm looking at it, not just from the flavor standpoint, but from the historic standpoint. To get back to your question: I wanted to use spruce tips, which are very traditional in Scandinavia. Some breweries in Alaska are starting to use them again because they are so tasty and traditional. They don't grow here, but redwoods do. I started chewing on the branches, and the springtime tips, which are very flavorful, very fun. Chewed on this year's growth, chewed on last year's growth. Once I understood the tree and the flavors it could give, then I decided to use this tree. My thoughts were of what can I do to showcase these flavors in it? That's ingredient based.

Nick: Are there general characteristics that you want all of your beers to have? Almost like your mark, or the marker of a good beer?

Brian: Balance is huge. However balance is one of those things that everyone has a different sense of what it means. My beers are well balanced to my taste, obviously. Drinkability is a huge one. I want you to drink a beer, and I want you to want another one, or two. Yes, balance and drinkability are key, but you know they are both so subjective.

Nick: Why do you think craft beer is booming right now?

Brian: It's kind of a perfect storm. People that wanted to have sophisticated tastes in our parent's generation went big into wine. Our generation is running the show now! And we're drinking beer!" That's a lot of it. I mean it's crazy. You watch the new drinkers, let's say 21 and up. What are they drinking? They are not even starting with Bud Light, They're starting with Sierra Nevada, and other craft beers. What you see is the people that are just coming of drinking age, not wasting their time with mild beers It's more about enjoying life than effortlessly getting hammered.

There was a time in the 50's, 60's, even 70's, when it was all about everyone having the same house, the same car, drinking the same beer, eating the same Oscar Meyer wieners. Everything was the same, industrialization was king, and diversity just went to hell. Now in the 2000s, it's all turned on it's head.

Nick: What haven't we talked about what you would like to discuss?

Brian: Beer styles.

Nick: Okay. Let's do it.

Brian: How legitimate are beer styles? The beer styles we have today are phenomenally arbitrary. They are artificial because they exist as a snapshot of what beers have survived through history until today. Beer styles derive from many things: climate, cuisine. Frankly the biggest thing is the water. For example, the water in Pilsen, Czech Republic is very low in minerals, that's why Pilsner style beer is so delicate. Where the water's very delicate, the resulting beer will be as well. Burton on Trent: "Burtonizing" water means adding Calcium Sulphate, to make the water and resulting beer taste drier and bitter. You want a true British bitter or IPA, it should come from Burton on Trent, or have the water from that geology in that part of England. Other parts of Britain have smoother waters.

Nick: You're saying that, because these styles are getting made, it's no longer geography driven, that these styles aren't appropriate for a beer?

Brian: Let's just say they were once very appropriate because that's the water that the brewers had available to them. When your water has certain mineral content that affects the flavor, as we know, that's going to affect the final beer. For a long time people didn't have bags of minerals that they could buy—people didn't even know what chemistry was until the last few hundred years. Damn, they do now. You use the water and yes today you can fine tune your ingredients to make the best beer you could with that water. You know why Dublin stout is so famous? That was the best possible beer style brewers could make with that water. You can't make Pilsner style beer with Dublin water.

Thinking more radically about beer styles, suppose barley and wheat were on this continent, and they had corn over in Europe. The classic beer styles would be from this continent! You would have Florida style beers, Cincinnati style beer, and San Francisco style beer. You'd have home brewers in Munich scratching their heads, "God, how do you make a Cascadian IPA? I can't get the water right."

Why are we trying to make those old European style beers over here? Just because they have been making them for hundreds of years because barley was native. What are the styles of beer that should be made here because of climate? We don't know, do we? This is because all the brewers today are oriented to follow recipes from some other places and other times.

> **"How legitimate are beer styles? The beer styles we have today are phenomenally arbitrary."**

Denise Jones
Napa Point Brewing Company

Denise Jones is the brewmaster at Napa Point Brewing Company in Napa. (Images were taken while Denise was still with Moylan's in Novato, California).

Nick: So, my first question to you is: Why aren't there more female brewers?

Denise: Why do bankers loan men more money for breweries?

Nick: Yeah. I completely agree.

Denise: That might be one of the reasons. Also, physical attributes. I don't expect any of my guys to lift a keg by themselves, but if fellows hire girls, they seem to want to throw that in there. . . . "Well, you can't lift 120 pounds." There's a "good old boys"

at Mervyn's Department stores. I worked in restaurants from the time I was a little kid.

Nick: So, looking back to your early days, do you remember that first experience when you realized you really loved beer?

Denise: My first experience with beer? I've always liked beer. My first experience with beer is when my dad let me drink Coors Banquet Beer out of a bathroom Dixie cup when we watched football and baseball. That's what we drank. I grew up in Bishop, California, and it was a big Coors town. That's pretty much what I learned to drink when I was a kid. I probably drank my fair share of domestics over the formative years—even then, when I would sneak them in high school, Henry Reinhard Private Reserve was a really nice, malty type of experience with a little hop base to it. It was a Pacific Northwest kind of a beer that was different from all the rest. I enjoyed a Lowenbrau dark. I liked beer with flavor.

At about 29 years old, I had already worked for the Postal Service, and I decided to either go to the culinary academy or the brewing academy. I decided to enter the American Brewers Guild program, and I served my apprenticeship at Great Basin Brewing Company. They hired me later as an assistant, so I spent two years with them, and brewed all sorts of different beers. The fellow who was the brewmaster there, Eric McClary, he and his partner, Tom Young, were accomplished home brewers. They won all sorts of awards. They struggled to open this little brewpub and they started doing fairly well. I wasn't their first assistant brewer, but probably two or three years into their opening the pub they hired me and I learned a lot from those two. I still do learn a lot from Tom. Eric has since passed away, but he left his legacy with me, and his vision of style and his vision that a beer can be a balanced effort. I think that's really where my stylistic value is . . . it's in balance. Although my beers haven't necessarily always reflected the most balanced of efforts. When you taste, say, a Caskhaven Brown XXIPA or a beer from my past like Hopsickle . . . if you really taste a Hopsickle, there really is balance in it.

I've been fortunate to be invited to be a beer judge for a number of years at World Beer Cup and the Great American Beer Festival, the California State Fair, and independent judging. That's really helped stretch my idea of balance and keeps me focused, and keeps my litmus in tune all the time, too. Judging's been quite an important aspect of my career as well.

After I left Great Basin, I took a job as head brewer and brewmaster of Blue Water Brewing Company, which was a brewery up in Tahoe. The guy was struggling up there, business-wise. I worked for him for about six months or so, but he ended up closing the business. That was devastating to me, to try to really hard for six or seven or eight months, making really good beers, and then all of a sudden you have a business close underneath you.

I finally landed a job with Third Street Ale Works in Santa Rosa. I was their brewmaster for eight years. I'm pretty proud of that project. I won numerous GABF and World Beer Cup awards with that company, and really established my stylistic endeavor. From there, I did some work over in Napa and then Brendan Moylan hired me at Moylan's in Novato.

club and there always has been. I've been fortunate enough to work for people that have never looked at it that way with me. They looked at the person I am, and I'm willing to work hard. It's a physical job and a lot of women get scared off from that, especially women who want families. A lot of women just aren't as physical, you know? I chose not to have a family, and that was my choice. I think that's why you don't see more women; it's because they, probably at some point in time, want to get married and have a family. I enjoy my career and I started my career when I was 30 years old. I'd already done physical jobs. I'd carried mail. I'd worked as a stock person and sales person

When I started there, I didn't really want to change anything out of the gate. It wasn't my intention to revamp his whole project, because they had already had beers brewed by Paddy Giffin and by James Costa and they were all very good beers. They bottled beers and Moylan's beers had been on the market a long time. Little by little, I guess, my influence was to tweak them into balance and to make them drinkable and more stylistically correct in some aspects. Some of them, a beer like Danny's Irish Red for example, should have been about 4.5%. Well, Brendan liked it 6.5%, so I had to dance a line of trying to make it to a stylistic standard, but with a greater amount of alcohol. A lot of the beers that were brewed there have a greater amount of alcohol, because that's the way Brendan liked it.

"If you find that you can be creative and still make good beer and sell the beer that you make, I think that's the ultimate goal, isn't it?"

Nowadays, I'm tasked with brewing exactly what I want to brew. My partners at Napa Point Brewing have confidence that my brewing style and experience are well suited for success. I'm working with a blank canvas. I know what sells and I know what I love to taste in my own beers so I'm creating new brews again. Having the opportunity to build new brands and develop a new following is something that I find quite exciting.

Nick: Would you say that you base your beers pretty traditionally on the classic parameters of each style?

Denise: I do, but I don't necessarily have to dance in the box, either. There's a lot of times I think it's necessary to really go after something specific. Then again, there are times that you do need to put a little bit of your own flair to it, too. I don't necessarily think that you can take just American domestic malt and make a true pilsner that tastes like it's from Germany. I don't think that you can make a true Australian pale ale without using Australian ingredients and Australian hops. I don't think that you can make a Canadian beer without using some really nice Canadian malt. I think if you're going to look for a style and be stylistically correct, you need to look for the ingredients that they use within the area that they brew that beer with.

Nick: As a brewer, do you feel more like a scientist or an artist?

Denise: You talk about creativity . . . you can be creative all day long with pumpkin seeds, rosemary, whatever you want to put in a beer, but is somebody going to drink it and then come back to drink your beers again? It could be technically correct, but it might not be exactly what's saleable. If you find that you can be creative and still make good beer and sell the beer that you make, I think that's the ultimate goal, isn't it? I mean, you can lean too hard on science, too—I've known guys that come out of Davis that wouldn't know the first thing about brewing a technically sound commercial beer. They might know all of the things to do and all the instruments to use to get the gravity and pH just right, but then you get them in the kitchen and you might have something that's just bland and simple. There has to be a balance between right brain and left brain. There have to be those days where you need to think on your feet and not necessarily read your instruments all the time. Then there are days that, if you don't have your instruments and you're just winging it, then the beer's going to reflect that, too.

Again, balance. You need to have a little bit of both in order to be successful with the beers that you have in your portfolio. If you don't have science, you're not going to be consistent, and have quality. If you don't have creativity, you're just going to taste like everything else.

Nick: What is it about beer that keeps you getting up every morning? What's exciting to you?

Denise: Beer is not just the blue-collar drink. It's actually being accepted as more of the white collar drink. Cocktails and wine were really the norm, but those drinkers have switched to a different product that doesn't cost them quite as much, that being beer. Beer has always been of high quality. It always takes a lot more effort to brew a beer than it does to make a wine, and I can get into semantics with different winemakers. They always say it "takes a lot of beer to make a good wine", and I tend to think "if it was wine it would be easy" because beer's just much harder to make, harder to maintain freshness. I love wine. Don't get me wrong. I know some awesome winemakers and I enjoy all sorts of different types of wine . . . quality wine . . . but it is a lot easier to make wine than it is beer. I'm not saying that raising your own grapes—the required viniculture, and those aspects of it don't come into play, but brewers are on shifting sands all the time. Our hops change. Our barleys change. Color, roasting changes. Our water changes all the time. Our yeast taxonomy changes all the time. We're constantly being held to consistency and that's the judgment of a good brewer: quality and consistency. A winemaker could say, "Oh, well, it was that vintage. Oh well, the weather that year did this."

Two crop seasons of barley, multiple harvests of hops, and brewing water are variables that could change from week-to-week, day-to-day, depending on what municipality you're dealing with. Yeast companies change what they do. Yeast, as it grows and develops over the course of years, changes a little bit. There are changes that we have to wrestle with, and I might

have to make a beer that tastes exactly the same 16 to 18 to 25 times a year or more, whereas a winemaker only makes that one wine once and he/she blends it out and tries to match it up year-to-year.

They have a built-in excuse, if you will, for their level of consistency, and we don't. We have a good number of things to consider to maintain our consistency. There's a lot more to it: keeping things cold, keeping things out of the light, keeping the carbonation in, and having absolutely no bacterial defect in it—unless that's what you're going for with different types of beers, but that's controlled bacterial function.

Nick: Are those the aspects you enjoy most?

Denise: That's part of what I enjoy about it. I enjoy that I've been a brewpub girl most of my career. I've been working in brewpubs, and one of the things that I do enjoy is seeing familiar faces day in and day out, coming in and enjoying my products. You're not just a hit-and-go kind of a business. You have to have that consistency and that quality for people to want to think about your beer day in and day out. It's not just the brewpub. I've always thought about the brewpub, but especially here at Napa Point Brewing, I also think about sending beers out to different states, different countries, and having people enjoy them just the same. That feeds the fire a little bit, too.

It comes down to the people you work with. It comes down to the challenge every day of maintaining your equipment and maintaining your quality with that. Those are challenges that I look forward to every day. It's hard work. I don't necessarily always like how many hours I have to work, but I do enjoy the fruits of my labor, and I enjoy my own beer. I truly make beer for myself, and I'm just really glad other people enjoy it.

Nick: Is there anything that you've never been asked in an interview that you've always wanted to say?

Denise: I've been interviewed quite a bit.

Nick: Do people always just want you to talk about being a woman brewer?

Denise: That question gets asked a lot. What's it like being a woman brewer, and again, I don't—

Nick: Is that a fair question?

Denise: It's not a fair question. No.

Nick: Why isn't it?

Denise: What's it like being a male photographer?

Nick: Yeah, I hear you.

Denise: I mean, do you find that you're looked on differently because you're a man and you take photographs?

Nick: No.

Denise: Are you a sissy boy? What? Come on.

Nick: No. No. No.

Denise: See, it's not . . . it has nothing to do with gender.

Nick: Exactly. This is your time—not to necessarily answer that question, but you can say why that question pisses you off. I would like to know that.

Denise: Because I'd rather be just regarded as a brewer of quality and consistent beer, and base my career on the fact that the proof's in the pudding. It has nothing to do with what I might possess as far as my body structure or size or what have you. It has nothing to do with gender. Obviously, I have opposable thumbs, so I'm lucky enough to be able to brew beer. I think that's really the genesis of it all. People will come up with "ale wife" and "beer wench" and some of these terms, things of that nature. Those are rather demeaning to me. If some of the gals out there want to call themselves those types of things, that's perfectly fine . . . the "beer bitch" or whatever you want

> **"I truly make beer for myself, and I'm just really glad other people enjoy it."**

to call them, but I just find that I just want to be referred to as a good brewer. I wake up every day knowing that I try my best to maintain the quality standards that I've set for myself. Anything less than that, I wouldn't be doing myself a service.

Don Barkley
Napa Smith Brewery

Don Barkley is the brewmaster at Napa Smith Brewery, with over 40 years of experience brewing in California, beginning with America's first microbrewery, New Albion.

Nick: Can you recount the Don Barkley story? What were your earliest experiences with beer and how did they get you here today?

Don: When I started making beer, it was 1971, actually the same year that I graduated from high school. I went down to Santa Cruz where my brother-in-law was making wine. I helped him make this wine, and at the end of the day I said, "Jim, when can we start to taste this wine? I'm all ready to have some of this wine that we just made." He says, "Well, that will be a year." No way! So I said, "Well if I'm going to be working this hard on something, I want to have a little bit faster results." So I went home and started looking into beer. At that time, it was illegal to make beer at home. I found a place in San Jose that sold malt extract and yeast and all the rest, and I made my first batch of beer from those ingredients. That was 1971.

Nick: So how did you go from there all the way to where we are here?

Don: I continued to brew as a hobby, and that was really fascinating. Eventually I realized that I potentially wanted to make it a career, because I got more and more into good beers, and they were all imported beers. So I started to look into various aspects of learning the trade. I visited my brother-in-law, who was going to UC Davis at the time. He told me there was a brewing program, how to make beer right at UC Davis.

I was living in the San Francisco Bay area, so it wasn't very far for me to go up to Davis. I was accepted into the brewing program at UC Davis in 1978, and went through that entire program—a four-year degree program—and graduated in 1981 with a degree in brewing science.

During the summer of 1978, I also started working at the New Albion Brewing Company. I worked there every summer from '78 till 1981, when I graduated from Davis. After Davis, I went on full time.

New Albion finally died in 1983. It was not able to raise the funds for expansion. So, in 1983, we jack hammered out the floors and took the New Albion Brewing Company apart. I moved lock, stock, and barrel with Jack McAuliffe and Michael Lovett, one of the other brewers, up to Hopland, California, where Michael Laybourn, Norman Franks, and John Scahill were all starting the Mendocino Brewing Company and the Hopland Brewery, which was the very first brewpub to open up in the United States. So we put that together and started the Mendocino Brewing Company.

Of course, at Mendocino we were producing Red Tail Ale,

Eye of the Hawk, Black Hawk Stout, Blue Heron Pale Ale, and all those. As master brewer, I developed all those recipes and production methods to make those beers. It was pretty interesting. Red Tail Ale was basically the first West Coast amber style of beer, which is all over the place these days. Very much a standard of the industry. Eye of the Hawk, one of the very

first big double ambers at 8% alcohol, was a very big, heavy beer, and that really made a splash.

The Hopland Brewery was a wonderful place because it was a brewpub. You could see exactly what people were drinking and their reactions to it, and it had a big beer garden.

In 1997, The Mendocino Brewing Company expanded and went to the 100-barrel brew house. We started in Ukiah, California, and from '97 until 2007, I continued as the master brewer there, after building that 100-barrel brew house. In 2007, I came down to the Napa Valley, and voila, we have the Napa Smith Brewery.

The family's been in the Napa Valley for five generations, so we've been around for a long time, believe it or not. Being able to be here, where the image of quality is so strong, is really great. And, knowing we could make a really good, solid beer that matches Napa's quality image, convinced us that the Napa Smith Brewery could be pretty successful.

Nick: Going back to New Albion for a minute: What was it like to work with Jack? And what did you learn working at the first microbrewery in the country?

Don: You know, New Albion was a fascinating place to start. Jack was a tenacious kind of guy because he really knew exactly what he wanted. He also understood the fundamentals of brewing beer, he stuck to them, and demanded that they be followed.

So, when I walked into the New Albion Brewing Company for the first time, the first thing you do is walk through a bucket of sanitizer. From there you could walk into the office, but if you were going into the production facility you had to dip your feet in buckets of sanitizer before you went to the bottle hall, before you went to the fermentation cellar, or anywhere. All of the

"People wonder what I'm doing making beer in wine country..."

floors in that brewery, as tiny as it was at 700 square feet, all of the floors were sloped drain floors. Jack understood, as well as Dr. Michael Lewis at Davis, that sanitation in a production facility had to be done a certain way and done right. That really got instilled to me.

Equally, Jack had a real fascination, not only with the history of brewing, but also with sort of a scientific approach to brewing. We had a very small lab, but we did yeast cultures and we did look for wild yeast and bacteria. We had our microscope and all those other things that are required of a larger brewery. Those were all incorporated into that tiny, teeny very first craft brewery. Jack demanded that be done. He was definitely a task master. He worked hard, and he did not put up with any kind of lackadaisical attitude toward his beer or the brewery. That's not to say he didn't have a lot of fun, because we had a great time there.

Nick: Sounds like Jack took a pretty scientific approach to brewing. Do you feel brewing is more science or art? Or both?

Don: I think that's a great question, because there is art and science in the brewing trade. I find I don't brew to a particular style, but I brew to a particular inspiration, if you will, and find a beer that fits that. I think I'm a pretty good mix between the two. There are certain beers that I don't prefer, I don't necessarily really have a great time with the sours or the strong Belgian style beers because those beers have all of the flavors that I've been trying to avoid my entire brewing career. I've made a lot of beers that taste just like that, and every one of them ended up in the

compost piles. I have a hard time getting through to some of those styles of beer.

There's a lot of creativity that's allowed in brewing and brewing styles, as well as the opportunity to have different herbs or different fruits in the beer. All those things are of interest and can add to the creativity above and beyond just malted barley, water, hops, and yeast.

Nick: That's not necessarily what you're after?

Don: I want a good, drinkable beer that I can just really enjoy. That's what I'm after. There's a lot of science involved with it, but the creativity comes in and is a great part, and really has a lot of the inspiration for my brewing as well. But I do also get a lot of inspiration by being able to just have a production facility that runs like a clock, that just runs smooth, regular, and efficiently. Those are all things that are neat to me.

Nick: Would you say that you're making the best beer of your life now?

Don: Oh, yes. Yes, I would say I'm making some of the best beer I've ever made right now. Not only the best, but some of the more creative, and at the same time maintaining that absolute drinkability.

Nick: Can you use an example of a beer to expand on that?

Don: Our winter seasonal, Bonfire Imperial Porter—that is just a fun beer to make, and I'm really proud of it. It's a great one. It has all the chocolate and all the coffee going in it, and the body that's there as well. Plus at about 8% alcohol, it's just a real winter warmer, just a delicious beer to have. I'm really proud of that one. That's a great beer.

Napa Smith Amber Ale is a really complex beer. We have seven different malted barleys, six different hops in it. So there's this whole layering of flavors. When we get into the Bonfire or the Napa Smith Amber Ale—where you have all these different flavors it's a whole different thing. For that matter, Grateful Dog, our barleywine, is an incredible beer that's made not only with the normal brewing techniques of a barleywine, but we actually

ferment it with both wine yeast and beer yeast, and we add some Simeon grapes that are completely infused with botrytis mold. Those go into it, and then at the very end, just before we bottle it, we blend it with some four-year-old barrel-aged Imperial Porter. Here's this beer that just has everything and the kitchen sink in it, and it has all these different flavors and characters that just roll over your tongue and make it something spectacular.

Nick: Do you think that in order to be noticed right now you have to go bigger?

Don: I think that those big beers are part of what get you noticed. If you want to be on the blogosphere and all the rest of that, then you're going to be making some spectacular beers here and there. Not that they're going to be beers that people are going to be drinking all the time, or drink more than one, maybe. You do need to have some pretty spectacular beers out there, just because of the competition. You do need to be noticed. You need to be able to jump up and say here's a particular style and type of beer, a double IPA or triple IPA. Without that notoriety in the market it's going to be a little tough.

Now, do I drink all those all the time? Not really. Do I love our pilsner, which is, at 5% alcohol, easy to drink and nice and crisp, and just a great beer? Yes. I'm just as proud making a beer like that as I am making something that's off the chart on bitterness.

Nick: Are there opportunities that being in the Napa region affords you?

Don: The thing about Napa, of course, is that it has an appeal worldwide. One of our biggest markets right now is Disney World in Florida, and a lot of that has with the fact that the Napa name carries a lot of weight, and a lot of marketing pizzazz, so that's really good for us as well.

People wonder what I'm doing making beer in wine country, but the fact is that, if you talk to any of the winemakers, they like quality. It doesn't matter who it is. They could be making the finest wine in the world, but they appreciate quality food, quality wine, quality beer, and quality spirits, I imagine, as well.

Nick: In terms of the industry, you've seen every change in the book. Are you enjoying where craft beer is right now? What do you think the future holds for it?

Don: I think the craft brewing industry right now is just a gas. It's really fun, really exciting. The number of different beers out there is just insane. The number of people getting into craft brewing is just insane. There's going to be a serious shakeout here some time pretty soon. It's happened before, it's going to happen again. It happens in every industry, especially when there are a lot of people that are getting in and hoping to make a living. They may understand how to make beer but they don't know how to run a business, or they know how to run a business but they don't know how to really make beer. There areall these different nuances that keep a business going.

Nick: Do you think it's going to come down to the beer?

Don: It always comes down to the beer, no doubt. If you can't make good beer, it doesn't matter how good a business you're going to run. Anheuser Busch, and Miller, and all the rest, they make a good product. It's all kind of the same product, all kind of generic, but it's a sound product. They're doing a great job.

What the craft brewers do, of course, is give you the flavor. It's not just white bread anymore. Now you've got the flavor and the nuances, and the passion. It's really fun to see the customers come in because they're excited about the beers that you're making. You can see the passion in their eyes. They recognize the excitement that the brewers have to make a special beer. It's funny to me to see the advertising that the big brewers put on TV, and whether its Clydesdales or frogs, or whatever it is, they're trying to instill passion by showing a Clydesdale, or the Rocky Mountains, or something like that.

> **"[Beer is] part of the fabric of humanity, and part of what puts it all together."**

Then you look at when a customer walks in to your pub and tries your beer, and they're excited about the different flavors and character, and they meet you and they catch hold of that passion, that's where it really happens. The craft brewers have a big advantage, that direct marketing and people recognizing that, hey, they're my neighbor, or the guy down the street is making that beer. That's a really special, and powerful thing.

Nick: Is there anything we haven't covered that you'd like to talk about or say?

Don: I think the main thing I've always tried to do with all of the beers I've made—be it at Mendocino Brewing Company, or here at Napa Smith Brewery—is to make that good, drinkable, social lubricant that works so well. Drinkability—keeping in mind that this is something that people are going to enjoy with one another—is a fascinating part of craft brewing and beer as a whole. It's part of the fabric of humanity, and part of what puts it all together. I think it's just a wonderful part of brewing beer, and I'm happy to be a part of it.

Tom Nickel
Nickel Beer Company

Tom Nickel has been a long-time brewer and craft beer bar owner in San Diego. He is currently the owner and brewer at Nickel Beer Company in Julian, California.

Nick: What was your first memory of enjoying craft beer?

Tom: My dad, he's always been the coolest drinker. He always drank two beers everyday after he got home. My family was not crazy about, "Oh, you can't drink till you're 21." If I wanted a beer or to taste something, they'd let me. I went away to college, where I started drinking lots of beer, but I didn't particularly like the beer I was drinking. There was a local brewery there: New Haven Brewing Company. I started drinking their beer. That's probably what prompted me into craft beer.

By the end of that first semester, I started home brewing. I vividly remember the very first time. We were in plastic buckets and I didn't understand anything about fermentation or CO_2 creation. I knew the airlock was supposed to bubble and had no idea what the yeast was actually doing. I got the first batch. I'm thinking, "It's going to smell awesome. It's going to smell like beer." I rip off the bucket lid and it's probably about six inches of air space in there, which I didn't realize. It was pure CO_2. So I dunk my head right in it and . . . well, it stops my brain from working. With the CO_2 inhalation I thought, "We can't drink it. We're going to die."

Sure enough, it actually turned out to be okay, because I just inhaled all the CO_2 right off the top. We bottled it and lo and behold, it was drinkable. We got involved in all-grain brewing very quickly because we realized for about 15 bucks we could make two cases of beer. It became an issue not only of availability, but economics.

I home brewed all throughout college and then came home after college. I wasn't sure what I was going to do with a degree in Medieval History, which wasn't really well suited to doing anything other than law school, which I didn't want to do.

Nick: You went to Yale?

Tom: I did. Yeah, I graduated from Yale in '94 with a degree in Medieval History. Like I said, there's not a lot that that was really pertinent to, but it's what I enjoyed studying.

I decided to come back to San Diego. I wasn't sure what to do. I started asking around at local breweries if anybody just wanted help. I was volunteering myself. There weren't that many breweries back then. There was a home brew shop. I wound up working there. About two months in, the guy who managed the shop moved out of state. I ended up taking his job and, what was supposed to be a summer job accidentally turned into a career. I spent about two and a half years at Home Brew Mart, and that was while they were opening Ballast Point. I managed the business of the store. I left to go to Pizza Port to work with Tomme Arthur. Colby

Chandler is the person they hired in my place at Home Brew Mart and we've always enjoyed that fact. I worked at Pizza Port only for about eight months with Tomme. That's where we started doing the festivals together. From Pizza Port I went to Oggi's and worked there from basically '98 to '05. The last two years I mostly spent in the new production facility in San Clemente. That's when they opened Left Coast Brewing Company and starting brewing beer for all of the non-brewery Oggi's locations. I left there in early '05. My wife and I had already bought O'Brien's in January of '03. I had two years of basically doing both before I decided I wanted to concentrate on the bar full time.

Nick: You and Jeff Bagby went to work at Oggi's at the same time?

Tom: We did, but never at the same location. Jeff was at Oggi's up until the end of '05. He had probably started there like '02 or '03. Together, we won the '04 Small Brewing Company of the Year award at the World Beer Cup. I didn't mention all the awards. I can give you a CV later if you like.

Nick: You talk a lot about things related to brewing as well as actually brewing. Things like festivals, getting the word out about San Diego beer, why did this become a mission of yours? Why is that important to you?

Tom: I've always enjoyed beer festivals. I remember when Tomme and I started the Strong Ale Festival, we were in Solana Beach. It just started because he was talking about his Santa's Little Helper Imperial Stout and then we started saying, "Oh yeah, this guy is going to brew this." There were 10 breweries back then. This was '97. You could pretty much name every single brewery, name every single head brewer. I was like, "Man, look at all these great Christmas beers that are going to come out," imperial stouts, barleywines, triples, whatever it was. That's what prompted the original Strong Ale Festival. It was just our desire to drink the other beers from every single brewery in one place so we don't have to drive downtown to San Marcos, to Carlsbad, to the San Diego Brewing Company,

drinking 10% alcohol beer. It was motivated out of our desire to drink the beers and nothing else.

Nick: When it comes to beer, though, it seems that San Diego has really turned into "Beer Town USA."

Tom: Which is insane. When we first got the Craft Beer Conference in 2004, I thought that was a real pinnacle, like, "Wow, we've really accomplished something here." The differences between the Craft Brewers Conference being here in '04 and then '08 and then 2012: the growth has been just exponential each time in terms of the number of breweries, the quality of beer, the number of bars, and local awareness.

Nick: You have a really unique perspective because you are not only a brewer, you're also a pub owner. What has that been like?

Tom: The beer industry is so tied to the pub owners that I feel like there's a lot of sympathy for what the pub owners go through. I feel that craft brewers and craft pub owners are significantly more closely aligned than the craft brewers are to each other. The biggest difference is some brewers, they just want to make the beer. The classic case would be John Maier from Rogue. He doesn't go out and shake hands or rally up the crowd. I mean, he is the exact opposite of Jim Koch from Boston Beer, who is the ultimate showman but not an expert at brewing. John Maier knows everything about beer, but he does not like to do public events.

> **"Craft brewers and craft pub owners are significantly more closely aligned than the craft brewers are to each other."**

To me, the biggest difference about being a bar owner is that you have to be the personality of the bar. You think about the Toronado in San Francisco and you associate that with its owner. You think about Hamilton's and you associate that with its owner, Scot Blair. O'Brien's is definitely tied to my personality and I think all of the best beer bars have a singular owner whose vision drives the bar.

I would say that same thing is true for the breweries, but the difference is the person who drives that vision for the breweries isn't necessarily a public figure.

Nick: Part of it is that you're also the guy that's bringing the beer to the people.

Tom: Absolutely. That's what I'm saying. You're much more of a liaison. Whereas as a brewery, to me, you can pull back and you can be an idea guy, you can be a driving force. Like Steve Hindy at Brooklyn Brewing Company. Most people would have no idea what he looks like. He can walk in to any bar in San Diego and people would be, "What can I get you?"

Whereas Garret Oliver, as the brewer, he walks into a bar, everybody knows who Garret Oliver is. Steve Hindy is the guy who actually drives that company, but nobody cares.

Again, for every person that knows Colby Chandler [at Ballast Point], there are probably a hundred that don't know what Jack White looks like. Colby is not the owner, Jack is. As a bar owner, you're much more of a public figure because you have to have that interaction with your patrons. If you don't, to me, your bar just lacks definition.

I feel like we're lucky in San Diego to have people like Scot Blair, like Ian Black [from Toronado San Diego] that are strong personalities tied to those bars that make these things work. There's no corporate marketing plan to make it work. That's one thing that's great about the best of the craft beer bars. There's no formula.

Nick: What is your mission in opening Nickel Beer Co?

Tom: I've just always loved it up here in Julian, growing up, camping up here and coming up here on trips. I've always liked the getaway aspect of Julian. I like trees, I like clean air, I like that it's only an hour from the city, because there are so many places you can go to get these things but then you're in Montana and what good is that doing you? I really like

> **"All of the best beer bars have a singular owner whose vision drives the bar."**

the aspect that in one hour I could be up here, or in one hour I could be stuck in traffic in the Gaslamp. To me, it's a luxuriously close getaway.

It's not a hard leap to imagine that most people are going to come up here and one of the things they do is they go wine tasting. So how hard is it to assume they would want to do a beer tasting? It's not like we're inventing the idea that you come to Julian for alcohol, we're just modifying it to be a little more "guy friendly." There are already a couple of good wine tasting rooms up here. What I wanted was a business that I really enjoyed running. Obviously I want it to make money but I like producing things, I like creating.

Nick: In terms of the beers you're brewing now, are there overriding brewing principles or elements that you apply?

Tom: I like good beer, and it's sometimes shocking that more people don't make good beer. I think more than anything, when I think about a beer, and no matter what I'm trying to brew, I think about something I want to drink. I drink a lot of hoppy beer, I drink a lot of dark beers. I would definitely say that hoppy and dark beers are probably an overall focus, but that doesn't mean I don't love the other things that we do.

I love a good pale ale, I drink a lot of our cream ale when it's warm up here. The last thing I'd ever want to do is brew a beer that I didn't want to drink, even if it's a style that's not my number one choice. I'm not a huge Hefeweizen fan, but when I brew one, I better enjoy it. It'll be flavor forward, clean—you don't want to muddy the beers. I think that Jeff Bagby and I have a very similar brewing aesthetic in that our beers are relatively simple, straight forward. We don't use a lot of crazy ingredients. If we do something, we try to do it so it's relatively style appropriate, maybe not always alcohol appropriate, but certainly flavor appropriate.

When you think about a beer, I don't want you to drink one and think, "OK, well that's interesting, but I'm going to have a pint of something else." I want you to drink it and think, "Man, I want another pint of that." Some people would be disappointed if somebody came in, ordered a pint of beer and then ordered two pints of the same beer. They'd think, "Well, you didn't try anything else." Well, who cares? He likes that beer and he wanted three pints of it! There's no failure there.

Nick: What is it, on a very basic level, about beer that gets you excited and inspired?

Tom: In some ways, I can't fully answer that. Why do chefs love to cook? Why do painters love to paint? To me, it's something that, in some ways, you have be a little bit predisposed towards. Ultimately, the thing I like about beer is that it's an everyday working man's beverage. There's nothing exclusive about it, there's always a social aspect to it, if done properly. You gather at a place and you enjoy beer with other people. There's a sense of belonging and togetherness that no other beverage really provides. Spirits? Nah. Wine? Wine is born on exclusivity. The more open and available a wine is, the more

people turn their nose up at it. Two-Buck Chuck is a perfect example. Here's a decent wine that everybody can buy cheap and people just deride it like crazy. Why? Shouldn't that be the whole point? Make something that's good and affordable. Think about the thousand-dollar bottles of wine, then think that the best bottle of beer probably costs you less than 25 bucks.

Nick: Is there anything we haven't covered that you'd like to talk about?

Tom: Well the only thing I'll say is: just don't let beer become wine. Don't let the fact that you appreciate craft beer ever make you think that somebody who doesn't drink craft beer is beneath you. Or that, just because you spent 50 dollars on a bottle of beer, that's going to make it better than a 6-pack of Sculpin in cans.

> **"Just don't let beer become wine."**

To me, it's the one concern I have about where a segment of the industry is headed in terms of that vinification of beer—where it's exclusive, it's expensive, and it's rare. From a business standpoint, do I love tapping Pliny the Younger? Yes. From a consumer standpoint, does it just fucking drive me crazy that people stand in line for two hours for a beer that's honestly not as good regular Pliny the Elder? In my opinion, yes it does. As a beer fan, I don't want beer to ever lose its everyday aspect, because that's what makes it so special, compared to a 10-dollar martini or a bottle of wine. Beer is something you drink everyday. It's something you drink with friends, and it's something you drink to relax and not worry about your problems. You don't drink it to impress people.

I don't want beer to ever lose its pub, working man, everyday, village sort of aspect. This is something that people have gathered to enjoy for thousands of years. It's an everyman's beverage. Wine hasn't been that, never will be that, never can be that. I hope beer will always be that, so there, no vinification of beer.

Evan Price
Noble Ale Works

Evan Price is the head brewer at Noble Ale Works in Anaheim, California.

Nick: How did you get into this whole thing? How did you start brewing?

Evan: I got into brewing from a trip I took to Europe with a couple buddies when I was 21. We went to England, Ireland, Germany, the Czech Republic, and Belgium.

One night, our train stopped in Belgium for some reason and we ended up having to sleep there overnight. We didn't even have the sense to try any Belgian beers, which is totally depressing now, because of how much I lust after those beers now. Apart from that, in all the other countries we visited, we drank classic beer styles straight from the source. It's been my benchmark ever since. Guinness was the first beer I fell in love with as a young beer drinker before taking that Euro-trip, but tasting fresh Guinness in Ireland was a beautiful thing. The poor shipping and storing practices of most European beers degrade their awesomeness pretty damn quick. If we were to ship the Noble beers halfway across the world, they would suffer in the same way.

When I came back, I realized that there was a slow building craft brewing movement going on here in the U.S. that I was completely oblivious to. My buddy Joe, who I went on the trip with, told me about how you we could brew at home, so we started doing it together, and we were terrible at it!

I ended up brewing a total of four or so batches before going to work professionally for a brewery, and every time, the beer never came out the way I wanted. I was getting really frustrated with home brewing, and couldn't figure out what I was doing wrong, so I interviewed with Owen Williams and he ended up hiring me as an assistant brewer at BJ's Brewery. I started out washing kegs, scrubbing floors, and asking the brewers as many questions as they would answer. I slowly worked my way up until I was brewing. BJ's slowly started phasing their breweries out, so I went from the Laguna Hills location, to Brea and lastly West Covina. I saw the end coming for BJ's breweries and knew I needed to leave so I took a job at Hangar 24 as their first brewer. During that time, it was just Ben Cook and myself. We took something small and continued to make it bigger and bigger. That was probably the biggest learning experience I've had in brewing, other than where I'm at now; working in that environment, ramping up a brewery, training, etc.

After that, I accepted the head brewer position at TAPS to work under Victor Novak. While at TAPS we were fortunate to get Brewpub Group of the Year at GABF, 2010 and 2011. Working under Victor, I learned to use the best ingredients I can get my hands on, which is the same philosophy I use over here to Noble.

Nick: Do you remember the first beer that you ever brewed?

Evan: I want to say it was a German Hefe, because I think that was the beer style that I was the most stoked about when I came back from Germany. When I got home, I went to Bev-Mo! and all these beautiful, delicate German beers were stale and oxidized, but I didn't understand why they had lost their charm at the time. All I knew is that I wanted to taste that beer the way it is supposed to be. That was a big reason why I started home brewing. I brewed that German Hefe to try to get that same full flavor and experience of that fresh brewed beer that I had in Germany.

I remember the first time I home brewed a beer that I was happy with, because it took me a long time. It was then that I started to get really excited about my potential with brewing. It was shortly after I had started with BJ's. I made a porter that I dry-hopped and, for the first time, I thought, "Man, this is awesome!" And I'm sure I would think differently now, but at that time in my life, I was so stoked on it that it was definitely the fuel that continued to fire my interest in brewing.

> **". . . tasting fresh Guinness in Ireland was a beautiful thing."**

Nick: What are the overriding lessons that you learned from your home brewing and early experiences?

Evan: Read! Most of my biggest failures, as a young brewer, would have been avoided if someone would have just recommended *How To Brew* by John Palmer. Cleanliness is extremely important if you want to see better results. It's something that I didn't get right when I first start home brewing. But other than cleanliness, one of the biggest things I focus on is trying to get the least amount of oxygen pick up in my beer after fermentation has completed. No one wants their beer to taste like wet cardboard. If you can avoid oxygen well (after fermentation), your beer will taste fresher for a longer period of time, which is really important for those hoppy beers. That's one of the bigger suggestions I can give. Also, really take the time to scrutinize every aspect of your beer. Act like it's someone else's beer when you drink it and try to find those flaws. Let's see . . . you can do a side by side tasting with your beer next to one of the greats within the industry like Sierra Nevada, Firestone, or Russian River. These breweries are creating absolutely incredible beers—the sooner you can learn from them, the faster you will be making better beer.

Nick: What's your thought process when creating a new beer? Do you have any general principles or philosophies that you always go to?

Evan: When creating a new beer, I don't set out to make another brewer's beer the same way they do but rather I think of ways to create something new. I picture the finished beer in my mind and the way I want it to look, smell, taste and then work my way backwards on how I can go about creating that. I think about every ingredient and how it's going to work in the beer. If I'm making an English beer, I use English malt. If I want more body in the beer, I use ingredients like lactose or oats. Every beer is made differently, so it always takes a few batches to really get it dialed in.

Nick: So, do you have a favorite beer to make or a favorite beer to drink? Any favorites?

Evan: My palate runs more on the dry side of things, so I almost always go towards that direction. Most of my favorite beer styles out there just have this awesome kind of dryness that makes drinking more interesting. With those kinds of beers, you take a sip, the beer wets your mouth but then all of a sudden dries it out and then your thirsty again, and you just kind of continue this never ending circle. I love that. Some of the beer styles I gravitate towards the most are the more sessionable ones. I love this new Session IPA kick that brewers are on, it's great! A good pale ale, a dry stout or a good pilsner. Oh, man. I LOVE Pils. We make a Czech-style Pils with New Zealand hops called Pistol Whip'd that I drink mass quantities of. Trumer is a benchmark. Firestone's Pivo Pils is one of my favorites for the style. TAPS makes 3 different kinds of Pils that are all delicious. A good Pils has everything I need; full flavor, an incredible aroma and then, they're just dry enough in the finish to keep you keep you thirsty and ready for that next sip.

IPA's and Double IPA's are not only great to drink, but are great for their aromatics. I could literally smell them all day. I can't get enough of the IPA's that Beachwood BBQ and Societe make. Also Orval. Oh man, Orval!? It's absolutely the best beer ever. And then, when I'm not drinking beer, I drink cocktails. I love cocktails.

Nick: What's your take on the current surge in the popularity of craft beers and all the craft breweries that have been opening up?

> **"I think Craft beer is only in its beginning stages of showing its real potential within our society."**

Evan: I think craft beer is only in its beginning stages of showing its real potential within our society. Right now, a new brewery is opening every day and craft beer is still only 9% of the beer industry! Yes, it's taken a lot of years to get some traction but I don't think it's going anywhere. Craft beers are more accessible then ever before. Bars, restaurants, liquor stores and even grocery stores are bringing on more craft beers into their line up either seasonally or sometimes even daily. The days of asking for a beer at a bar and only having the choice between Bud or Coors is dying off fast. The craft brewing movement is extremely exciting to me not only because I'm a brewer, but because America has never seen anything like it before!

Nick: Not since like the 1850s.

Evan: It's so crazy! As brewers, we're able to really push the limits on whatever we want beer to be. I mean, take The Bruery, who makes some of the most out of the box beers out there, and those guys are coming out with a brand new beer almost every week! People line up from down the street to try them. It's incredible to see the creativity that continues to pour out of craft brewers and how it is one of the biggest driving forces of this industry.

Nick: What do you think the next five years looks like?

Evan: I think we'll see more breweries open, some close their doors and most will be able to continue or even expand. As time goes on, we'll continue to see more places support craft beer. We're already seeing a lot more bars opening up that pour delicious craft beer right out of the gate and don't think that will be slowing down any time soon. I don't want to be overly optimistic in any way, because I don't know how it's going to play out but if we were able to grow craft beer within a recession, then what are we capable of when the economy is actually doing well?

Nick: What does the next five years look like for Noble, do you think?

Evan: Well, the last two have been crazy and during that time we quadrupled in size, but the next five? It's hard to say. I know that we're running out of space quicker than we ever thought we would and at this point, we don't quite have room for many more fermentation tanks, unless we get REALLY creative. We'll most likely have to move our entire brewery to whole new location. Our never-ending goal is to try to make the best beer we can. From a systematic trial and error process, to talking to other brewers, to reading as much as we can on any given subject, we just want to be known for our unwavering quality of delicious beers. I definitely see some good things for this place. A lot of good things, especially with the team that we have over here. Like Jerry, the president. He's the nicest guy.

Nick: Well, it seems like he's giving you a pretty great opportunity here to basically take the reins.

Evan: Yeah, you know—

Nick: Can you tell me a little bit about that?

Evan: Jerry and I were friends before I started at Noble. He would come down to TAPS, where I was brewing at the time, and use our keg washer to wash kegs for Noble. When the previous head brewer left, Jerry called me the next morning and told me, "I can't think of anybody else that I want for a head brewer" but I had to give it a lot of thought because Noble didn't quite have the best reputation at that time. I ended up taking it on after Jerry told me I could have creative control to brew whatever beers I wanted to. So yeah, it's been incredible and I'm having a great time with it.

Nick: What are you most excited about doing here?

Evan: You know, I get the most excited about changing the way that people see beer. Some of the fun stuff that we've brewed so far is a Gose with a magnolia scented Oolong tea called Gosebusters, a golden milk stout with coffee added, and then served on nitro called Naughty Sauce. We did a brandy barrel-aged American Strong Ale with brettanomyces and a whole bunch of figs called Fig Poppa, a California IPA with buddha's hand zest and pommelo zest called The Messenger, and an orange creamcicle beer called Everything But The Stick. We're really stoked on this single hop double IPA series that we've got going on right now that showcases a different hop variety, with each release in order to show what each single hop variety smells and tastes like. Hops are glorious! Let's see . . . we've also done collaboration brews with The Bruery, Beachwood BBQ, Three Weavers, and we have a bunch of others coming down the line. We also want to continue to focus on lagers a bit too, which is a bit confusing when your name is Noble Ale Works. But who's really going to call us out on that? Looking into the future, we just want to continue to add some diversity to our line up and keep things fun. As much as we love hops, we don't want to be a one-stop shop for hops. We're planning to increase our barrel-aging program as well as adding a few five-barrel fermenters to be able to experiment with for our taproom.

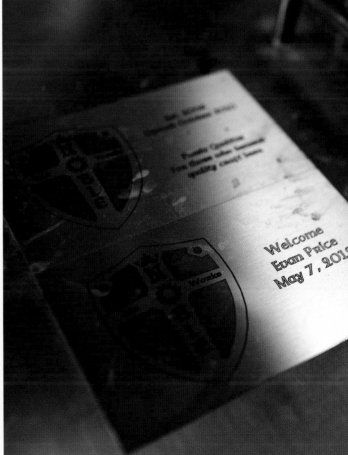

Mark Ruedrich
North Coast Brewing Company

Mark Ruedrich is the president, brewmaster, and co-founder of North Coast Brewing Company.

Nick: When do you remember having that "a-ha" moment about beer? And how did that lead to where you are right now?

Mark: I grew up in New York, so my earliest experiences with beer were the old New York breweries—Ballantine, Rheingold, Piel's, and fairly well-established regional brewers. This was in the 50's and, of course, and nobody knew those breweries would end up going under in consolidation in the next 10 or 15 years.

> **"Our friends felt it was their obligation to teach me about what beer really was . . . Everybody knew that Americans had no idea what good beer was."**

I graduated from college in 1973, at a time when there wasn't much choice for American beer consumers. In 1977, I moved to England with my then girlfriend, my now wife, Merle. We moved to Devon in the southwest of England and into the bosom of her family and friends there. I began to get an education about beer in a completely different context. Beer culture in England was even stronger then than it was over the next 10 or 15 years. Our friends there felt it was their obligation to teach me about what beer really was, because they knew. Everybody knew that Americans had no idea what good beer was.

That was a very comprehensive focused education, in some respects. I learned about what pub life was all about and how beer fit in with day-to-day life in England. I also learned what beer could taste like. Actually, one of the most interesting aspects of my experience was to become aware of the fact that breweries didn't have to be gigantic corporations. There were some regional brewers there that I learned about that were actually some very small breweries. There was a guy, a single guy, who had a brewery a few miles away from where we lived, which was way out in the country. His brewery was located in the barn behind his house. It was the Blackawton Brewery, he brewed Blackawton Bitter and sold it to my local pub and to a lot of other pubs around the area.

That was a revelation to me, that beer could be connected to a community by a single guy. I guess that idea stuck in my head and changed the way I would approach beer later on.

We moved to Fort Bragg in 1979. I wanted to get back to California. We'd been living in San Francisco before we left. Of course, in Fort Bragg in 1979, there were five different beers that were available. I remember there were a couple of imported beers—Watneys Red Barrel Ale, Bass Ale, and Guinness, of course. It was a pretty small selection of imports.

It was very soon after we moved back here that I began home brewing. I had a buddy from England send me a book about whole grain brewing. I was familiar with the concept described in the book because I have a degree in zoology, so the biology was all pretty straightforward. I brewed regularly at home. I had a number of beers that I liked to make. Our Old No. 38 is one of the first beers that I made at home in my kitchen.

By 1986 I was working as a construction foreman when my future business partner Tom Allen told me about the Roaring Rock Brewery opening in Berkeley. Roaring Rock would later become Triple Rock. Tom thought it would be a great thing to do here on the Mendocino Coast and wouldn't I be the perfect guy to brew the beer. My knees were starting to give me problems. I was a ripe old 35 at that time and thought, "Well, there's no way I'm going to last in construction. Maybe this would be a fun thing to do." I began doing some research. I went to the Craft Brewers Conference in Portland along with about 75 or 80 other people. It was a very small group. There were probably 10 people at the trade show. Actually, the group that was

there at that time was a collection of breweries that started up when we did in 1988. They were all doing their research at the same time: Rogue, Great Lakes Brewing, Goose Island, Deschutes, Wynkoop in Denver (John Hickenlooper's Brewery), the Vermont Brewery and Pub, Greg Noonan's Brewery—a good group of guys. It was my first experience networking with a lot of other people who were really trying to do something that had largely not been done yet.

I found out about some equipment that could be had in England. The little tanks called Grundies, which were being surplused by the big brewers there. These are little seven-barrel tanks. So I made a trip with my brother Dean. Tom, another business partner and I threw some seed money together. I went to England and bought our first group of tanks. We began to put together a business plan, gathered some investors together, and over the course of two years, found our location for our brewpub. And I learned. I went around, at least to the extent that I could, visiting any place that was open and operating to learn what other guys were doing. I often wonder how the hell we did it without the Internet.

We made friends. Brian Hunt; we consulted a lot with Brian in those early years. He had experience in a big brewery and of course, he had been instrumental in the start up down in Santa Rosa of Excelsior Brewing. So, that's how it all began. We had no idea what we were getting into, but we had a lot of the elements that were necessary to succeed.

> **"The beer begins as an idea, and sometimes not an idea based on something we've tasted."**

Nick: How do you think your English education in beer influenced the way that you guys brew here now?

Mark: I certainly learned what a good beer tasted like. I understood from the beers that I drank in England how important balance was. Really, the guys that I would go out to the pub with—three guys who lived in the village—we would go to the local pub, The Pig and Whistle, for an evening of drinking. This was serious, serious volume drinking. The beers were relatively modest in their alcohol content, but we would do two rounds with four guys, so that's eight pints—and those are imperial pints, of course. That's 160 ounces of beer that we would drink in the course of an evening, which was just a prodigious amount. Had we been drinking really hopped-up beers or really strong beers, there's obviously no way we'd get through an evening like that.

This was a very good illustration of the principle behind how breweries succeed if you want to sell a lot of beer. It has to be a beer that people can drink a lot of without ending up on the floor. Or having their taste buds overwhelmed. That was certainly one lesson. These were really well-made beers. They were the product of professionals, guys who had apprenticed and grown up in the trade working in breweries, some of which had been around for hundreds of years. There was a tradition that you were certainly aware of. That certainly informed my early efforts.

Nick: So, how do you go about formulating a new recipe now? Do you think more about emulating a specific style, or is it more ingredients based?

Mark: The beer begins as an idea, and sometimes not an idea based on something we've tasted. I think that this is the beginning point for what has happened over the last 35 years. It's led us to where we are right now. For me, I can see with every beer that we have produced since the very beginning that there has been an evolution. Some of the beers that we've made were influenced directly by other beers. Old Rasputin was inspired by Bert Grant's Imperial Stout, which, at that time, was the only imperial stout in America. I know now that Samuel Smith's had an imperial stout but that wasn't something that was available to us. I can remember drinking Bert Grant's Imperial Stout in 1986 and the memory of it stuck with me.

We first brewed Old Rasputin in 1995, so nine years later. I had an idea of what I wanted an imperial stout to be. It was derived from that taste memory that I had of Bert Grant's beer, which, at that time, was the best thing that I've ever tasted in my life.

You look at the other beers that we've done—we introduced PranQster, which was about the same time. There weren't a lot of American breweries that were brewing Belgian-style ales. My thinking on formulating that beer, and some of the other Belgian-style beers that we did later, was based to some extent, on experience with classic beer styles.

Nick: Do you think a general adherence to the classic styles is a key to success?

Mark: I don't know really. There are a lot of guys who are very experimental in their approach who have been very successful. My approach, and the approach of the brewers here, has been very conservative in some respects. We don't use fruits and spices in the beer. We use all-traditional raw materials and yet we've created a very broad spectrum. Our portfolio is pretty wide.

If you look at our beers, there's sort of a continuum. The connection between them is clear to me because I know how the ideas for each of them evolved. In some cases, one beer grew out of another one. We really liked that there was a little bit of this tart character in one of the yeasts that we used for PranQster, and we really wanted to accentuate that because I was very interested in the idea that you could get away from the balance created by maltiness and bitterness and have a beer that was balanced by maltiness and the acidity produced by these certain yeast strains. We found a strain that we liked a lot and we used that. This was during the run up to brewing Le Merle, our saison. In a beer with the strength of Le Merle, you got this nice little tangy finish in there.

We took that idea, of having the maltiness balanced by acidity, to the next level in our 20th-anniversary ale, which became our Grand Cru. This is the beer that has almost no hops in it at all. The maltiness is balanced by the acidity that's produced by this particular yeast strain. I don't know of other beers that do this particularly, but typically the Belgians will use bacteria or wild yeast strains to achieve this sort of result. In that respect, it's not completely out in left field. . . .

Nick: In your branding, the name North Coast is very small, almost hidden, while the beer name itself is much more predominant. Is that on purpose? To let the beers speak for themselves?

Mark: Scrimshaw, Red Seal, and Old No. 38 were the first three beers we opened with. I think that our idea was that we needed beers that covered a spectrum and that would appeal to a broader cross-section of consumers. They were all formulated with that in mind. Anyway, I think that strong branding demands that the beers themselves have an identity. A brand like Scrimshaw has a much stronger identity than "North Coast pilsner." I know other breweries have been very successful bringing different styles underneath one strong umbrella, but we chose another path. If you look at the English beers, a lot of them have distinctive names. The brands that stand apart have their own name.

That principle extended to a decision that I made early on in choosing the way the beers would be made. I chose the yeast strain, actually, one that I'd been using for a long time as a home brewer. I had been propagating it at home, and it allowed the other ingredients to shine. It's a very neutral yeast strain, so you could use the same yeast to produce a wide range of beers and have each of them taste very different. The beers reflect the malts and the different hops rather than one yeast in particular. I think that was a very important part of what we did early on, having a yeast strain that sat in

the background. We use the same yeast strain to brew Old Rasputin, Red Seal, and the Blue Star wheat beer. They are all obviously very different flavor profiles and they reflect the malt and hops.

Nick: What's exciting you about the beer industry today?

Mark: The thing that excites me most is seeing that the work that the brewing community has done for the last 30 years to educate the public is finally starting to pay off. You see a general acceptance now of our products in a way that, even 10 years ago, you didn't. When we began 25 years ago, we had to convince distributors to give us a try. It's been such a long process. No distributors wanted our beers. Every step of the way was a fight for us to gain acceptance for what we were doing. Now, those challenges are much less. Though we still find that people are having to learn, it's not the same. That's the most exciting thing to me—to know we're able to take advantage of what we've done now, and that we really have come to a place where we can fully express our ambition. That means putting these beers that we conceived and have brewed for all these years in front of a gigantic audience. That's exciting.

This is definitely a team game. One person doesn't get everything done. The people that I work with have really participated in this completely—they are my partners in this endeavor. That obviously includes Tom Allen, and my present business partner, Doug Moody, who handles our sales efforts around the world. And my wife Merle, who has worn a number of hats over the years. The head brewers, Pat Broderick and Chuck Martins, have been with me since the early 90's. They share a vision for what we're doing that includes producing great beer and doing it in a consistent way so the consumer knows that every time they open one of our beers, they're going to get the same thing that they got the last time.

> **"Beer consumed responsibly in a social setting is a very important part of who we are."**

Nick: You've been doing this for a long time and obviously there's something about beer that excites you on an emotional level. Do you know what it is about brewing and beer that keeps you going?

Mark: Again, there's an idea. It's not just about the beverage. It's about the place that the beverage has in history. In communities, the brewer historically has been a very important person in the town. There are the social aspects of drinking. Nowadays, it's important, I think, to clarify and say drinking responsibly. Beer consumed responsibly in a social setting is a very important part of who we are. For me, it's obviously not a simple thing, because a lot of my identity is tied up with what we do and what we've accomplished here in this little town.

Ignacio Cervantes
Pizza Port Brewing Company

Ignacio Cervantes, who at work is better known as "Nacho," is the head brewer at Pizza Port Ocean Beach.

Nick: Tell me a little bit about how you got started in this whole thing. How'd you start brewing?

Ignacio: I kind of just fell into it, really. I got pretty lucky. I started working at Pizza Port in Solana Beach in 2004. At the time, I was just flipping pizzas and doing any type of restocking work. From there, I picked up on the whole craft beer thing that was going on. Before I knew it, I was bartending and learning about all these crazy beers, and seeing all this crazy stuff that was going on in San Diego at the time. At one point, there was an opening in Carlsbad, so they offered me a position mainly to be kind of like the "gofer" of the crew—to wash kegs, drive stuff around, and so on. I worked my way up and eventually a few new locations opened up, moving some of the other brewers around. I got moved up to assistant brewer, and after Jeff Bagby's departure, I became the head brewer at the Carlsbad location until I moved to the Ocean Beach brewery, where I am now.

Nick: Pizza Port has played a pretty significant role in San Diego's craft beer history. Can you just give me a general overview of all that?

Ignacio: As a company, the first location was at Solana Beach. Vince and Gina Marsaglia, brother and sister, are the owners of the whole enterprise now. I believe that they opened in 1987. They didn't start brewing until 1992, when they pretty much dug out a big hole in the restaurant, put in some brewing equipment, and started brewing. That was the original Pizza Port.

The Carlsbad location is the second location, which opened, I believe, in 1997. They started brewing right off the bat. After that, you have San Clemente, which started in 2003. Then there's Pizza Port Ocean Beach, which opened up in 2010, and now the newest and largest location is in Bressi Ranch. That opened in 2012. That's a quick brief history right there.

From there, you also have Port Brewing and The Lost Abbey, which are an offshoot that started 2006–2007. They're kind of like a sister company, I guess.

Nick: Do you remember the first beer you ever attempted? Did you home brew at all before this?

Ignacio: No. I like to say I went to the school of Pizza Port brewing. I just learned everything here. I literally didn't know anything or what I was doing. The guys I was working for were really helpful in showing me the ropes. I picked it up pretty quickly and it just went from there. I think the first beer I got to brew was just an offshoot of our Poor Man's IPA. I think halfway through the brew, Jeff decided to go a whole different route because we had some visitors from Rome. He decided to turn it into a black IPA and it just became this big old monster. I think right off the bat I knew that brewing here had a similar tradition to home brewing—in a way, my home brew roots came from working here. It's a pretty popular place, a pretty busy place, but at the same time we get to play around, as most home brewers do.

Nick: Do you have any overriding philosophies or strategies that you use when you go about creating a new beer?

Ignacio: Most of the time, when we come up with something, it's just that we've gotten bored with the same stuff after a while. So it's like, "All right, let's come up with something new." My approach, of course, is literally to just look at the timetable of what I have brewing, and what, at the time, I haven't made.

> **"I think right off the bat I knew that brewing here had a similar tradition to home brewing—in a way, my home brew roots came from working here."**

Usually I think, "Oh, we haven't ever made a beer like that. Let's make that." With one of my newer double IPAs, I definitely wanted to go a different route, take a different approach towards it. We're known for all these IPAs, and they all taste a certain way. I think our IPAs are great—people have a general idea of what they taste like. I want to experiment, try something new, go for a different approach, try different malts, different hops. We have all this back stock of all this great grain and hops, so it's great to be able to experiment.

I also just ask around—I ask some of the more experienced brewers if they ever tried a particular kind of beer and what their thought process was. Usually their feedback is, "Just go for it. Just try it and use your best judgment." For the most part we just, I don't really want to say "wing it," but at times we kind of do. I like to have a pretty good understanding of what I'm getting from each ingredient. I know what I want from a certain malt or a certain hop or a certain yeast. I know what I'm going to get from those ingredients. It's just really about fitting it all together, coming up with the right calculation or percentage, and going from there. Hopefully it works out and the end result's a good one.

Nick: Do any beers come to mind as recipes you're most proud of or that you really love to drink?

Ignacio: Not really. I like a lot of different beer. I never really stick to one. I feel the same way about some of the beers I make. With some, I might be a little more sentimental, because it may have been the first beer I got to make on my own or so on. At the same time, I like other ones that I come up with. I like some of the lighter-drinking, lager-tasting beers. I like those just as much as the bigger crazy ones I've made. I can't really say there's one in particular at all.

Nick: Do you have any general advice or words of wisdom for someone who is just starting out, either this industry or home brewing?

Ignacio: It's like our philosophy here at Pizza Port, at least for us as the brewers: just experiment. At the same time, pay attention to detail and what you're doing, even when you're trying something new. We write everything down, take notes on what steps we took to make a beer. We're really serious about being clean, sanitizing, and so on. We're really careful with our yeast. We always try to use the freshest yeast we can. Same with the ingredients. We try not to hold on to our grains for long periods of time. If we know something needs to be used, we'll try and make a beer out of it. Don't hold onto [ingredients]. So, I guess the main advice is: don't let stuff go bad, just be clean and sanitize, and pay attention to what you're doing. Also, take rigorous notes in case something turns out really good and you want to go back to it, so it's all written down and all there.

Nick: You've done pretty well with the World Beer Cup Award and other awards you've received. Can you talk a little bit about some of the accolades that you're most proud of and what you attribute your success to?

Ignacio: The World Beer Cup was actually the first competition I was part of.

Nick: You won two awards, right?

Ignacio: Yeah. It's really a team effort. I have guys working under me. They're a big part of it. Their role is a big part of why we're successful. I've been a part of a team—I was already brewing under Jeff when we won the last three [Large Brewpub awards] at the Great American Beer Festival. I felt like I was a big part of those awards as well. All those awards were great. My thought process is: It's great to get recognized in that manner and it's good for the company, but in the long run, I think the response from the regulars that come to your bar is almost more important to me. I want those guys to come back. That's like my core. Those are the people that come here all the time. I'm happy for everything we won, and it's great for the company, but it's not really why I'm brewing.

Nick: What do you attribute all the success to?

Ignacio: I don't know. I always look at what everyone's doing that's different. Beer: it's the same process for everyone. It's four ingredients, the same. To me, it's just the way that we're pretty meticulous about them, and like I said, paying attention to our ingredients, being clean, and so on. I know there are some things we really concentrate on and really try to keep

track of. What is it we're doing different? I have no idea. We've just been lucky enough to make good beer and lucky enough that judges in those competitions like them as well. It definitely gives us something to strive for. Kind of keeps the ball going.

Nick: How have you and Pizza Port experienced the current boom in the craft beer industry?

Ignacio: I noticed it a lot in this county, when I first jumped into brewing. When I joined the brew crew here, there were proba-

bly four or five well-known breweries, brewery pubs or bars, and in a very short amount of time it's expanded to maybe 20, 25. It's definitely grown. It has to do with the fact that the educational side of it has really worked in connecting with consumers. A lot of younger people are coming on board or have become fans of the whole craft beer scene and the beer itself. I think it's just a combination of all those things. I guess the success helps, too. It just has that cool factor, that artisanal side to it.

> **"For the most part we just, I don't really want to say 'wing it,' but at times we kind of do."**

Nick: What is it that gives craft beer that "cool factor," do you think?

Ignacio: There's kind of like a "ma and pa" feel to it, I guess. An anti-big-company feeling that I know lures a lot of people. I think people in this area really go out of their way to help out the local businesses. I think that's part of it. I think the biggest part is just the increased beer knowledge and culture. You go to bars and you talk to one of the bartenders and they'll explain a beer to you. It's a trickling effect for sure. It's just that you hear it from one person and then it goes to the next. Here in this town, it's just really taken off. Saturation might happen. It might happen here. For the time being, I think there's room. The one thing that impresses me is how willing every company, all the breweries, all the brewers, and the home brewing community are willing to work together to participate and promote and help each other. We really go out of our way to help our neighbors, to help our fellow brewers out. That's probably one reason that it really hasn't felt saturated yet. It hasn't really been hurting other breweries or businesses. I think obviously there have been some breweries that have opened up and their product hasn't been up to par with some of the others, and those are probably the ones that have suffered. It's just the way of the world, you know.

Nick: What do you kind of see going forward for the next five or ten years? Do you see the craft beer boom being sustained?

Ignacio: There was a moment there when I thought it was becoming too much and it might affect the whole industry. But the more I watched it, the more I realized that it's not going away,

and it seems like it's picking up. I don't think it's really going to be an issue, at least not in this area. It's a big, growing city. That's pretty much just going to draw more people to the craft beer scene. It might affect some other parts of the country—like up-and-coming brew cities, but for this region I'm pretty sure it's going to be fine and we're going to have more places opening up. The city's willing to work with the breweries to make it easier for people to maintain and keep their breweries up and running.

Pizza Port is definitely expanding. It's good for the business, good for the owners, good for them. Me personally, I like the situation I'm in. I like the whole brewpub side of the craft beer scene. I'm still waiting to see what happens. I have mixed feelings towards growing too big. We'll see what happens. I'm sure there are a lot of people who know of our brand and can't get a hold of our beer who are excited that they now have a chance to see our beer come around their way.

Nick: My last question for you: Is there anything that no one's ever asked you in an interview that you've always wanted to say?

Ignacio: You're going to like this one, Nick. This is my first interview.

Nick: Really?

Ignacio: So, all the questions I got today.

Nick: That's awesome. Then is there anything I haven't asked you?

Ignacio: You popped my cherry, what can I say?

Steve Dunkerken and Owen Williams
Ritual Brewing Company

I'm Owen, I'm the janitor. I'm Steve, co-janitor.

Nick: So, where did you guys come from? And how did you get to where you are right now?

Owen: Well, when I had past life regression therapy—I guess I was a brewer for Ramses III. That's where it all started. Then in this life, I wound up being a home brewer with my dad, at the house. We figured we could make better beer at home than you could buy at the store, and sure enough we could. Well, "Reader's Digest version," my consumption surpassed my production abilities. . . . Legally.

I had to volunteer as a brewer, or schlepper, in a brewpub, called Riverside Brewing Company. I left there and went into BJ's and was there for over eleven years. I opened up eleven breweries and eighty-six restaurants for them. Then I needed to go out and start doing my own thing. I was a consultant for a while, taught at Cal Poly for a while; and then I met Steve, and that's when the wheels started—

Steve: The downward spiral.

Owen: Yeah. Things really started clicking and started working. I know we wouldn't be where we're at today without Steve.

Nick: Great! Steve, how about you? Tell me your first experiences with craft beer and how you fell into home brewing.

Steve: My gateway beer was Pike IPA, back when I was working for Price-Waterhouse in Seattle. I had some clients up there and it was the first time I had a freshly brewed, freshly dry-hopped IPA. I was totally captivated by the beer, but I had no idea how to make beer.

When you work for a big consulting firm, you have no life, so I continued to look into home brewing, what it was about, what it took, and I didn't actually do it until I left the firm a couple years later. I literally took a couple weeks off between jobs, went down to the local home brew store, and bought all the stuff: converted keg kettle, immersion chiller, glass carboys, everything.

Nick: Do you remember the first beer you home-brewed?

Steve: A honey-brown ale. Turned out pretty good. I surprised myself.

Nick: What's the concept behind Ritual?

Steve: I think wanting to get great beer to as many people as possible. That's really the goal. We want to have fun, and one of our values from day one, we said, "If the beer's not great, nothing else matters."

Owen: Yeah, that's exactly it. Great beer for great people. We drink our share and sell the rest. We really like the beer we produce, and we are consuming it ourselves. That's the inspiration behind the single rye IPA; wanted to see what this base malt would do with the different hops, and play with it that way. That's been really fun. It's a hobby gone wrong, and we're looking to make some money with it while we're doing it.

And some good beer.

Nick: The name, Ritual? Is there anything behind that?

Steve: That came from my end. We actually had a focus group with a whole variety of names, and I loved it because it spoke not only to the process itself, in coming out of home brewing—I always equate it to a very long, prolonged version of making your coffee in the morning—where you're mashing the grains, and you experience all the aromas through the production process—but also the finished product is used to celebrate. . . .

It's all those little rituals in life that mark our passing on this earth; from a birth, to an anniversary, to a Friday at the pub with the guys. You raise a glass right and left, so it's not only a little bit of ritual involved in the making, but it's used to celebrate those little rituals in life. That's where it comes from.

> **"It's all those little rituals in life that mark our passing on this earth; from a birth, to an anniversary, to a Friday at the pub with the guys."**

Owen: Yeah, you know, I like the rituals of life. You brush your teeth, you get ready for bed, you get up, breakfast, lunch, dinner, you kiss your significant other, and whatever else it takes. . . .

Steve: Go home and have a beer.

Owen: Go home and have a beer; that's exactly it.

Nick: What do you think it takes to be a brewer on a production scale?

Owen: Gosh, so many different facets to that. Passion. Honesty. You have to be physically able and you have to be smart enough and all that other kind of fun stuff that goes along with it, but those are the big things. You have to be passionate and honest. I say honest because if you do make a mistake, you want to know exactly what the mistake was, and there's a lot of mistakes that are now really, really good beers. Black Tuesday was a mistake, and so you have to be able to replicate that. As long as you're honest with doing what you're doing, I think you're in good shape.

Nick: Steve, you did a bunch of home brewing before transitioning into a production level. What was that transition process like?

Steve: Well, I brew a little bit here. Owen and I, in a way, we divided and conquered; we both love beer, we both do a lot of things together. He spends more time in the back, I spend more time on the business end, and we have Oscar and the guys in the back to do a lot of the heavy lifting. Ironically, the first batch we ever did here was a recipe that came out of my portfolio, and Owen had jury duty.

So, here I am, I had gone from a 28-gallon vessel to a 30-barrel system and, at first, I thought, "Wait a minute, how do you do this? How do you do that?" But really, it was fine by focusing on what the ingredients need to do: the mash temperature, the pH, the consistency of the temperature, the consistency of the mash, and checking your gravity and everything going across. It's the same. The ingredients need to do the same thing.

Nick: When you're talking to other home brewers, are you noticing any big mistakes that you find are general things that home brewers do that maybe they shouldn't be doing?

Steve: Boy, where do you go with that?

Owen: Don't suck on the hose.

Steve: I think there's a natural cycle to everything. Some people started out wanting to educate themselves and they got more obsessive going into it. I'm that way by nature, so that's where I started. And other people learn by their mistakes. That's the whole beauty of home brewing; it's a small batch, it's your beer, you can do whatever you want. I think there's a progression there where people figure out pretty quickly the importance of sanitation; they figure out pretty quickly the importance of temperature control and fermentation, that comes parallel to it; I think after that, people switch to all-grain.

If I'm talking to home brewers, I say switch to all-grain in your brewing, otherwise you're just making beer. It's like making mac n' cheese out of a little tear-open envelope and calling yourself a chef when you're really just warming up something that's pre-made. If you really want to brew, get to all-grain, where you can control and do everything. It's not as hard and complicated as some people make it out to be. That's my only recommendation there. I think more people need to do that and not be afraid of it.

Nick: So, what's the story of how you guys met, how you clicked, and how this whole thing spawned?

Owen: You tell it better than I do.

Steve: You want me to tell it again?

Owen: Yeah, tell it again.

Steve: Tell me if I screw it up. Toby, who Owen mentioned, was a mutual friend. Anyhow, when I first started brewing, he literally tasted that first home brew. I wanted to re-create that Pike IPA flavor. Toby helped me. There was no recipe or anything. He helped me get going in the right direction, which meant I went to all-grain brewing by my third batch.

Enter Mitch Steele, the current brewer at Stone. Great guy. It's when he was new to California and to Stone. We had an event at my house and Mitch came. It was Mitch who got Owen over to my place. Owen walks into the garage, and I have one of the big beer systems with all the bells and whistles. It caught his interest, so he came over a couple times to brew, and I'm thinking, "Okay, this guy's been around the block, he's pretty respected, he's made a lot of beer." I give him some of my beers and I'm asking him, "So what do you think?" And he would say, "Oh, it's great." "Well, what do you think about this?" "Oh, this is fantastic. This is a great beer." I got absolutely zero feedback. No constructive criticism whatsoever.

Leading up to that, I'd had a hundred people or more ask me, "Hey, Steve, this is great beer, have you ever thought about opening a brewery?" The verbal answer was always

> **"If I'm talking to home brewers, I say switch to all-grain in your brewing, otherwise you're just making beer."**

no, but you always think about what comes next. Going from home brewing, to brewing professionally, or working in a brewery, or owning a brewery is natural. I'd had a great executive position, a challenging job running a multinational manufacturing group of companies, so why am I going to go bail and try to make beer on my own?

So, one day Owen walks into the garage with a little twinkle in his eye, and he asked me that question, "So, you ever thought about opening a brewery or brew pub or something?" And for the first time I said, "Let's talk." So we started talking and it slowly evolved over time. We started putting some models together.

What I liked about Owen as a partner was, yes, he's a brewer and he's an accomplished brewer, and he knows how to put some of the equipment systems together. But the biggest strength for him: he was a director, a senior guy in a publicly traded company. At this point in our lives, we're running our business, it's about the bottom line, we're not a couple of guys going, "Dude, we're going to make beer! And we'll figure out how to pay the bills later."

Nick: When it comes to creating a new recipe, do you take an ingredient-based approach, or do you have a concept in mind and work backwards from there?

Owen: I know for me, as far as my recipes, if I like a beer that's in front of me, I'll try to analyze it and see if I can't copy it or come close to it or something. Or try to find the style. That's always kind of fun. And then do your own little twist on it. For example, there was an extra-special bitter that I was pretty fond of, and I threw a lot of extra dry hops into it. That was fun.

Steve: My approach, which came through years of tinkering in my garage, was really focused on flavor. Obviously, there were beers I was influenced by, but it was literally finding the best flavor profile. So I'd brew beer and look for a little something I was missing. Maybe it was just changing a grain, or using a different maltster. Things like that. It was a little bit at a time. I focused on getting the flavors I wanted and the balance I wanted to see.

Nick: Then, are you writing down more recipes first before you brew them? It sounds like what you're doing is more flavor-based, and you're more figuring it out as you're brewing along.

Steve: I think with the more experience you have, the more you understand those flavors, the easier it is for you to do just what you said. Once you understand how the different grains and hops work, and how they play together, putting something together is much easier to do. You can just sit down and say, "Let's put these together," and have a higher level of success.

Owen: Yeah. Because you also want something at the end of the day that the consumer's going to like and they're going to buy. It doesn't make a difference what I want to do as far as a recipe. If consumers don't like it, what good is it? I'm home brewing again.

Nick: What's your take on our so-called current "Craft Beer Revolution"?

Owen: Little bit of history: Back in 1880, we had over 4,000 brewery concerns in the United States. Then, because of industrialization and so forth, the bigger boys started picking up and buying the little guys. Jump forward to where we're at now, we just surpassed 3,000 breweries for the United States, and I think there's plenty of room for more breweries.

For a long time we didn't even do an IPA, just because we said, "Well, that's not who we are." You know, we didn't want to do that at the beginning.

Steve: We got our ass kicked every day for not having an IPA.

Owen: Finally, we did an IPA and everybody's happy now. So . . . I don't know, I think there's plenty of room for all kinds of growth.

Steve: I have a little bit of an alternate view. It's getting a little crazy out there and I think it'll change a lot. I think craft is here to stay. I don't think craft beer is a trend, I don't think it's a gimmick, I don't think it's a bubble, but I think the growth rate will slow down and I think it might shake out a little bit.

I agree that we can support more breweries and stuff. But there's a lot of small, inexperienced, undercapitalized concerns out there, especially with the nanos; you can have a ton of fun in there. If you get a good crowd coming, there's some good cash flow there, but there's a ceiling on how much money you're ever going to make at that, and I think some people are just going to get tired of coming in and brewing small batches over and over.

Nick: What excites you guys now in brewing, in the industry, and in your company?

Steve: I love Belgian beers; we do three. We want to be very true to style, and we want to do a lot more Belgian sours. We want to do some legitimate wild ales, not just something with a little brett, and "here's our sour beer." There's a lot of breweries that are in trouble, a lot of breweries that are really just calling it sour—the alleged sour thing. We want to get there, but we want to do it right.

Scott Cramlet
Rubicon Brewing Company

Scott Cramlet is the brewmaster at Rubicon Brewing Company in Sacramento, California.

Nick: How did you first get your start in craft beer? And how did you wind up where you are right now?

Scott: My start with craft beers was shortly after I graduated high school and was living in San Luis Obispo. I had a bunch of other friends from high school that were going to Cal Poly, but I wasn't. I was going to the junior college. We were sitting around and got to talking about making home brew. A few months passed and I finally figured out there was a home brew shop in town, so I got some old how-to brew books and some malt extract and started trying to make home brew. It was pretty primitive back then. Some results were better than others, but I was barely 18 at the time. I didn't even know if it was legal for me to buy a bag of hops or anything, so I remember we lied about our ages to the home brew shop.

That's where I got my start with pale ales and stouts and porters and all that sort of stuff. A few years later, I moved up here to Sacramento and was a member of the local home brew club, the Gold Country Brewers Association. One day, we were out at a club campout up by Folsom Lake, and the original brewmaster from Rubicon—Phil Moeller—was looking for help and was kind of looking at who was out there from the home brew club. Eventually, the finger got pointed at me and, literally, I got a tap on the shoulder asking if I might be interested in coming down and helping out. I came in and talked; I don't even know if you call it an interview, but I talked to him about a week later. I started a few days after that and have been working here ever since. I think my start date here was September 1, 1990. My career is a one-shot: home brew to commercial brewing and one location.

Nick: What are the advantages and disadvantages, do you think, of being in one place for so long?

Scott: Well, it certainly brought a level of continuity to what we make here. When someone calls me an old-timer now it's kind of weird. I don't know exactly when I became an old timer, but I have. I think it's good to have someone here that has a sense of our history and a sense of history of the industry as a whole. Straight from home brewing to commercial: some of the negatives, I think, even though I know an awful lot about brewing and brewing science, I don't have a formal degree. So I kind of regret the fact that I didn't get a formal education. I was too busy doing it instead of learning how to do it. I have no regrets, really.

Nick: What's your recipe development process like? Do you look to create a specific style, or do you get inspired by particular ingredients?

Scott: Historically, I come up with an idea. There are a number of ways of looking at that question. I get a flavor in my head, more of a concept about what the beer might be, and then you kind of brainstorm on the flavors and the parameters. You come up with a beer after that, but it starts in the head with an idea. You can look at it a little bit like if you are a good cook in the kitchen, you don't necessarily have to get out the cookbook and follow it. If you know basic ingredients, basic techniques, the palate of spices you have to work with, you can come up with that different pasta sauce or that novel dish. Of course, we are brewing on a commercial level, so you have to have some confidence that you are going to hit it. Back in the early days, we would do a 5 or 10-gallon home brew to test out concepts, but now we just throw a full batch in. We're a 10-barrel brewery—there's 310 gallons in a batch, or about 2,480 pints—so you have to be relatively confident that it's going to be something that the public is going to enjoy. We are just the first part of the equation. The public is the big part. They have to accept it, buy it, drink it, and hopefully come back for more. Otherwise, it's no fun if you have a batch of beer sitting in your tank for 6 months saying, "Well, it seemed like a good idea at the time."

So, you do come up with recipes in your head, but they are also ingredients driven. When I was at the Craft Brewers Conference, one of the German Hop Grower's Associations had some experimental hops out, and one of them was a super-high alpha acid. It was like 25% alpha, and I know a lot of people were looking at that. They had one that had mandarin-type notes to it, but they had one that they called "melon" and it had cantaloupe and honeydew-type characteristics. That one kind of caught my eye, and I began thinking about how to create a beer if we can get our hands on some of those. That's an example of a new ingredient, a new hop variety where I am thinking about making a beer based on some of those flavor and aroma concepts. So that's driven from the other side—ingredients driving the process.

Nick: Are there general characteristics that you hope that all your beers end up with?

Scott: The main characteristics are drinkability and balance—or, for a real simple term that a lot of people use, I look for "more-ish"; that is, do I want more? It's all fine and good if you get someone to drink a pint of beer and enjoy it, that's great. Ideally we want to create beers where someone doesn't even have to think. The waitress comes up, and, "Do you want another one?" Yes. It's not, "Hmmm, let me think about it." We make a variety of different beers, but that's a good measure of a beer, where someone doesn't even have to think about it. Our flagship beer here was the IPA, which we started producing in 1988. It was pioneering at the time. Even if a small brewery made an IPA, it wasn't necessarily their flagship. Back in the

> **"My career is a one-shot: home brew to commercial brewing and one location."**

day, people thought it was crazy, it's so strong, it's hoppy, it's bitter, but nowadays we certainly enjoy it. The level of IPAs in this style have eclipsed what we do, so we refer to our IPA as a truly "old school IPA."

Nick: Has Rubicon had to change as the general public has become more educated about craft beer?

Scott: We have pretty much stuck to our guns for better or for worse. Of course, our beers have evolved somewhat, but our decor inside looks pretty much the same as it did in the early 90's. A lot of what you will see on the menu board will be very similar. We are kind of a photograph from the past, I suppose. We haven't really tweaked it that much. Certainly, there is a whole new wave of consumers and brewers out there. Shoot, there are commercial brewers that weren't even born yet when we opened up. There are breweries, certainly like the Belgians, that just do sour beers or Belgian-influenced stuff and, again, they aren't really doing Belgian. That's where they got their start and they have created whole new categories of beers out there. We tend not to chase trends, even if it may be a good idea. We could do a good job. People ask, "why don't you have this because that's a really popular style?" We can't spend our time necessarily chasing what the trend of the day is. We are the tried and true.

> **"For a real simple term that a lot of people use, I look for "more-ish"; that is, do I want more?"**

Nick: What is it about brewing a beer that engages and excites you, do you think?

Scott: I have always had an interest in the arts and sciences and, in hindsight, brewing is a fantastic blend of art, science, and mechanical skills. There is a certain physicality to it, working with equipment. I was a kid that was always taking stuff apart trying to figure out how it worked and didn't always get stuff put back together.

Nick: You've been around the brewing scene for a while. What do you think about what we're seeing today, in terms of the explosion in craft beer popularity?

Scott: We have seen the ups and downs. When we opened up in 1987, it was just at the beginning of the curve, and shortly after—even 1988, 1989, and 1990—there were a lot of breweries that opened up and a lot of them that aren't here anymore. I think the first shakeout going back was 1994/1995. Back in the early 90's, you had a lot of other folks like professional restaurateurs and some of these chain restaurants that were looking for any edge they could get so a lot of them got into the game. There was a shakeout in the early 90's and then it kind of laid flat for a while. Now, we are seeing this huge growth.

San Diego County; they have 200 breweries in planning or 150 breweries in planning. We have the nano-brewery craze, which is kind of cool. I'm not sure if it makes economic sense all the time, but heck, if you can pull it off, or even if you can't pull it off, whatever, that's on you. It sure is cool to see a lot of people out there trying to get their foot in the door. Here in Sacramento, we have lost some of our brewpubs, but we are seeing some of these micro-breweries with tasting rooms opening up and it's quite a popular trend.

Nick: It seems like you and the Rubicon brand are one now. What's it like having that identity?

Scott: I don't mind it. I don't know any different, though. It's been pretty much my entire adult life. I think it could be pretty cool to have worked at a bunch of different places and have different experiences, but I'm not that flighty. Now, I have my roots in place. It's definitely home, and it's something to be proud of as well.

Nick: What advice might you have for a young home brewer who was looking to up his game or even considering going into production brewing?

Scott: When I started making home brew, I think my first book was Dave Line's *Big Book of Beer*. My first home brew, I crushed my grain a half cup at a time in the Oster blender—I didn't know any better, we weren't told. Certainly now, someone entering the home brew hobby, gosh, the depth of information is out there with the Internet and other resources. Boy, what an advantage coming into the hobby now, versus when I stepped into it. As far as someone thinking about transitioning from the home brew to a professional, boy, it's not all fun and games. Brewers are certainly a fun group of people. It's a great, fun career. It's a great community. Lots of early mornings, lots of hard work, sweat and tears, sometimes blood. It's lots of cleaning.

Nick: So, what is it about brewing that still excites you?

Scott: What is it about beer that is so beautiful? After all the years and all the beers, it's still amazing you can go somewhere and have a beer that you haven't had in years and it can evoke memories of a time and place in your life, or you can still be surprised. New flavors. At the Stone anniversary party I had their Russian imperial stout and it was aged in an apple brandy barrel. The first one I had for breakfast that day. It was—still after all these years—I took a little smell of it, and took that first little taste in my mouth, and gosh, it just makes you stop and think. It's like, "How can I make something like this?" There is still inspiration. It's never ending. You can never say I've done it all with this career.

Nick: Is there anything you have never been asked in an interview that you've always wanted to say?

Scott: I'm just proud for the career I've had and the association with Rubicon, not being the original brewer, but carrying on a long legacy of what was started before me. I'm proud to be carrying the torch, but adding a few other spins along the way, certainly stuff like the Rosebud have been some fun ones. Kind of interesting; that was supposed to be a batch of Irish red, but that day I heard Jerry Garcia died. So I threw in a bunch of the stuff from the Irish red, and the pale malt, some of the crystal malt, and then just started looking around in our grain bin for what looked good. A bag of wheat, a bag of this, some rye left over from another project. That's how that beer was created; total improvisation, and we have been making it every year since. Every year it's a little bit different, but it's still the same beer. It was just going to be a one-off thing, kind of a good tribute for Jerry. Some liken it to how the Grateful Dead played—it's still the same song, but it's different than it was last time. They played it differently or they accented this differently. You still recognize it, but it's still different every time. The career is certainly something to be proud of—carrying on a legacy, it's one of those things.

> **"What is it about beer that is so beautiful? After all the years and all the beers, it's still amazing you can go somewhere and have a beer that you haven't had in years and it can evoke memories of a time and place in your life."**

Vinnie Cilurzo
Russian River Brewing Company

Vinnie Cilurzo is the co-owner and lead brewer at Russian River Brewing Company in Santa Rosa, California.

Nick: So, when and how did you fall in love with beer? And how did you make your way to where you are today?

Vinnie: Well, my parents had a winery down in Southern California, in Temecula, so I grew up in the wine industry. The winemaker, she was into home brewing, so I tasted her home brew. That was probably my first taste of a good beer. She would also go down to this little brewery in Fallbrook called Bolt.

After I moved to San Diego to go to college, I started home brewing, and my roommates were already into good beer. My first craft beers were Sierra Nevada, of course, Anchor Liberty Ale, Anchor Steam, Sam Adams, and Pete's Wicked Ale. At the time, those were real tough to find, and being in Temecula, we would have to drive half-an-hour down to Escondido just to be able to buy good beer.

Eventually, my hobby got out of control and, in 1994, I started Blind Pig Brewery in Temecula with a couple of business partners. We made a barleywine four times a year, and we made a double IPA. In 1994, it was the first beer we ever brewed out of Blind Pig. That was an accomplishment right there, brewing double IPA. At that time it hadn't really been done before, so they say. I was there for about three years before I worked myself to death and decided to sell my part of the brewery.

When my wife Natalie and I moved up to northern California, Korbel was opening a brewery and we had learned about their project. Once I showed up, they hired me as a consultant. Six years later, I was still brewing for them, but they decided to get out of the beer business. So, instead of shutting the brewery down cold-turkey, they decided to sell the brand to me and Natalie. In lieu of severance, I took the brand. Natalie and I raised some private money and built out, and we opened the brewpub. That was 2004—four years after that, in 2008, we opened the production brewery where we sit right now and where we're at capacity.

Nick: Regarding your general brewing philosophy and goals, are there characteristics that you hope to incorporate into all of your beers?

Vinnie: You can see some consistencies, but because we make such different beers, it's not like—I think the best example is Sierra Nevada. When you taste Sierra Nevada, there's an overlying flavor in all their beers. It even crosses over from their ales to their lagers, although it's very evident in their ales—their yeast just has such a distinct character. In our beers, we have session beers at the pub that are all 5.5% or under, and then we've got all of our barrel-aged beers and those are funky and sour. Then we've got our line of hoppy beers, our IPA, which is what we're most known for, and then we've got a line of Belgian beers that aren't the funky, sour ones. We really have four different kind of families of beer that we make, so you've got these four very distinct beers and you can't make the funky beers taste like the IPA. There are yeast characteristics and yeast driven characteristics. Take the beers that get sold at the pub, the IPA, those definitely have some overlying character. But nothing is going to taste like the barrel-aged beers. Even the Belgian beers, the yeast that's used to ferment the Belgian-inspired beers, well that's typically the same base yeast that ferments out the barrel-aged beers. By the time the barrel-aged beers go through an entire barrel-aging process, they get hit with brettanomyces, they get soured, and at some point they get hit with fruit. At that point, you can't even tell what the base yeast was to begin with. In fact, when you make barrel-aged beers, the base yeast almost doesn't matter, you can use anything.

Most of our beers in general are very dry, so that's definitely an overlying character of all the beers. Even our quadruple finishes probably lower than most Belgian dubbles do. We make a Belgian dubble, but that finishes dry, so we've really taken styles and just made them the way that we like them. Luckily, people drink them. We also found, in the early years, that when we started making Belgian beers—'99, I think,—the first Damnation was pretty sweet and over the top. It was too sweet and too malty and we had to make it drier and more bitter, otherwise, it wouldn't sell. It's like figuring out what Americans want compared to what Americans maybe think Belgian beer is, even though Belgian beer isn't sweet. It's usually dry, but it's very fruity, so people confuse the fruitiness with the sweetness. We definitely figured out that we needed to make those beers a little hoppier.

> **"That was an accomplishment right there, brewing double IPA in '94, it hadn't really been done before, so they say."**

Nick: When you set out to create a new beer, would you say your development process is more ingredient based or is it more conceptual?

Vinnie: It's normally starting out with an idea of what I want the end beer to taste like and then working backward into it, knowing what hops will do what. It's rare that we just throw stuff into the pilot kettle. We've got a little half-barrel system, it looks like a home-brew system. We normally start with an end goal in mind and then work backwards. In the case of Brux, our collaboration with Sierra Nevada, that was a process-driven beer—less ingredient driven, pretty basic malt, pretty basic hops, the brett obviously was unique, but Ken didn't want brett all over his brewery. Ken's son, Brian, and I had to figure out a way to

get the brett added to the beer without basically contaminating all of Sierra Nevada with brett.

I had this idea for years about injecting brett on the fly in the bottling line. Between Brian and Ken and myself, we built the first-ever in-line bottle injector, at least the first we know of, to get the brett added. That was definitely an equipment-driven component. It was process-driven, as opposed to ingredient-driven, in that we still only used the four traditional ingredients: water, yeast, grain, and hops. We just happened to throw in an extra strain of yeast, we injected it in a certain way, and we also adjusted the water chemistry in a direction that you normally wouldn't do. We basically broke every rule in brewing on that beer. Eventually, Sierra tweaked it so it fit their actual 200-barrel, or 100-barrel brewery. That was a two-and-a-half-year project from the time that Brian and I initially talked about it to when the beer got bottled or released.

Nick: It seems like innovation is important to you. Why do you think California supports so much brewing innovation?

Vinnie: Probably because the consumers are willing to buy it. To be honest with you, I don't know if that holds true anymore. Craft beer has taken hold everywhere in the United States. I think it used to be a West Coast thing, but I think now you've got innovation going on all over the United States, in every state, and in all kinds of craft breweries. One brewery that's been doing it the most on the East Coast—using a lot of unique ingredients and processes—is Dogfish. Then you know, you've got Allagash up in Portland, Maine, doing spontaneous beers. And there's Ommegang up in Cooperstown, New York, that's been doing Belgian beers for umpteen number of years. We know of at least 200 breweries making—not bourbon stuff—just funky, barrel-aged beers.

Nick: What is it about that style that excites you? What got you started on the barrels?

Vinnie: That started when we were at Korbel, it was 1998 or so, maybe '99. I wanted to take what was, at the time, our only Belgian beer, which was Damnation, and add it to a barrel. I wanted a locally sourced barrel and I wanted to take my favorite component out of it and put it into the beer, which is brettanomyces. I wanted to just use brett, no bacteria with the beer in the barrel, and to see what happens. We ended up

winning an award at GABF. It tasted really good, but I couldn't sell it all because no one was buying that stuff. We couldn't even sell it in the deli at Korbel, which was our tap room. We literally bottled it and drank it all ourselves, or sold it to Toronado in San Francisco. They were literally the only bar in our area that sold this type of beer. After Temptation came Supplication, which is the brown ale. Yes, we have them in three-core lines, Temptation, Supplication, and Consecration.

Nick: You've probably been asked this about 1,000 times, but Pliny is obviously one of those beers that just caught everyone's attention. Did you ever see Pliny becoming this successful?

Vinnie: No, it was just another beer for us. We had been making Pliny since '99, going back to our Korbel days. Back then, it was a seasonal brew. When we opened the brewpub in 2004, we made it a year-round beer. We'd been using pretty much the same recipe. I mean all beers get tweaked along the way, but it's always been a Simcoe hop-focused beer. It was one of the first beers ever to use Simcoe. We were actually using Simcoe at Korbel when it was an experimental hop. Weis DR014 was its experimental number. Weis DR stands for Yakima Chief Research. Yakima Chief was the hop company that had a breeding program that bred Simcoe. So, when we made a double IPA, it was sort of a carry-over from when I made a double IPA back at Blind Pig.

When we made it full-time at the pub, it was purely organic that it became popular. It picked up this cult-like following. You can't point to one month or one year and say this is when it happened. We just started selling a keg a day, and then it became two kegs a day and then three, and then four, and it happened very slowly. Now it's tough to keep up with demand at the pub and we're now shorting distributors their orders to make sure the pub doesn't run out. We've got people traveling here from all over the world, it has become a destination. Sonoma County—as much as it's a wine and grape destination—has become a pretty big beer destination. With Bear Republic, Moonlight, Lagunitas, and us—the four of us—it's a pretty nice trip if you're flying into Oakland or San Francisco.

Nick: Explain the concept of Pliny the Younger, and how did that idea come about?

Vinnie: We were already making Elder at the pub year-round. Doing some research historically, we figured out that the Elder had a nephew and adopted son, Pliny the Younger. It was said that the Younger had chronicled the Elder's life once Pliny the Elder had died during the eruption of Vesuvius in A.D. 79. We thought it would be cool to make a sister beer, and we had two ways to go. Either make it a lighter alcohol beer, which would actually make the hops pop even more, or go the other way and make it a bigger beer, where you can just keep piling more hops in and it becomes more of a balanced type beer. We went with the bigger version. Why? Because we thought it would probably be a little more appealing. That's one thing that America is not quite in tune with yet: low-alcohol beer that's got big flavor.

We decided to make this bigger version that was triple—where Pliny's was a double IPA, the Younger would be a triple IPA. That was the idea. The first year that it really got out of control, we sold 20 barrels—so 40 half-barrels—40 kegs in eight hours. The following year, we decided to do no-growler 10-ounce pours only at the pub or kegs through distribution. Basically, if you wanted to drink Younger, you either had to drink it at our pub or go to one of our few accounts that got it. That's how it's stocked now and it's worked really well. People travel from all over the world to get it. It's become a vacation for them. It affects the rest of the businesses around downtown, they gain from it. Third Street Ale Works, the brewpub next street over from us will tell you that's the biggest week of their year now is Younger, or two weeks, Younger Days as we call it. It's been nice, too because it's affected local hotels in a positive way, local restaurants, other local stores and that's probably the best thing we can do for our community is bring more business to our neighboring friends.

> ## "We were already making Elder at the pub year-round . . . we figured out that the Elder had a nephew and adopted son, Pliny the Younger."

Nick: Do you think that term "Craft Beer Revolution" is apt for what we're experiencing right now? And do you see sustaining?

Vinnie: The crystal ball question, everyone's asking: Can it be sustained? It probably can for a while. The one thing that I'll always say is that it's got to be quality. If any brewery, new or old or whatever, is not focusing on quality, then they're in the wrong business, because that's what this industry is about. Even the big three—Bud, Coors, Miller—you may not like what you taste, but quality has always been their focus. And consistency. I don't think that can be stated enough that it's got to be a quality driven mindset and you've got to be willing to reinvest in equipment that will analytically show you what quality is.

Nick: Why no major expansion for you?

Vinnie: Because it makes us nervous, to be leveraged that much.

Nick: Do you just like being small?

Vinnie: Yes, small is beautiful, but we're not that small. It's a relative term. We're going to do about 14,000 barrels this year, compared to Brian [at Moonlight] who's what, maybe going to do a couple thousand? The thing is, we have been growing. We've actually averaged just under 20% volume growth a year, not dollar growth.

Nick: What is it about beer and brewing that excites you most?

Vinnie: Definitely the hops. I love hops. It's the creativity, that's the main part of it. It's always challenging, but how bad can it be? You're making beer for a living. It's brings joy to people, that's for sure.

Ken Grossman
Sierra Nevada Brewing Company

Ken Grossman is the founder and president of Sierra Nevada Brewing Company in Chico, California.

Nick: Thinking back to your beginnings, what got you really interested in beer? And how did you wind up where you are today?

Ken: I was actually first exposed to home brewing in the mid 60's. I had a buddy who lived a couple of houses down. His father was a very accomplished home brewer, and a home wine-maker. He was one of the founders of the Maltose Falcons, which was the first Home Brew Club in the United States, so it started down in Southern California. I was exposed to his brewing on weekends. As a kid, I would go to his house and he was always brewing something up, whether he was crushing grapes or making beer on the stove. So the process was something I was very familiar with at a young age.

I started home brewing around 1969, and moved to Chico in 1972. Back in those days, there really wasn't a good supply store for home brewing ingredients. In 1975, I decided to open my own home brew shop in downtown Chico called the Home Brew Shop. I did that for a number of years. I was studying chemistry—initially at junior college and then later at Chico State. I decided after a couple years that I wanted to open a brewery. In 1978, I went on a bit of a pilgrimage—I had visited Anchor before, and I went down and visited New Albion, which had recently started up. I saw what Jack was doing and made the decision that it was something I wanted to do with my life.

> **"I saw what Jack [at New Albion] was doing and made the decision that it was something I wanted to do with my life."**

I sold my home brew shop in '78, wrote a business plan to open a brewery, and started building and fabricating all of the equipment myself. By 1980, I made my first batch of beer. My original brewhouse was home-built equipment—I was brewing 10 barrels at a time, and grew to a little less than 1,000 barrels in our first year. We were up to about 14,000 barrels in 1987, when I started to build on the site where I am currently.

At the end of '87, beginning of '88, we started brewing here. In the first year, we did a little over 20,000 barrels, next year 30,000 barrels, year after than 45,000, and year after that about 60,000. That was all I had designed the second brewery to do. We pretty rapidly started to expand that plant and, by 1997, we were at nearly 300,000 barrels. We did a pretty significant expansion with what you see today—with the 200-barrel brewhouse, which was built by the same German company—Huppmann—that had built my original used one.

I also purchased my third brewhouse from them to install in North Carolina. It's also a 200-barrel system.

Nick: Let's talk a little bit about your process. When you're coming up with a new beer, are there any overriding principles or philosophies that you always employ?

Ken: Recently, we've gone in a range of directions. We've done things with Russian River, using brett. We've done a collaboration with Dogfish Head using a range of different kinds of syrups and sugars from trees. I don't know if you've seen our research brewery, but we have a small ten-barrel brewery where we brew a wide range of stuff.

We're very eager and we enjoy experimenting with that little brew house. We've been a hop-centric brewery for our whole existence. I like hoppy beers, and so we've done a lot around that arena with a lot of hop research. We've worked closely with breeders and growers for many years. We've had our own hop fields for nearly ten years.

That being said, we've been branching out and doing things that are completely off in a different direction with malts and other kinds of sugars and styles that are fun to play with. As a home brewer, I did a lot of experimentation. We did a lot of lager brewing. I used to malt my own wheat and roast my own grains back in the late 60's, early 70's, before a lot of that stuff was widely available. Experimenting with brewing and using different ingredients is something that goes way back for me.

Nick: I've rarely met a brewer on this project so far that hasn't told me that Sierra Nevada Pale Ale was their "A-ha! Moment" in their beer evolution. What does that mean to you, to have created something like that?

Ken: I've had that feedback from a lot of brewers. It's a great honor to hear that from great brewers—there's a lot of great brewers in this country today. I do think we were somewhat instrumental in getting more extreme styles to be more widely accepted. When I was first starting, when we were producing four or five thousand barrels, I remember saying, "If I could only ever get to 12,000 barrels. I think that's probably the limit in America for hoppy bottle conditioned beers." I figured my understanding of what the consumer would accept was very limited, based on what most people were drinking, which were very light, fairly flavorless, lager styles. I thought having yeast in a bottle was a turnoff to a lot of people—that and having a fairly aggressive hop profile at that time. We haven't changed our hopping since we started.

Nick: Did you ever imagine being as successful as you are?

Ken: If I was lying, I'd say, "Yeah." In reality: no, I had no clue. I had very modest aspirations back when we started. 3,000 barrels was what my business plan called for. Again, there were no real models or other people who had done what we were planning on doing, which was going from nothing to creating a new brand and doing it in a way that was not mainstream.

> **"I do think we were somewhat instrumental in getting more extreme styles to be more widely accepted."**

To predict that we could have grown too 100,000 barrels, 200,000, or a million would have been a completely outrageous claim back then. For us, getting to a point where we could make enough money to live on was sort of our goal—and doing something we're passionate about, which was brewing beer. I think we've accomplished that. Obviously, our success has been much greater than I ever imagined.

Nick: Can you talk a little bit about your partnership with Steve Dresler? How do you guys work together to create new recipes? How influential has he been in the success of this company?

Ken: Initially, I brewed the Pale Ale, the Porter, the Stout, our Celebration Ale, and our Bigfoot. Those were all brands that I developed and came up with. Now we have a research brewery and we're doing Beer Camp. There has been a huge amount of input from Steve and Scott Jennings, who runs the pilot brewery. Actually, a lot of our beer campers have come up with some pretty interesting ideas.

I don't limit where the direction for the next beer will come, and Steve has been involved in a lot of that, as has Scott and the pilot brewery. It's fun. It's like, if you're a chef, you wouldn't want to be limited to only making a few different food types everyday. Having that creative ability is something we encourage in the brewers. They come up with some amazing beers.

Nick: Your son is very heavily involved in the business. As you move forward, is this something that would you like to remain a family business?

Ken: We would, it's not only my son who is involved. I have two daughters as well. They've been involved in various levels and they're still involved in various levels. It would be great to see the company continue on into the future and still produce great beers under our family's direction.

Nick: Talk a little bit more about the industry. What do you think about what people are calling the "Craft Beer Revolution."

Ken: We've seen some other periods where there's been some pretty accelerated growth in the acceptance of craft beer—not to the degree we're seeing today. I'm one of the people who've pointed to various reasons why they think it slowed down before. Was it too many non-authentic beers and breweries out there? A lot of contract brewing? I think people were a little turned off by the lack of authenticity and also the lack of quality coming from a lot of the breweries that were around in those days. They had some challenges producing consistent beer. I think that caused, somewhat, the lack of growth for a number of years in the industry.

Today, there's a huge excitement. There's an explosion of new breweries coming into the marketplace. A real niche has opened up for the rest of us who are producing unique, distinctive, and handcrafted beers. These are places where you can talk to the owner and get close to the brewers and the brewery. I think there's a difference in how the consumer perceives a brand like ours, or Sam [Calagione at Dogfish Head], or Vinnie at Russian River, or [Greg and Steve] at Stone. There is a personality behind them that people connect with. I think that's part of why we're seeing this renewed interest in what we're doing.

Nick: Do you think the term "Craft Beer Revolution" is appropriate?

Ken: Yeah, I guess it's a fun saying associated with the brewing industry. I think the consumer has become a lot more aware of beer and beer styles. A lot of what's driving the brewers is coming from the consumers. The brewers are driving a lot of the innovation and pushing the boundaries with hoppier and hoppier beers, and sours, and brett beers, but all those things wouldn't be possible if there wasn't a consumer acceptance.

Nick: Tell me a little bit about the North Carolina facility. What are some of the challenges?

Ken: I started thinking about a second site years ago. We've agonized and struggled over the concept of having a brewery that I can't touch and feel everyday. I'm very much a hands-on person. The thought of having a plant far away that I couldn't just walk in at any hour and see what's going on—It was a challenge for me to deal with. My son is moving back to North Carolina and I'll be back there probably every other week for a number of years spending several days a week.

Our Eastern growth has become a more significant part of our operation, and shipping beer from Chico, California, and getting it in good shape to the consumer has been vital and very important for us.

Having a second site closer to our consumers made sense. We looked at a lot of areas, hundreds of cities. We studied geography and shipping and growth patterns. We did a lot of analysis and due diligence on where a good location would be and then we narrowed it down to a handful of cities. I spent time in all of them, made several trips to a bunch of them. We fell in love with the Mills River community, and we like mountains. So having a great outdoors area was important, but equally important was having a supportive community. We found that in North Carolina.

Nick: Environmental sustainability is incredibly important for you as a company. Why have you made that such a priority?

Ken: Going back to when I started 30 years ago, we had so little money, and being frugal with resources was really what we had to do. With the original brewery nothing was brand new. Everything was used or was re-purposed from something else. We realized we were a big consumer of water and energy. It was very important that we figure out how to get by with the least amount of that—and that we consider the cost from an environmental stewardship standpoint.

As we grew in Chico at this new facility, we put a lot of those things in place. As we had more resources, we started to look at even more environmentally conscious solutions and that's

when we added solar panels. We have more than 10,000 solar panels on the facility now. We have a mega-watt of fuel cell power, which I put in there about nine years ago. We were fairly early adopters of some of the green technologies. We're trying to bring the brewing process as full circle as possible.

Nick: You've been doing this now for more than 30 years. Take it down to a base level for me; What is this all about for you?

Ken: As I alluded to earlier, there's a science aspect of brewing, which is how beers are made. There's a lot of science behind it. I've been fascinated with science since I was a little kid. I think that intrigues me. There's an engineering aspect of it—I've studied engineering and that's also sort of a passion of mine. I like the nitty-gritty and nuts-and-bolts of being involved in the technology and engineering side of brewing. I still do a lot of the design and get involved in a lot of process stuff.

Then there's the art of taking that science and that engineering and working with biological processes of fermentation and enzymes and trying to draw all of those things into producing a great tasting beer. The whole package is a fun challenge—creating a product that you can enjoy consuming, one that gives you a lot of pleasure and satisfaction. It's an intriguing business to be in—it offers a lot of challenges and a lot of satisfaction when you master it.

> **"What happened in the U.S., in beer, in brewing over the last 30 years is nothing short of amazing."**

Nick: Is there anything you've never been asked in an interview that you've always wanted to say?

Ken: What happened in the U.S., in beer, in brewing, over the last 30 years is nothing short of amazing. When I started, there were less than 40 brewing companies operating in the U.S. Most of those are now gone. What happened in America with our craft brewing revolution has really spread to the rest of the world. It's had a big influence on what's happening with beer in countries like Germany, which has a great brewing tradition.

I was in Germany recently, where I visited a small brewer who is brewing IPAs and doing things that would be unheard of by a German brewer not long ago.

We've opened up their eyes to the fact that beer can be a lot more, and a lot more exciting than the direction it had been heading. The German beer industry was heading the same way as the British brewing industry. They were being lost, and now I think we've opened the eyes of the rest of the world to what beer can be. They're looking at what happened in America saying, "Wow, maybe my industry could be that healthy and robust again."

Douglas Constantiner and Travis Smith
Societe Brewing Company

Douglas Constantiner and Travis Smith are the co-founders, co-owners, and brewers at Societe Brewing Company in San Diego.

Nick: Okay, Doug, let's start with you. What was your earliest influence in craft beer and how did that lead to where you are right now?

Doug: Okay, so first craft beer experience: I was pretty young. I remember it was Rogue Chocolate Stout, actually from Japan. My aunt is Japanese so she brought some back and I was lucky enough to taste it. I've always loved chocolate and the fact that beer could taste like chocolate, it absolutely blew my mind. After that, my mom was nice enough to go out and start buying some beers—she let me take little sips of them, so I explored that way. I started home brewing in college; that's what really took me from just drinking the beer to saying I want to do everything I possibly can with beer, including making it.

My mom bought me a kit, I started making it, I fell in love with the brewing side of it. I brewed throughout college, left college, and moved to New York to do investment banking with the hopes of one day starting my own brewery. It was going to be later in retirement, but I got too antsy. Less than two years out of college, I thought, "Screw this. I'm going to move to San Diego." So I saved up some money, moved out here, and the plan was to become a professional brewer.

I took jobs at a bunch of places just part time, whatever I could do. Bottling line, assistant brewer internship, bottle shops, just anything to get myself in the industry. I ended up landing a job at The Bruery; it was part time keg washing. That's where I ran into Travis. I worked my way into fulltime cellerman and then eventually brewer. At that point, Travis had left and it was a couple of months afterward that we said "let's do our own thing together." So that's when we started Societe.

Nick: Okay, Travis, you're up.

Travis: All right. I guess, starting in college, I started drinking lots of beer and it happened to be craft beer. Being in Sonoma County I had a plethora of good options. Russian River Brewing Company wasn't open—it was only at Korbel—but I could get it in bottles. Third Street Ale Works was my favorite place to go—that really got me into craft beer. Then my wife—who was not my wife at the time—got me a home brew kit, which I was thoroughly interested in. I started home brewing and got way interested in making beer.

I went to school for criminal justice, I worked for the Sonoma County Sheriff's Department, and had tons of opportunity to go into law enforcement, but instead, I took a job at Russian River Brewing Company. I started as Vinnie's first brewery hire. Throughout the 5 years there I ended up handling almost all of the operations in the brewpub as the production facility was being built. That's where I developed my true understanding of how to make beer, a combination of mentoring by Vinnie and Brian Hunt, who I was very close friends with. I became very opinionated about good beer and stuck in my ways.

Doug: When I left The Bruery, Tyler King jokingly said, "I'm happy you're leaving because now we can bring in a brewer who's not corrupted by Travis."

Nick: That's hilarious.

Travis: I left Russian River to take the job at The Bruery, then moved down to Southern California, brewed there for a year and a half. About six months into brewing there Doug came on and we instantly fell in love. It was just like . . .

Nick: Fireworks.

Travis: Fireworks, yeah. I left, he stayed on for another six months or so. Then we started Societe.

Doug: It was like, okay, failure is not an option, that's why we say, "starting Societe." It wasn't like we were working while trying to start something part-time. This was full on.

Nick: Travis, how did working with Vinnie Cilurzo and Brian Hunt affect you personally and professionally? And did they influence the beer that you're making now?

Travis: Brian Hunt is an eccentric individual, and so am I. He has views on beer that I absolutely agree with, and some that I don't, but his idea of what beer is supposed to be is something that really influenced me. I mean he's a tremendous mentor for me and really focused. Then, working with Vinnie for five years, I really learned what good beer was and how to make it.

Nick: How would you say that those experiences impact the beer that you make today?

Travis: The beer that we make today is a culmination of our life, it's not just what I learned at Russian River, it's not just the influence from Brian Hunt. It's all based on what we want to drink and what we've learned in the past. It all helps us to create the beer that we know what we want.

Nick: Are there any single pieces of advice that either of those guys gave to you that kind of resonated?

> ## "The beer that we make today is a culmination of our life."

Travis: There's a lot of advice that they gave me. Brian Hunt—when he talks about styles of beer, that's something I agree with. If you're going to call something a style, a certain style, it should be that. It doesn't all have to fit into a box—certain beer doesn't have to—but don't call it that style if it's not that style. You can still make it, and it can still be awesome. Death and Taxes, if you ask Brian, "What is it?" Is it a stout? A porter? He says no, it's just a dark lager and it doesn't have to fit into a box to make it a beer. But if you say it's in a box, it better fit in that box.

Nick: Do you have beers like that?

Travis: Well, The Harlot doesn't really fit into a box and so we don't try to force into a box. The Harlot, stylistically, it's a Belgian Extra, which comes from that little-known border between Belgium and the Czech Republic (a place called Germany). It's something we made up because it's a very clean lager-like beer, but it's brewed with Belgian yeast and it has more complex characteristics because of that. It doesn't really fit in a certain genre, truly.

Doug: We don't want people to put it on the menu as Belgian blonde or Belgian single, because we don't want someone to order it and say it doesn't taste like a Belgian blonde. So we're not going to put a name on it, just to make it easy.

Nick: What did you guys envision the mission of this company to be?

Doug: It really stems out of pure selfishness. "How can we make a living making beer that we want to drink?" and that's it. The beers that we want to drink are the beers that we're making, and it's one of the things where, if we like to drink it, hopefully you do, too. If you like to drink it then we could keep making it. The Harlot, The Apprentice, The Pupil: those are beers that we envision as ideal beers for us to drink. That's really it. It's pretty simple. We like beer that tastes like beer.

Travis: I fell in love with beer because it tastes like beer. I didn't fall in love with beer because it tastes like something else.

Doug: We're not into spicing beers or doing crazy flavors. We have nothing against it, but that's just not what we want to do. We're head-over-heels passionate about everything we do here. I'm sure we can make a good or acceptable pumpkin spice beer, but if I don't absolutely fucking love it, how can I make it to the best of my ability?

If I absolutely fucking love West Coast style IPAs, I can devote all of my mental energy and creativity to this beer. I'm not saying it's going to be the best one, but it's going to be exactly what I want. If I don't care that much for pumpkin beer I'm not going to put that much effort into it.

Nick: When you think about creating a new beer, are there overriding principles or philosophies that you incorporate into that process? Is the process more style based, or is it ingredient based?

Doug: Probably everything under the umbrella. New stuff comes up, our palates align probably about 95 to 98 percent of the way—so just enough to agree but also that small gap where we disagree enough to keep challenging ourselves or keep each other on our toes. For example, this new English IPA idea didn't cross my mind, but Travis proposed it and I wasn't sure. Then he showed me a recipe, gave me the breakdown of what he was thinking, and I said, "That sounds great, absolutely." It was the same thing with The Butcher, our Imperial Stout. It was not something Travis was ever into, or has ever really craved, but I pitched it to him. I explained that this is what I'm looking for, this is what I want to do, here's why I like this beer and we can hopefully get others convinced about why we're doing it.

Travis: We do focus on certain styles. We break our lineup into four different categories, generally, and we have what we call our "Out West" beers, and it's all San Diego IPA driven. We have multiple beers of varying strengths and different hops. Then we have our "Old World" beers, which are Belgian-inspired beers. We don't really call them Belgian ales because they have our twist to them, like The Harlot. Then we do a line of stouts and we have our sour barrel-aged funk program.

Nick: So, what would you say are the key elements in making great beer?

Travis: It is attention to detail. It's what goes into the beer, and that's not just the ingredients. It's the process, and the process is probably more important than the type of grain or the type of hops that are used. You can have a fantastic recipe, but you can screw it up in the process. Likewise, you can have a pretty shitty recipe and still make a decent beer out of it, if you do it right.

Nick: What's exciting to you guys right now?

Doug: We'll start bottling the sours. You'll see our "Old World" beers in bottles. We've said from the beginning that our IPAs will likely never be bottled. I don't want to say never, but we have zero plans or desire to bottle those.

Nick: Why don't you guys want to bottle your IPAs?

Travis: IPA really needs to be consumed fresh. Putting it in a package, like a bottle or a can, you're guaranteeing that someone out there is going to taste it well past its deserved shelf life.

Doug: Absolutely, I think it can be done. Obviously, Seirra Nevada does it with great success. Firestone does it, probably better than anybody else, in my opinion. We don't have the technology to do that. That's not what we want to focus on right now. You only have so much energy in this business and you've got to really budget where you're going to focus that. I've had bad IPAs—a bad bottle of all of my favorite IPAs. If I want Pliny the Elder, I go down the street to O'Brien's and get it. Same thing with Alpine.

Travis: As a beer consumer, I never buy bottled IPA because it always lets me down. I think Sculpin is a fantastic beer on draft, then you go have it in a bottle and it's like, "Well, why did I spend that much money for the bottle when I could go to the bar and get it fresh and tasty?" I don't want people to drink our beer from a bottle and think the same things.

Doug: The simple answer that I tell people is, "I don't buy bottled IPA. If I don't do that, why would I put my own product in a bottle?"

Nick: What is it about San Diego that you think makes it a great city for you guys?

Doug: I think we could have started in another city and done a total belly flop. The beer drinkers in San Diego are so primed and accustomed to the beers that we like to drink so, if we make them, it's going to fit in perfectly. It's going to align with a lot of people's palates here. It's really the consumers out there, like Travis said; they end up liking our beers. You see more of the real beer fans going for the IPAs, and we've got the foodies and industry chef types all going for the Belgians. It's really been them—they've given us a good name. We're terrible at branding and marketing ourselves. We have

no PR, we're good at one thing and that's . . . well, actually I shouldn't say we're good, but we focus on one thing and that's making beer.

Nick: What is it about beer that you love so much?

Travis: Beer is fucking awesome. Pretty plain and simple. Beer is fantastic, it's something to be passionate about. It is worthy of passion, worthy of my attention. It's a huge part of my life, it's a huge part of many of our lives and it brings a lot of joy to me here.

Doug: Beer is my number one love in life. I'd put it ahead of all other things, and I love my fiancé to death, that's different. I wake up in the morning and I think about beer, I go to bed and I think about beer. It's everything in the world to me. I'm not religious but I've had . . .

Travis: Religious experiences.

Doug: Religious experiences with beer. I mean I can probably name 90 or 95 percent of the beers I've ever had in my life and I have had a lot of different beers. I fucking love it.

Nick: What haven't we talked about that you want to mention?

> **"Beer is fucking awesome. Pretty plain and simple."**

Doug: I'll tell you what's worrying me right now is the snob level that I'm starting to see in beer. And that scares the shit out of me. That will destroy this community and this industry faster than we know. People get into beer because it's not intimidating and it's welcoming. Just like with comic books or heavy metal music, you instantly bond with somebody else over your love for it. The second someone starts pushing people away because they're not worthy, we're all screwed, we're all fucked, and what we have right now will be terminated.

Nick: Travis?

Travis: My focus is on making our beer . . . and I try not to think about much else.

Doug: Good answer.

Mitch Steele
Stone Brewing Co.

Mitch Steele is the brewmaster at Stone Brewing Co. in Escondido, California.

Nick: Can you tell me how you first got into beer and how you wound up where you are right now?

Mitch: I was a college student at Cal Davis. I was looking for a class to take and a counselor recommended that I take "Intro to Winemaking." The quote, I remember it to this day:

He said, "You cannot go to UC Davis and not take this class." I took the class and I just fell in love with the whole idea of making wine. As I started getting into it and started majoring in it, I found out about the brewing science program that was at Davis. I gravitated over to that, and so I had a fermentation science degree from Cal Davis with an emphasis on brewing science and also winemaking.

When I graduated from Davis, there weren't any jobs in the brewing industry. This was before craft brewing. Sierra Nevada was open, but that was about it. And Anchor. So I ended up getting a job in the wine business. I worked that for several years, living in Hollister, California.

When San Andreas Brewing Company was looking to open, I met Bill Miller. This was in '88 or '89, I believe. He had

At the same time, I was still keeping up with what was going on in craft. We had a real good Master Brewers Association in New England. In 2006, Stone put an ad for a head brewer out on the Brewers Association forum. I admit I was kind laughing about it with my wife. Then she kind of prodded me into sending a resume, because she knew things weren't going great at Anheuser-Busch. She said, "What's the worst that can happen? They can say no or they could say yes, or whatever."

When I came out here, I just fell in love with the company. I came out here to interview, and they had the distribution company here—selling 30 other breweries' beers. I really loved what they were doing to promote the craft brewery business. I thought, "Oh my God, these guys are all about this business and they're not just in it for themselves. They have vision."

Nick: Have your experiences brewing in other parts of the United States given you a unique perspective on California?

Mitch: Yeah, living in other parts of the country has influenced me. One very specific example is the Black IPA that we did for the 11th anniversary. That was inspired by a beer I had in Boston. I'd never had a Black IPA before. I think it was still kind of a fledgling style. I'd never seen one, I'd never heard of one. I had one at the Beer Advocate Extreme Beer Fest. It was brewed by Shaun Hill. It turns out, as I've researched the style, the first ones were brewed in Vermont. It was Greg Noonan's Vermont Pub and Brewery in the late 80's or early 90's that brewed one. Shaun was inspired by that, and I was inspired by Shaun's beer. I kind of pushed for it to be our 11th Anniversary Ale, which became Sublimely Self-Righteous Ale. I West-Coasted it up a bit. I'm a West Coast guy. I've got a pretty strong love for the West Coast hop profile and approach to brewing IPAs and things.

Back to living in different parts of the country. . . . Living in Colorado in the early 90's didn't suck. That was pretty cool. They approach brewing a little bit differently. They tend to be a little bit more malt-centric, as opposed to the West Coast thing. New England brewers tend to be a little bit more traditional, I think. I was excited by a lot of the beers in New England. There were some really good IPAs being brewed there.

> **"I thought, 'Oh my God, these guys are all about this business and they're not just in it for themselves. They have vision."**

a 14-barrel brew house and he wanted to brew English-style ales, particularly low-alcohol ales. He hired me as a part-time brewer. I was still working at the winery, but I was able to come in and brew on the weekends. I did that for four years, until I decided to try to get a full time job brewing. I ended up getting hired by Anheuser-Busch in Colorado. I was the shift supervisor at Anheuser-Busch for three years, basically running the day-to-day operations in the brewhouse, fermenting cellar, and the finishing cellar—the filter cellar there.

After three years, I got promoted to the new products group at Anheuser-Busch in St. Louis. I did new products for AB until about '98, '99. I worked in the St. Louis brewery until I got transferred to Merrimack, New Hampshire in 1999. I worked there until 2006 as an assistant brewmaster.

Nick: How do you go about creating a new beer or expanding on a beer that's already in your lineup? Do you have specific philosophies or guidelines?

Mitch: The approach can be either way. We could have an end product in mind or goal in mind, or we could just say, "Let see what would happen if we do this." There are several instances of each. Collaboration brews—we've never pilot-brewed a collaboration brew. We always just put together a recipe and brew it, and whatever we get is what we get. With beers like the Vertical Epics and the Anniversary Beers, we have more of an end goal in mind. We actually try to pilot brew some of it at, just to make sure that the recipe is sound. It may not replicate what we get on the big system, but it's close.

> **"Greg and Steve instill in the whole team . . . , "It's got to be great, it's got to be amazing. Don't half-ass it."**

Sometimes you just come across a new ingredient and say, "You know what? I'd just like to brew with this, and brew something that really highlights this new hop," new malt, new yeast strain, or something like that. Let's brew a beer that's going to allow this new ingredient to really come through and showcase it." The one thing that Greg and Steve instill in the whole team is, "It's got to be great, it's got to be amazing. Don't half-ass it." We always have that in the back of our mind. They encourage us to take risks, and sometimes the risks don't pan out exactly the way we want to. You learn something from that and move on.

Nick: Do you find that this is more of a creative process for you or a scientific process?

Mitch: Recipe formulation for me is all about creativity. It's not scientific. I approach it more from an art and creativity standpoint. I tend not to worry about what the color of the beer's going to be, for example. If we want to—if we're going to brew an amber beer, we just put together some malts and say, "This is going to work. This is going to have a nice flavor profile." We're not trying to actually hit a certain color target. We have general guidelines for what we want to try and do, but we're not formulating the recipes to hit the color, IBU targets, or even alcohol targets. We want to be within a certain range, but we get what we get. That's been a lot of fun.

Now that we've got our core brands dialed in, we have started applying science to them. If we have changes in crop years and hops and things like that, that's where the science comes in. We try to keep the creative process really creative, allowing for some variations from what we originally set out to do.

Nick: How is working at Stone different from working at AB?

Mitch: At AB we had to have . . . (laughter) My God, is it different. Number one, I think at AB it was very marketing driven. Anytime a new beer was going to be released, the marketing department had to suggest it, not the brewers. That was the biggest difference. Then, of course, we had to hit the color targets. If it was one or two degrees off the color target, we had to make some sort of adjustment. We had to fix it. Bit-

terness, alcohol, all the same. Alcohol was easy at AB, because they'd brew everything at high gravity and then added water to hit the alcohol targets. It was a little bit easier to deal with. Here, we're relying on our brewing skill to hit the alcohol target, and making sure that our brewhouse processes are right in line and everything else. It's actually more difficult.

Nick: The marketers came to you and said, "This is what the poster is selling—guys from New York City. . . ."

Mitch: Yeah, the focus groups. They might have an area where a certain beer was doing really well and we needed to brew something to compete with this particular beer. "You can't have your own beer. It's just got to be like this one." That part of it always kind of sucked, to be honest. Instead of being able just to create something that was good on its own merits, it always had to be what they call a "competitive brand" or a "reactionary brand." We had to brew a beer that was a pale ale to compete with Sierra Nevada, instead of just creating our own pale ale, which we all wanted to do.

Nick: You wrote a book on IPAs. Why is that style particularly important to you?

Mitch: It's a great honor actually, to have been able to put this book together on IPAs because it's been my favorite style ever since I tasted one.

Nick: What's the best thing you learned from working on the project?

Mitch: The biggest thing that I learned from it was that in the 1800s, Burton-on-Trent IPA was aged for a long period in barrels before it ever went over to India. It first went through an extensive barrel aging process, then it went through a secondary fermentation in the barrel, and finally it was put on a boat to India. It was not a fresh IPA; it was a 7 percent 17 Plato type of beer. It wasn't much different from what people are brewing today. The ingredients were different. Specialty malts weren't around, for example. They used the widest, lightest color malt they possibly could. They wanted the beer to be very pale in color. Of course, the big thing is that most beer historians today don't feel like IPA was invented by anybody. It was just something that kind of happened, as part of a standard pale ale that was being shipped to India that tended to do well.

Nick: Let's talk a little bit about Stone's marketing approach. The company's tactic—its marketing tactic at least—is kind of like, "We're arrogant bastards. We're going to make some really kick-your-ass beer, and you're going to love it." How has that image affected your beers? Is that the mantra that you guys go off of?

Mitch: Yeah, I think with Arrogant Bastard Ale, it definitely fits. The idea being to brew this beer that was just so aggressive and that people weren't used to. It was about having something with flavor that people were going to be taken aback by it. Of course, the name fits the beer. Greg likes to say that the beer named itself. That's great. People that know us know we're not really arrogant. I think as a rule, Greg and Steve and I, and the brewing team, we like a lot of flavor in our beer. It doesn't necessarily have to be aggressive to the point that people are going to be put off by it, but we want a beer that's got a lot of flavor. If it's got a certain ingredient in there, we want people to be able to taste that ingredient.

Sometimes subtlety works in certain beers. We've used subtlety before, but, in general, we tend to approach it like, "Hey, if it's got Calypso hops in it, you're going to be able to taste the Calypso hops." That's been liberating for me. I've totally embraced it, because that's the way I brew at home.

Nick: Stone is the tenth largest craft brewery in the U.S. and is still growing. What do you attribute the success to?

Mitch: Our success, I think it's a lot of things. I think we have good beers. Our regional reps are really good. They're really into beer. They're not just sales people, they're beer people. They're craft beer people. They know it. They live it. They can talk about the beers intelligently, and they do a great job. I think that's a big part.

We also try to keep our beers fresh, and I'm not talking fresh beers, as in young beer. We try to keep what we do new, kind of inventive, and try and be fresh with new ideas.

I think our core brands are solid. We're not afraid to go back to the drawing board if we think it needs to happen. I think just the fact that we promote the industry and we're very active . . . you can't underestimate the social media

aspect of it. Our website is probably one of the most visited brewery websites out there. Greg's on Twitter, we've got Facebook pages, and—even though we don't advertise, we market. We've got a very strong identity and we stick to that in everything that we do. Who we are, our philosophy, are very sharply defined. We don't veer from that. I think that's helped us.

Nick: What is it that gets you up and out of bed every morning?

Mitch: For me it's a couple of things. That's a hard question to answer, just because I like so much about this business. I think doing something new is fun. Tasting a beer that we've made, when it delivers is just like, "Yes." It just makes your day. The Ruination 10th anniversary IPA was like that. When we tasted that one, we were just like, "Yes, yes! We nailed this!" That's a lot of fun.

We've got such a great team here. I just love working with our brewing team. We've got a very young team and a very energetic, creative group of people. I just love to see them do things and try different things. Knowing how I started out and how important that creativity part is, it's nice to be able to give them those opportunities to do that and see the pride they take in the beer.

It's never going to be dull here. That keeps me going as well, because I'm challenged as a brewer. For me, that's a big thing. I want to be challenged. I want to be learning new things. I want to be able to try different things and learn something about ingredients or fermentation techniques or aging techniques. I'm just soaking it all up and trying different things, and that's awesome.

> **"It's never going to be dull here. That keeps me going as well, because I'm challenged as a brewer."**

Victor Novak
TAPS Fish House & Brewery

Victor Novak is the brewmaster at TAPS Fish House & Brewery in Brea, California.

Nick: What's your first memory of being interested in craft beer? And how did that lead you to where you are today?

Victor: So, all of us have that epiphany moment. Mine was back after I graduated from UC Berkeley in late 1988. Back then we were drinking wine coolers and other crap since there wasn't much awareness of craft beer yet. I brought this gal home that I was casually dating and we opened up the fridge. She says, "Oh, your roommate drinks good beer." I said, "What do you mean good beer?" I looked down and saw Sierra Nevada's beautiful hop green label, which still makes me salivate. I love that beer. So, we cracked one open, of course. I essentially stole one of my roommate's beers and that was the moment. Had it been an Imperial Russian Stout or big, hoppy IPA back then, I'm not sure I would have been so blown away. It was the balance of that beer. It's still one of the only bottled beers I prefer over the draft version.

Anyway, we dated awhile and she ended up getting into grad school at U Penn. We moved to Pennsylvania, where we couldn't get Sierra Nevada Pale Ale, and that Christmas she got me a home brew kit so we could clone it. That was our sole goal at the time. I had no intention of turning that hobby into a career until I read Michael Jackson's *World Guide To Beer;* then I was hooked.

I had studied Cultural-Political Geography at Cal, primarily dealing with human rights, land and water rights issues, writing papers on Israel–Palestine, the Yanomami in Brazil, Native Americans issues here in the U.S., etc. So, when I read the *World Guide To Beer,* it encompassed so much of what I had studied at Cal—history, tradition, culture, geography, etc. That's because every beer has a story behind it and a sense of place.

So six months later, in June of '93, I applied for a job at Dock Street Brewery and Restaurant in Philadelphia. I got a job waiting tables with the intention of becoming a brewer and within a year and a half I worked my way up to assistant brewer. I trained under an English brewmaster and learned to brew the classic styles of England, Germany, and Belgium on a little 8-barrel JV Northwest system with open fermenters. I also traveled to England, Germany, Ireland, Scotland, Belgium, and the Czech Republic to "research" and taste the classic styles at the source. Unfortunately, a change to Pennsylvania's liquor laws meant that my position was going to become part-time so, with no job or prospects in Pennsylvania, I decided to move back home to California. (I'd split up with my girlfriend at the time.)

I soon ended up at a place called Doc's Brewpub in Simi Valley, owned by a couple of doctors. Unfortunately, they had very little restaurant experience and it was only open from May to October of '97. Then, in December of '97 I went and met Joe Manzella, the owner of TAPS Fish House & Brewery,

on a recommendation. We met over a beer at BJ's in Brea and basically agreed that I was going to be his brewer starting around April of 1998. We ended up not opening until September, 20, 1999, but he's been true to his word—that I could brew whatever I wanted as long as it sells. Knock on wood, everything's worked out great for fifteen years.

Nick: I want to talk a little bit about your Philadelphia experience. How did working in beer on the East Coast influence the beer that you're making now?

Victor: There used to be much more of a distinct difference between West Coast and East Coast beer. Overall, what I've found is that, hop-wise, here on the West Coast it was more about a punch in the mouth. Back East there was more malt character to balance out the hops. Initially, when I was brewing here in California, I brewed my IPA with more malt character complemented with some hop presence. I was using Fuggles, East Kent Goldings, Styrian Goldings, among others. People would say, "It's OK, but where are the hops?" Fortunately, I was roomed with Matt Brynildson while judging at the Great American Beer Festival one year in the mid 2000s and he turned me on to Hop Union's Hop School. So I went the following fall, learned more about the West Coast hop varieties, and made my hoppy beers more in line with West Coast tastes.

> **"There used to be much more of a distinct difference between West Coast and East Coast beer."**

I still think here at TAPS we're a little bit more of an East Coast brewery, in that we do more lagers and traditional European styles on a regular basis. You rarely see Kolsch, Alt, Hefeweizen, Doppelbock and Schwarzbier; so many German styles are on at the brewery here. They are not boring styles at all. To me there's a transparency that helps demonstrate the brewer's skill. Any off-flavor—fermentation issues, lack of balance in hopping, those will show up. So when you nail those styles, it's very satisfying.

Nick: When you go about creating a new beer or interpreting, do you have specific principles or philosophies that you always use?

Victor: It would depend on the style, like when we did Schwarzbier. We always alternated Porter, Oatmeal Stout, and Imperial Russian Stout, but I didn't do a Schwarzbier here for ten years because I was worried it wouldn't move well. We only had eight beers on tap initially, but now we have twelve so I have more room to play.

To do a Schwarzbier, a classic style like that I had brewed in Philadelphia, I had to go back to my recipes that I still have from Dock Street, and use that as a foundation.

Obviously, like with any chef, if you come from a great restaurant, that's your foundation. You do what you know.

Then of course, you're going to do your interpretation of it. So I remembered what I did at Dock Street, Schwarzbier-wise, and then brewed my interpretation of it. Fortunately, it worked out well and we've won a Gold Medal at the Great American Beer Festival and a Silver Medal at the World Beer Cup.

You don't want to brew strictly for a competition. It's gratifying when you win a medal, but you really want to stick with your intuition and your instincts and say, "OK, this is what I feel the style is." We've made our name in many ways brewing true to style.

Nick: What's the balance between science, technique, and creativity for you?

Victor: For me, in many ways, it would be the perfect marriage of all three. You really need to understand your ingredients, which helps you be creative with the recipe.

> **"Understand your ingredients, which helps you be creative with the recipe."**

Having gone to UC Berkeley and having dined at Chez Panisse, I realized how important the ingredients are. The quality of the ingredients is huge. We use Weyermann Pilsner for our base malt for Cream Ale and all of our German styles. Then we use Crisp and Simpsons malts for the British stuff because the malt character is absolutely essential.

You want to use beautifully fresh hops; to know when you're going to add them to get the aroma, flavor, and balancing bitterness you're looking for in your pale ales and IPAs.

Then for, say, a Helles, you use German Perle and some German Hersbrucker to get that German hop character.

Know your yeast strains. We use about twelve different yeast strains because if you're making fifty different beers and you only use two or three, a lot of the beers start tasting the same. So, by using twelve different yeast strains, you get the yeast character that's very specific for that style.

Then, of course, there is the science in terms of what mash temp we're going to hit, achieving the right pH with certain mineral salts, knowing how fermentation temperature will affect the yeast character, etc. And then you have to understand your processes and techniques in the brew house, fermentation, dry hopping, when to dump yeast, venting off excess CO_2, conditioning, fining, filtering, and carbonating, etc. All of these factors affect how the final product is going to taste.

Nick: What's your take on the current explosion in craft beer in America?

Victor: It's like the mid-90's. A lull and then a second kind of wave. I think the trend is fantastic. Beer is my passion. I've been doing this for almost twenty years so it's great. It comes down to education. You look at coffee back in the 80's. You had Peet's around. You had Starbucks. But my parents weren't drinking it, you know. Then the 90's and 2000s hit. There was a Starbucks on every corner and Peet's. Then you get places like Portola Coffee Lab, Blue Bottle, Intelligentsia, etc. So now you've got your craft or artisan roasters that are focusing more on the kinds of beans and the right roast level to bring out certain characteristics.

Beer is the same way. We've got a little more of a head start. I mean, thirty years at Sierra Nevada and Sam Adams for example. I was around in the early to mid-90's with the first explosion. Sort of like with coffee, a lot of people got into it, I think, for the money rather than the craft. They died off.

Now it's up again. I just think that people are becoming more educated on the flavors. I mean, it could be partly due

to marketing. It might also be partly due to the big boys getting in. With Blue Moon, Shock Top, and others.

Belgian Whites are massively up, and they are perfectly fine. Are they my favorite Whites? No. But do I respect them? Sure. Their brewers are phenomenal. Their knowledge and consistency is amazing. I always tip my hat to the big boys. When you're making billions of dollars off Bud Light, what are you going to do? Why would you not make it? I would. I would make other things as well, which they're doing with their Michelob line.

> **"It's about creating something that you love, where you look out and people are drinking and they're stoked on it."**

What I find is, for me and a lot of people we know, we drink really well but we drink less. The idea, of course, is to drink great beer and to enjoy your beer, preferably with food. We do beer pairings as well. The idea is to not to get hammered. If you want to get hammered, drink tequila or vodka.

And it's not only on the coasts now. You can go to Des Moines. You can go down to Savannah, GA, where I was last week, and have a great craft beer. So it's not only that there's more awareness, there's just more of them. The south used to be a wasteland for craft beer. Now in North Carolina, I think there are more than thirty breweries, which seemed crazy twenty years ago.

Nick: You've been doing this for twenty years. What is it that keeps you getting up every day and coming in here? What keeps you excited about beer?

Victor: You've said it. It's excitement. Everyday, I mean, I hate to speak in clichés, but they are there. I turned basically a hobby-passion into a career. So when I go to work, it literally isn't like going to work. I mean, yeah, I've got some admin stuff to do and the paperwork is kind of boring. I need to balance that with brewing today. If I'm not in the brew house, I'm not happy. It is that physical labor, the creativity, the creation that keeps most brewers going. If I get out of the brew house too long, and I'm wearing a suit, then I lose the reason why I got into the industry in the first place.

When you're brewing, it's back to those early days of home brewing and your first brewing gig. Honestly, it's about making people happy. It's about creating something that you love, where you look out and people are drinking and they're stoked on it. That's the gratification and the reason to get up. It really is.

Nick: What's the one thing you've never been asked in an interview that you've always wanted to say?

Victor: The perception of wine versus beer will always be extremely high for wine and very different for beer. There are a lot of disparities there. Beer has come up in prestige. Here, we had Prohibition. Our beers got lighter and lighter and there's a good reason why Bud, Coors, and Miller are the way they are. You get consistency, but not as much flavor. When you go to Europe, the reverence for beer, say in Belgium, is unbelievable. I mean; just using the correct glass. Rinsing the glass. The pour. Everything, down to the bottle shape, the glass shape.

We're getting there more with American craft beer today. For me, to see what craft beer has become is honestly very gratifying and I want to keep it there. I don't want to knock it back down to it's pre-Anchor, pre-Sierra Nevada days. I don't think we should go back there. I think it's funny. There's always a great sense of humor with the brewing industry and I love that. That's the thing, I think, that differentiates it from the wine industry. We don't take ourselves as seriously. It's not as pretentious. I love that about it.

Alexandra Nowell
Three Weavers Brewing Company

Alexandra Nowell is the brewmaster at Three Weavers Brewing Company in Inglewood, California.

Nick: Do you remember the first time you enjoyed craft beer? How did that moment bring you to where you are today?

Alexandra: It was Sierra Nevada Pale Ale. I was in college. I lived in Florida; that's where I'm from. It was kind of a beer desert, as far as craft beer was concerned. Lots of big macro lagers everywhere. I had just actually started taking a brewing science class at my school and I think it was the course that exposed me to all of the different styles, options, and small breweries that were out there. I started ordering pale ales and they were so good and complex. At that time, I thought, "What is this in my mouth? This is really interesting," because it was pretty much my first exposure to the hop.

I really enjoyed the brewing science class. When I was done, I was offered an internship at Sierra Nevada Brewing Company, which was very cool to me because I was coveting their pale ale. It was right around when Torpedo had come out and I just thought, "This is the coolest thing ever. I get to go and walk through the hallways of Sierra Nevada and belong there." So I moved to Chico and I was a training development intern there. I wrote a training course for brewery staff on Sierra Nevada's traditional methods from grain to glass. I was there for 6 months.

I met Denise Jones, formerly of Moylan's, at an event at Beer Revolution in Oakland. [Denise and I] were talking for a while. She tried my home brew. She was really nice about it. She gave me some constructive criticism and, at the end of the conversation, I said, "So when are you going to give me a job?" She said, "How about you give me a call in two weeks?" So I followed up and moved to Berkeley about a month after that. I started in the cellar in packaging at Moylan's. That's where I cut my teeth on production work. It was a really small, little brewery with a lot of staff. They turn a lot of beer out of a very small place.

It was a good learning experience, but didn't quite have the upward mobility that I was looking for in a job, so I started reaching out to my friends locally. I had built up a decent-sized network in the Bay Area because there are so many breweries there. I was sitting at the bar at Triple Rock one night with Rodger Davis and I said, "Hey man, I'm not really feeling Moylan's any more. Do you think you can maybe help me out with a job somewhere?" He thought Drake's might be hiring, and at that moment the operations manager from Drake's walks in, Dave Rowe. He's says, "Rodger, could you do me a favor? I need four people to interview for this brewery position at Drake's." Rodger just points at me. He's says, "Well, you could start with her." I interviewed, got the job, and spent three years at Drake's. I started out as a brewer. There were only four of us there. We were doing maybe 4,000 barrels a year. By the time I left as lead brewer we broke 20,000 barrels brewed.

I saw Drake's through a huge amount of growth and it gave me my first chance to take a crack at recipe formulation on a larger scale. I took over a lot of the creative side of recipe formulation there, and I ran the barrel-aging program. After some time I reached out to Ting Su at Eagle Rock and asked if they were hiring, because I'm a huge fan of their beers.

She said, "No, they're not hiring, but I know this brewpub in North East L.A. County called Kinetic. They're looking for a new head brewer." I interviewed and was only there for 8 months, but during my time there I was able to revamp all of their recipes, bring them into a more commercially competitive position. Their beers weren't quite competitive enough to be in the L.A. market, especially when you're up against San Diego IPAs. I reformulated a lot of their stuff, and won a couple of medals at the Great American Beer Festival with them, but I needed growth in a position. That's what was so appealing about Drake's to me and that's why I left Moylan's. I started itching to do something more and it was around that time that I was introduced to Lynne Weaver. She had this idea of opening a production brewery on the West Side of L.A. I thought, "Sounds kind of cool. Let's talk."

We got along really, really well, and we found that a lot of our ideas were directly parallel to each other. We saw eye to eye on so many different things that it seemed it would be a really easy kind of partnership to work through.

Nick: So, what is the concept behind Three Weavers? And what's the approach to the beers you make?

Alexandra: We don't go with any sort of overarching theme or style. We just want to be associated with quality. Certain breweries, you know—when you order a Firestone Walker beer—are pretty much always going to be really good. You don't have to worry about it. I don't want people to feel like they're taking a chance when they order a Three Weavers beer. They know it's going to deliver every time. That's just kind of the brewer that I am. I'm a purist at heart when it comes to brewing. I like my beer to taste like beer. That's not to say we won't play around with different kinds of agriculturally-available products because California is so rich in agriculture, but I just want our beers to be solid, maybe not exactly to style, but clean, flawless, beers you're going to want to drink more than one of.

The idea behind Three Weavers itself is very much Lynne's child because she had looked at the current brewing industry. There are a lot of great breweries out there, but L.A. was lacking in what she saw as an overall package of a brewery. She wants to base this a lot on the community. That's where we saw eye to eye: on having a purpose behind our brewery. Other than creating really high quality beer, we also wanted to build a community around the brewery itself, so we're doing a lot of public outreach, non-profit work, and are bringing artists into our tasting room. We want to give other people exposure because beer is a really awesome social medium. It brings people together.

Nick: What do you think you have brought to Three Weavers from your varied experiences at all the other breweries?

Alexandra: I think that I'm still developing into who I am as a brewer, even after five years in this industry, because every job offers you something different. There's a different dynamic with your employer, with your employees, with the beers that you're making, with the people that are drinking your beers. Kinetic was a really awesome learning experience because it allowed me total creative freedom to do whatever I wanted. It was such a small system, and the beer was gone really fast. If it doesn't work, it doesn't work. If it does, you brew it again or you make it better.

Nick: That leads right to my next question: What's your approach to creating beers? Do you tend to be more style driven or ingredients driven?

Alexandra: It's not the same all the time. If there's an ingredient out there that really intrigues me, that I want to work with, I'll base a recipe on that ingredient. Like the Mosaic hop. I have used Mosaic in a mild and it was very subtle. We wanted to draw out the blueberry notes of this hop and piece it together with this really nice kind of crisp toasted English malt character found in Golden Naked Oats that I really love. Or, if I want to emphasize Golden Naked Oats in a beer, I'll start with that and then determine the best application for it. Now, I'll pack a beer with three times as much Mosaic just to draw that really super dank tropical hoppy note out of it, but it's just being able to discover the breadth of an ingredient and how many different uses you can have. There are so many ingredients available to us as brewers. It can be overwhelming. So many hops, so many malts, and the combinations of them are virtually endless.

Sometimes, though, it may be like a market demand. If I'm asked to brew an IPA, I'll ask, "What kind of IPA do you want? Do you want old school North West resonance? Do you want these new straight 2-row base mango hop bombs?" Sometimes, you're told what to brew. With Three Weavers, I will have a lot more freedom to do that, but then also we have to satisfy a market.

Nick: Can you talk a little bit about the role of women in the beer industry? What are your thoughts and observations?

Alexandra: Well, we are seeing an increase in diversity. Stone has three or four female brewers. Devon Randall is the brew-

> **"Other than creating really high quality beer, we also wanted to build a community around the brewery itself."**

master at Solana Beach. There's several. Kim Lutz at Saint Archer. It's a hard job. More and more women are being exposed to the production side of things. I think it's taking time because there has been this—I don't know how to put it in a positive way—like a "good old boy" mentality in Northern California. But that's been changing.

Brewers are getting younger and younger, and so are brewery owners. I think they're a little more open to bringing people in who may not physically look like they can get the job done, but they absolutely can. If you go into places like Colorado, there are a lot of female brewers in Colorado now. I was surprised. Every time I go to a Pink Boots national meeting, like the GABF meeting in Colorado, they're all there.

I don't have an issue any more with my gender and my profession. At first, I did. It was hard to gain people's respect because they just look at you as a "girl," which is unfortunate, but I think now it's more of a novelty thing. People think it's cool because craft beer has become so mainstream in the U.S. You look at a Sam Adams commercial or something and everyone has got big beards. And then you look at me and I don't have a big beard, but I am very much a brewer. I think we're just debunking the myth that all brewers are big, burly, bearded men. I don't think it's really that hard for us any more.

Nick: So have you seen more opportunities for women opening up?

Alexandra: Absolutely. There have been several women who have blazed the trail for women in the brewing industry. It's just become more normal. We're not as much of a —I like to say "unicorn," like kind of the rare, special object in an industry. We're no longer the unicorns of the brewing industry. I'd like to see more ethnic diversity now. Get off the topic of gender diversity.

I really applaud Drake's because they didn't care. John Martin always hired women. Like Teri Fahrendorf, one of the first female brewmasters in the United States. One of her first breweries was Triple Rock in Berkeley and John Martin didn't even bat an eyelash at hiring her. No problem. He's always been that way and now there are several women on the production floor at Drake's.

Nick: What's your take on the L.A. beer scene? Is it going to become like the Bay Area or San Diego, do you think?

Alexandra: I'm new to L.A., but I think it's similar to what happened in Florida. In Miami, where I'm from, things just hit there later. Trends may be created in L.A., but perhaps the city is more resistant to letting outside trends in. It's just been very much a macro lager town and it's taken a little while to break through that.

It's such a spread-out town, too. It's hard to get around. You have to drive everywhere. It's maybe not the friendliest for the alcohol beverage industry.

As far as beer trends go, L.A. is a little bit behind the curve, too. They're really getting into these weird over-spiced, complicated, complexly-flavored beers where other places are like, "Yeah, we did that five years ago. Let's move onto session beers and things that are clean and well made."

It's exciting though—just to be positive about the L.A. craft beer scene. It's super exciting. It's a massive market of people. So many people are now thirsting for more craft beer, so essentially we can probably do whatever we want.

66We're no longer the unicorns of the brewing industry.99

Nick: So, what are your soapbox issues? When people ask you about beer, your job, and the industry, what do you like to talk about?

Alexandra: There's one thing that I pride myself on in my craft: it's maintaining a connection with the people who produce the ingredients. It's important. I visit hop farms every year. I see the hops growing. I hand select my hops. I get to know the growers, the farmers. I try to keep my thumb on the pulse of the agricultural elements that are responsible for the beer I make. Overall, I think that makes you more thoughtful in what you do and how you approach these ingredients. It helps you respect the ingredients.

You can look at someone like Brian Hunt. He gave me some really awesome advice a few years ago. I said, "I'm making this cask beer and I want to make it like this imperial stout and I want to put like vanilla beans and cardamon and all this stuff." He said, "Choose one of them. One thing, so you can actually pick it out and evaluate this flavor and this beer. Be simple about it. Respect the ingredients."

Nick: On the most basic emotional level, what is it about beer that speaks to you?

Alexandra: The community. The people. Absolutely. The family that revolves around the craft beer industry. Just the brewing industry, in general, are the best people I've ever known. No matter what city I live in, I know that there's always a community there for me. Moving to L.A. was easy because there were brewers here too, and they just welcome you in. We're all crazy enough to do this for a living, so we have at least that in common.

Jeff Kimpe
Triple Rock Brewery

Jeff Kimpe is the head brewer at Triple Rock Brewery in Berkeley, California.

Nick: What's your first memory of enjoying craft beer, and how did that lead you to where you are right now?

Jeff: The first time, I was underaged, but I have a proud Belgian heritage. When I was plumbing with my uncle and cousin, who are also very proud of their heritage, we would always have Budweisers and stuff. But then, when we would get paid, my uncle would go and get a 4-pack of Duvel. I remember him pulling out these wine glasses and pouring it into the wine glasses. There was all this preparation, with him explaining to me, "When times are good, this is what we'll drink. This beer should be treated differently." That was my first time thinking beer was not just beer.

I remember drinking Saison Dupont, all the Charles Finkel, Merchant du Vin, those guys, anything they were importing. Then it just evolved into home brewing. I have to credit Michael Jackson's books. I was a big fan. He made reading about beer really interesting. I loved the photos—the old photos of the history of it. I just kept home brewing like crazy. That started around 1994. Then I moved to L.A. with a girlfriend. Just being a blue-collar Midwestern kid from Detroit, living in L.A., it was really hard to meet people. I had no social circle. I just had a bunch of books, beer books, and more books. I had this job delivering high-end wines, like allocated wines. I'd go around to all these stores and find even more beers to taste and more beers to brew.

That's when the hobby really took off. Like I said—lack of social circle, just really seeing lots of bands. But when I wasn't doing that, I was brewing. After seven years of living there and home brewing like crazy, I looked into going to school at Davis and Siebel. I went and talked to—I'm sure some of these guys don't even remember—Vinnie [Cilurzo], when his brewery was at Korbel. I was a total beer nerd. I took my beers with me. I said, "What do you think?" And, "Should I invest in school?" I talked to him. Then I went to [Peter Zien] at AleSmith, I really liked him. Everyone was pretty cool. They were like, "Try to take a chance and find a job." Get in where you can fit in, that kind of thing.

I cold-called at Pyramid—I cold-called a lot of breweries in the Bay Area. It was funny, because a lot of those guys I called, I'm friends with now.

At Pyramid, I got about three interviews. I was pretty excited on the third one. Not until my first day of being on the brew deck, a 125-barrel system, did I realize, "Wow, I'm here. I'm here to do this." Then I just kept my nose down and worked as hard as I could. I showed up every day. I didn't want them to know how much I really liked it, because I thought I'd never wanted to be cocky, always be humble. Eight years later, I received an opportunity to go work at Drake's. That's when I thought that Pyramid was definitely fear school for me. They

had no time for mistakes. It's like boot camp. I've seen a lot of guys flushed out of there, so I'm pretty proud to have gone through that. Being a cellar guy, you're hungry. They're doing six knock-outs a day. So I learned a lot of solid practices there.

Over at Pyramid, guys would come over and say, "Hey, what do you think about this grain?" That's when you know you had kind of arrived. That was maybe six years in, when somebody actually asked me about recipe formulation. When they're asking you, you better have an answer. Otherwise, they're not going to ask you again. Drake's was a whole new experience. That's the first time that somebody [took my direction], like, I said, "I think we can up the mash temperature a little bit." They're like, "Really? Okay." Those guys are administrative brewers, and they don't have a whole lot of time to be thinking about other things. You're the hungry guy that should. That's why they're paying you to think. So, I learned a lot about that.

Then the opportunity came to work here. I decided to take the bull by the horns and call the owner and say I wanted to put my name in the hat. It was real casual and John's a great guy. I met him for a beer. Then we met another time for another set of beers. He told me, "Hey, I was thinking about some of the stuff you said? What do you think about re-upping the lineup for Jupiter and see how that goes?" Again, going back to when somebody asks you to make a change, you better be ready to do that. So I'm pretty proud of that, being ready to answer the call, because the raw materials were pretty limited for that project. I think some good beers came out of it. There's a brown ale, and a winter warmer, and a barleywine. They're all pretty solid.

Nick: How do you see yourself fitting in to the great Triple Rock heritage?

Jeff: Triple Rock was started in '86. From what I know, back then, they had guys like Rick Warner. Twenty Tank still existed, but Triple Rock was the first one. You had all these brewers doing really big, multi-big, strong beers. I wasn't around, so I can only look at the old recipes, and believe me, I've gone back and looked at them. I think they were doing really cutting edge stuff for the time. You can see how things have evolved from Shaun O'Sullivan, how playing with hops the way he did was on the cutting edge of things. Then Christian came here, doing coffee beers, some Belgians, and then Rodger Davis just took it to a whole other level. He decided to change a lot of things.

Rodger was also an employee at Pyramid, so we have the same kind of mindset. We just do the same things.

Nick: Do you feel like you have really big shoes to fill?

Jeff: Yeah, I there's definitely big shoes to fill. What I'm most proud of is this brewery can brew five days a week. For a brewpub, that's a lot.

The institution, it's iconic. The thing I'm really proud of too, is John Martin and Reid Martin, the two owners, they've basically just handed me the keys. They're involved. They're flying at 40,000 feet, but that's when you know things are okay. It's been pretty much a sink or swim kind of thing. I think I'm

> **"I don't take my job for granted."**

tackling it. But then again, I'm pretty humble. I don't take my job for granted. Being a brewer, I think you have to be so neurotic about things that it's hard to get an assistant who is going to deal with this neurosis. You don't want to be micromanaging, but you want to make sure that everything is done right.

Nick: Tell me a little bit about your brewing styles and philosophies. Are there general characteristics that you like all your beers to have?

Jeff: Absolutely. I like the beers to be balanced. I like beers to be dried out. I'm more about hop flavor, hop aroma, than hop bitterness. I like all the late kettle additions, dry hopping like crazy. Sometimes people will think that the beers are out of balance, but that's what we do in the Bay Area. It's all about the hops. Right now, we're doing a pound per barrel on average recipes, and for some of them, there's 10 pounds for a 7-barrel batch. For a double IPA, it's even more. The Belgians; those are the ones where I stick to style. Here, saison should be dried up, bone dry. You don't want to muddle it, or try anything weird with too much spice. If the drinker, if the people out in the public say, "I can tell there's coriander in this," in my opinion, you've overdone it. You want to leave them head scratching, because the yeast will have interplay with the spices. In Belgian ales, to me, the yeasts are the main player. Let them do their thing. Whereas California, pale ales and stuff, hops are the main player.

Nick: When you create a new recipe, is that primarily ingredient driven? Or is it style driven, and then the ingredients follow?

Jeff: I think that brewing is 97% really hard work, and the 3% of creativity is what I really enjoy. Usually, I know the yeast strain I'm going to use. It just stems from that. You have an idea, and then you think, "What do you want it to be like?" I want it to have a lot of dark fruit. That will come from the yeast strain. But you can also do an interplay of some specialty malt. A lot of the Belgians should be digestible. If you use too much malt, they're too heavy. That's the way it works for me.

Nick: Would you say it's more of a scientific process for you, or a creative process?

Jeff: Creative process. I'm a hack. I know the equipment that we use and what I need to go with. I think that stems from working at a big brewery, where you had a lot of bean counters walking around all the time. You had marketing people making beer, as opposed to brewers. Now, you're in complete creative control. You can do those beers that are crossover beers for people, but you can also do ones that are head scratchers, where people are like, "I don't know if I like it. I can't figure this beer out." There are ones where people will empty the tank in five days. Then you know they love it. Unfortunately, those ones, you really can't keep up with because the hop varieties are usually very hard. You can only use Citra and Amarillo so much. You're going to run out.

Nick: Do you think California embraces new beers, new styles, and innovation more than other places?

Jeff: I think it's the new frontier. It's America. It used to just be, for a while, a lot of the guys from San Diego, or up here. Now, you're getting some guys in my home state of Michigan that are doing really well, and guys from the Midwest. When you look back, when you answer the question about California, it seems more is better. People cannot deny the IPA or double IPA. There's a trend now, and you cannot deny the people that like IPA or double IPA or triple IPA.

Nick: I think Europe's a bit stuck in their ways in terms of brewing. You have Stone, who wants to open a brewery in Europe to have fresh beer there, and also to give the industry a kick in the pants. What's your take on that?

Jeff: I think it would be great for them to do that. Anything that's good for American brewing is good, worldwide. Those guys are definitely one of the brewers that should do that. It would open up a whole new avenue. Those guys [in Europe] are hungry for beer, too. Maybe that would be good for the industry, having an American company come in with a great marketing like Stone has. Who knows? Anything that's good for American brewing, I'm cool with.

Nick: What is it about beer that turns you on the most?

Jeff: It's the drink of everyday people. There's a lot you can learn about a city when you go and you see what kind of beer selection they have, how much a pint costs, things like that. I don't know. I just like everything about it. Good people, a good industry to get into.

> ## "I think it's the new frontier. It's America."

Somebody asked me this really great question once. He's a builder, a carpenter. He asked, "You work on a seven-barrel system, and how long does an average beer stay on tap?" I said, "Anywhere from two weeks to 10 days." He said, "How does that feel sometimes, when you put in all this creative effort, and the beer's gone in 10 days? You can't make that for another year, or maybe not ever." I thought, "That's a great question." He builds these buildings, and he gets to go back and look at them. The cool thing is you have these memories from people that come over to you, and it makes you feel really good. You'll be out somewhere. You take the good with the bad. Sometimes people will pan you. Sometimes people say, "Hey, man, I had that beer or I had this beer, and it was great." And it lives on in people's memories. I think sometimes because it's not around, it's even bigger than it was. That's when you know you have a winner. It's legendary.

Nick: So what's the best advice you can offer a home brewer who maybe wants to make better beer or even get into the industry?

Jeff: They've made a good choice in starting a great hobby. I would say the same thing I was taught: Do the same recipe over and over and over, until you get it right, no matter how boring that seems, until you have somewhat consistent results. If you don't have the right kind of equipment, meaning if you can't regulate your fermentation temperature and things like that, it's probably not the best idea to go out and do a bohemian pilsner. You're not going to get the right results. You find a style, like a good English bitter, which would be a good beer to make. These are beers that a long time ago, people made at home. You can make those beers at home. That's the kind of advice I have. Also, have fun.

As far as getting into the industry, don't be too sensitive. Always be persistent, but be professional. There is a big difference between being a professional and being an enthusiast. It's great to be really excited about what you're doing, but I think when you're doing something as a living, you have to remember that there's a level of professionalism. It is a job.

Nick: Is there a question you've never been asked that you've always wanted to answer?

Jeff: I just wish my dad was around to see what I was doing. He'd be really proud of me. That's one thing. With that being said, I have an eight-year-old son, and he's really proud. He's always saying, "My dad makes this beer. He used to make this beer like Drake's." There's a lot of pride in our family, a lot of that kind of stuff. It would have been cool for my dad to see what I do. That's one thing.

Shaun O'Sullivan
21st Amendment Brewery

Shaun O'Sullivan is the co-founder and brewmaster of San Francisco's beloved 21st Amendment Brewery.

Nick: Take me through your brewing history. Start off with your earliest memories of enjoying beer and bring me up through where we are today.

Shaun: I was living in Los Angeles in another lifetime. My initial passion was photography and I shot punk rock and political photos for a local weekly, which was pretty amazing. I remember covering the L.A. riots back in 1992 and the club scene in Hollywood. I also worked for a stint at CNN as a producer, which didn't really pay the bills, so I sold out and took a job as a paralegal at a big New York law firm's office in Los Angeles. I was in my mid-twenties and they would fly me around the country and take very good care of me. That experience was where I had my first craft beer.

I remember after work we'd go across the street to this classic suit bar and I'd have a Red Hook ESB. It was amazing. That was one of my first craft beers along with Anchor Steam. I lived near Santa Monica and there was a place called Father's Office, and back then it was an old man bar with saw dust on the floor, a pinball machine, a cat and 20 craft beer taps. That was back when no one was doing multi-tap bars. It was an amazing place and although it's still there it's changed quite a bit since back then.

Nick: Young hipster?

Shaun: Yes I suppose. You could get a beer and take it next door to a barbershop through the backdoor and get your hair cut while enjoying a Pete's Wicked Ale. I think they were one of the first places that poured every single Anchor Brewing beer available on tap. Only there and next to Judy Ashworth's Lyon's Brewery in Dublin, California.

It was about that that time I began homebrewing, which I found fascinating. The idea that you could craft your own beer. Pretty cool stuff. At the time I was disillusioned by the legal world and didn't know what I wanted to do so, I thought about attending law school or business school and came to the realization that wasn't for me. I then decided to move north to the Bay Area. I ended up in Berkeley, and got a job at Triple Rock Brewery within the first nine months of moving here. I went in one day and I told the bartender, "Hey! I just want to come in and brew one day. How do I do that?" The bartender said, "Just give the head brewer a call." So I called up Sandy Savage and he said, "We're going to start at six o'clock in the morning tomorrow come on in." I went in the next morning and we brewed all day long and it was incredible, just amazing. I wasn't wearing a suit and we were playing the Grateful Dead and talking beer, other brewers were stopping by to chat. I was hooked. At the time Shawn Donnelly was the assistant brewer

and we tasted beers most of the day and went mountain biking afterwards. I'll never forget that day.

Then I just started going to Triple Rock to volunteer. Shawn would call me up and say, "Hey, I'm filtering today," or, "I'm brewing today. You want to come in?" I just worked for free for about seven months. I ate it up, I was a sponge. Then when a position opened up I jumped at it and they hired me. For two and a half years, I was the assistant brewer making $6.20 and hour and had a part time job in downtown Oakland that would pay the bills. The Martin brothers owned Triple Rock and also a brewpub in San Francisco called "Twenty Tank Brewery," a well-known brewpub in San Francisco brewing history. It was right across from the music club Slims and the two brewers at the time were leaving, so it was my job to go over and learn the system. I had already been hired around the same time to work at Steelhead Brewing Company, which was opening a pub at Fisherman's Wharf.

Early on, when I was working at Triple Rock, my business partner, Nico, had moved to the Bay Area for the same reasons that I had and started working for the Celebrator beer magazine. He had gone out to UC Davis to take brewing courses and writing about these one-week courses they were offering on brewing science and such. We met there and became friends. One day I invited him back to Triple Rock to brew with me and we had this conversation. He said, "What are you going to do with the rest of your life?" I said, "I want to open a brewery." Nico had been a theater major in his former life and was in Los Angeles doing what struggling actors do, working and managing restaurants, so he had that background and skill set. He would run the front of the house and I would be the brewer. We set out to write a business plan and start to raise the money and look for spaces in San Francisco in the South of Market area where leases were cheaper and there were buildings large enough that could house a production brewery and a restaurant. We started the process and found our location in 1998. That took a long time and getting the money was even tougher. We opened up in August of 2000—the same year the San Francisco Giants' ballpark opened their new park.

The first two years were pretty rough as it was the end of the dot-com era and business were failing. 2001 brought 9/11 and then the economic downturn. We almost went out of business a handful of times. What really kept us alive was the ballpark as we had those 81 games a year in our backyard. The neighborhood started coming around and had more people coming back to work and live near us. Residential units started sprouting up everywhere and we just realized that we were probably going to make it.

> **"The first two years were pretty rough as it was the end of the dot-com era. . . . We almost went out of business a handful of times."**

Nick: Let's talk about brewing, your process, and your philosophies on that. When you are brewing a new beer, what's that process?

Shaun: I first get an idea about a beer, and think about what I want it to taste like and maybe focus on a particular style. From there I see if there is a twist on that style involving unusual ingredients and I then create a recipe. I might home brew a small version or try it out on our 12-barrel brewpub brewery.

A good example of that is our Hell or High Watermelon Wheat beer. The inspiration for that beer was a recipe that Nico home brewed in his San Francisco apartment. It's a beer we brew with real watermelon juice. The first year we opened, he suggested we brew that beer and I said "nobody is going to drink that beer." It was a pretty interesting combination with beer and brewing with watermelon. Then the second year we were open I brought him to the back of the brewery where I had cases and cases of watermelons stocked and surprised him. I said, "We're going to make that beer." It ended up being one of the most popular beers we make. Everyone loves that beer, so refreshing.

That's an example of using an odd or different ingredient in a way and you're not really sure how it's going to be in the end.

Nick: Was there lot of trial and error, though?

Shaun: No. Not really. Not so much. It was maybe how much watermelon to add, but my philosophy on brewing is simply this: it is the marriage of science and art. You're essentially scientists in the kitchen. The great thing about brewpub brewing is you can serve your mistakes as long as there is not something terribly wrong. That venue really allows for experimentation and to try new things. I love it.

Nick: You talked about the marriage of science and creativity, but how important is tradition for you?

Shaun: Our industry is steeped in tradition, especially when you look at the mass produced beers that are on the market. I love to acknowledge that tradition, but the great thing about craft beer is you can try new things that hopefully the public

will enjoy. For instance we make an imperial IPA, our Hop Crisis, but we age it on oak spirals and the nuance of the toasted spirals complement the aroma of the hops and the tannins add bitterness complexity. You also see it in our Sneak Attack, a Belgian-style saison, as well, where we add cardamom that gives a spicy flavor and aroma. A slight twist on a style.

Nick: Are there certain characteristics that you like your beers to have, generally?

Shaun: Yes, that is a great question because I'm a big believer in the flavor arc of beer. Let's use IPAs as an example. When you drink an IPA you typically know what you're getting because it's labeled an IPA and that sets you up from the start for your flavor experience. If you are drinking out of a glass you see the golden color, your senses become heightened when you smell that beer and take in that rich hoppy floral aroma. With an IPA I want to hit people over the head with that hop aroma. Most of what we taste is with our nose, where we can detect over one trillion scents versus the tongue that can only detect six different flavors. Your nose knows. Then when you take that first sip of beer, you get that little bit of sweetness, and bitterness, but it has a malt backbone to support that bitterness, otherwise you have a very bitter beer with no structure. It should then finish dry and that's my big thing. I want the beers to finish dry because I want you to drink another one, and another one. If it's too sweet in the finish, it's cloying and it's a hard thing to stomach. All beers should be about balance even if the style calls for the beer to lean toward bitter or sweet.

Nick: Tell me about the name 21st Amendment.

Shaun: The 21st Amendment in the Constitution is the repeal of the 18th Amendment, Prohibition, which occurred on December 5, 1933. Before Prohibition, there were something like forty-five operating breweries within San Francisco. Prohibition took that all away. When we were looking for a name we looked at old San Francisco yellow pages for old brewery names. Those old brewery names weren't really that interesting. They were pretty generic. It just dawned on us as we were looking in that era that we should call ourselves the 21st Amendment, the amendment that brought back the legal manufacturing, distribution, and sale of alcohol.

The idea and the philosophy behind our pub is the return of the neighborhood gathering place. Historically the pub was a communal place where you would meet and discuss the day's events. Pub is short for public house and it really was the original social network. Before the repeal of Prohibition, citizens had to hide and drink in speakeasies; the 21st Amendment is about celebrating the end of that dark era.

Nick: Let's talk a little bit about the industry because, in the past five years it's experienced the next wave of popularity. People are calling it the "craft beer revolution."

Shaun: Again.

Nick: Do you think that's what we are seeing?

Shaun: Yes definitely. There are hundreds of breweries in the planning stages right now, that's a lot and maybe a little worrisome. My concern is—where is this beer going to be sold? There are only so many tap handles spaces and spots for packaged beer at grocery and liquor stores. I think success in this industry is going to come down to quality, good business practices, marketing and sales. Quality is going to be priority one—many inexperienced people are getting involved in craft beer, and opening breweries. There is a concern that the lack of quality will turn off beer drinkers. As an industry, we are experiencing explosive growth and as Paul Gatza, the Director

of the Brewers Association, said at the 2014 Craft Brewers Conference in Denver, "Don't fuck it up. Make quality beer."

Nick: Why do you think in the past five or so years we've seen this big spike?

Shaun: Craft beer is the art of making something with your hands and that has an effect on people, it resonates with our core to create and enjoy. In many ways craft brewing has spawned other artisanal industries—from micro-farming, cheese-making, chocolatiers, and other culinary arts. A renaissance is taking place in craft beer and by extension is being played out at weekend farmers' markets around the country. The bland soulless beers designed by marketing teams are being replaced by beers made with more flavor and interesting ingredients and it's resonating.

Nick: What motivates you to get up every morning and come in here to brew beer?

Shaun: Well, it's in my blood. I feel like the luckiest guy in the world that I get paid to do this. Although I don't brew every day at our pub as I once did, I design the recipes for all the beers that we produce and distribute.

> **"Beer is alive, this is what it's about. Don't call it "product." Call it beer!"**

When you make a beer, and people get excited about it, and they tell you how wonderful it is, whether you're reading it on a social media site or they're telling you in person, it's pretty heady. And it is what drives me. We currently distribute our beer in sixteen states and that is growing. By the time this book hits the shelf we will have opened our new production brewery in the Bay Area. We will have gone from our small 500-square-foot brewery in San Francisco to a state of the art 100-barrel destination brewery just across the bay in San Leandro.

Nick: Ok, last question: what have you never been asked in an interview that you've always wanted to say?

Shaun: Don't use the word "product" when you talk about beer. We're not making ball bearings and we're not making cocaine, we're making beer, a living and changing beverage.

Nick: Expand on that.

Shaun: Sometimes, when I talk to business people and distributors they use the word "product," or "liquid' and I cringe. I preach it all the time and I've said it before, It's water, malt, hops, and yeast, and there's a whole lot of love behind this and we are not just churning it out. Beer is alive and dynamic from when it's being made and fermenting to packaging. It's as big of a time as it gets. Don't call it "product." Call it beer!

INDEX